PSYCHOLOGY OF LEARNING AND DEVELOPMENT

ES-332

For

Bachelor of Education [B.Ed.]

Useful For

IGNOU, Nalanda University, Kurushetra University, Lalit Narayan Mithila University, Andhra University, Pt. Sunderlal Sharma (Open) University (Bilaspur), Annamalai University, Bangalore University, Bharathiar University, Bharathidasan University, HP University, Jamia Millia Islamia, Kakatiya University (Andhra Pradesh), KSOU (Karnataka), KOU (Rajasthan), MPBOU (MP), MDU (Haryana), Punjab University, Tamilnadu Open University, Sri Padmavati Mahila Visvavidyalayam (Andhra Pradesh), Sri Venkateswara University (Andhra Pradesh), UCSDE (Kerala), University of Jammu, YCMOU, Rajasthan University, UPRTOU (UP) and all other Indian Universities.

--: Hindi Edition Also Available :--

GULLYBABA PUBLISHING HOUSE (P) LTD.

AN ISO 9001:2008 CERTIFIED CO.

Developed and Produced by:

GullyBaba Publishing House (P) Ltd.

Regd. Office:
2525/193, 1st Floor,
Onkar Nagar-A, Tri Nagar,
New Delhi-110035
Landmark: Kanhaiya Nagar Metro Station

Branch Office:
1A/2A, 20, Hari Sadan,
Ansari Road, Daryaganj,
New Delhi-110002
Ph. 011-23289034

E-mail: info@gullybaba.com, Website: GullyBaba.com

Edition: 2013
Author: GPH Panel of Experts

ISBN: 978-93-81638-03-3

How to Get GPH books Home Delivered?

To get the books by VPP/COD, Email/SMS your complete address, telephone number, subject code of the books.

To get the books by RBD/Speed Post/Courier, Pay in advance by Bank Draft (in favour of "Gullybaba Publishing House (P) Ltd.")/ Money Order/ Online Transfer/Cash Deposit. In case of DD/Cheque add ₹25 extra. In case of cash deposit add ₹110 extra in total. And email your payment details.

To know the current postage charges visit Gullybaba.com.

Order online through GullyBaba.com.

For more information dial:- 09350849407, 09312235086, or email us at gphbooks@gullybaba.com.

Preface

This book is mainly targeted for the exam of Psychology of Learning and Development for all Universities. It has been introduced in market after seeing the huge demand of ready to grasp material for exams with high level of quality, and its un-availability in market. We the GullyBaba Publishing House took a step ahead to publish the quality material focusing on exams at the same time giving you indepth knowledge about the subject.

GPH Book is the pioneer effort that provides a unique methodology so as to perform better in exams. If your goal is to attain higher grade use this powerful study tool independently or along with your text.

*On the Web : **www.gullybaba.com** is the vital resource for your exams acting as catalyst to boost up your preparation. Now you can access us on the net through **www.doeacconline.com, www.ignouonline.com, and www.astrologyeverywhere.com.***

Feedback about the book can be sent at **es332writers@gullybaba.com.**

New Delhi

Constructive criticism is always welcome as it will add to our knowledge. You can email at feedback@gullybaba.com.

Topics Covered

Contents

Question Papers

Understanding the Development of the Learner

Q1. Explain the meaning and concept of Growth and Development and differentiate between them. **[June-06, Q1]**

Ans. The term growth and development are very often used interchangeably but it is worth while to keep in mind the distinction which is made between them or at least to understand why they are so often used together. The term growth implies an increase in size. When a body or any of its parts is described as having growth it usually means that it has become large and heavier. It is thus that we speak of growth of arms, brain, muscles or the body in general. The Difference. Growth means increase or addition in size, height, length or weight and can be measured. Development means change in shape, form or structure so as to improve in working or functioning. Development implies certain qualitative changes or changes in character leading to maturity of improvement in functioning. Arms grow large but also they develop by undergoing certain changes which equip them for better work.

The difference between Growth and Development in tabulated below : -

Growth	Development
1) Growth is used in purely physical terms, it generally refers to change in size, length, height and weight of an individual. Changes in the quantitative aspects come into the domain of growth.	1) Development implies overall changes in shape, form or structure resulting in improved working or functioning. It indicates the changes in the quality or character rather than in quantitative aspects.
2) Growth is one of the aspects of developmental process.	2) Development is a wider and comprehensive term, it refers to overall changes in the individual. Growth is one of its aspects.
3) Growth describes the changes which takes place in particular aspect of the body and behaviour of an organism.	3) Development describes the changes in the organism as a whole and does not list changes in parts.
4) Growth does not continue throughout life, it stops when maturity has been attained.	4) Development is a continuous process.
5) The changes produced by growth on the subject of Measurement. They may be quantified.	5) Development implies improvement in functioning and behaviour and hence brings qualitative changes.
6) Growth may or may not bring development. A child may grow (in terms of weight) by becoming fat but his growth may not bring any functional improvement (qualitative change) or development.	6) Development is also possible without growth as we see in the cases of some children that they do not gain in terms of height, weight or size but they do experience functional improvement or development in Physical, Social, emotional or intellectual aspects.

Q2. Write down the various Principle of human development? What are its various stages. [Dec-05, Q1] [June-05, Q1]

Ans. Development is a continuous Process, throughout life. It represents changes in an organism from its origin to its death but more particular the progressive changes which take place from origin to maturity. Development is a product of maturity and learning. Human development involves changes. Here we shall discuss the various principles of human development with suitable example :-

1. Continuity – As we know that development is a continuous process. A human beings development can be of various kinds link body development, development in behaviour, interests, needs etc. It does not stop but exists in whole life. As for examples first of all an infant learn 3 to 5 words only as mother, father, bread, water etc. according to his needs. But this process of development continues till death and he/she earns many new words day by day. His body also develops continuously. Various organs of his body make development without stopping. As for example an infant knows only weeping after his birth but gradually he learns many ways to perform many works as laughing, seeing, understanding, sitting, standing, walking, running etc. This process of learning and development continues till death. It means life is the other name of various changes and every person learns something new everyday in his whole life.

2. Sequentiality – Development is sequential or orderly. Every human being follows a sequential pattern in development process. It follows a certain kind of order in development. Development has a relation between organism and environment in a transaction or collaboration. Individuals work with and affect their environment and in turn the environment works with and affect them. A development pattern has one stage leading to the next. As for example first of all an infant learns small words combined with one or two letters, after it he learns some large words after it sentence. In other example, an infant first of all develop art of sitting and after it walking and running. We cannot find that a child learns walking first and standing after it. Or a child develop running habit first and after it habit of sitting. It means every human being follows a fixed pattern or sequence in his process of development. This development cannot occur without order.

3. Generality to specify – Development moves from general to specific. In every area, human being learns general habits, continuously these habits become specific. For example first of all an infant feels fear from every strange things and begins to weep to demonstrate fear of all kinds. Gradually, he/she moves from generality to specificity, he becomes specific in feeling of fear then he does not fear with every strange thing. In other side he/she does not express his/her feeling to fear mere through weeping but instead of it he develops many other ways to express his feelings of fear such as crying, turning away, hiding or pretending to be not afraid. With other example infant calls every edible thing by the name of 'mammam' generally at starting stage. But gradually he begins to call them by their special names like milk, bread, biscuit etc. Thus every human being makes development according to the principle of generality to specificity.

4. Differentially – Development does not occur at same pace. Individuals differ in the rate of growth and development. Each part of the body has its own particular rate of growth. The feet hands, nose reach maximum development early in adolescence while the lower part of the face and the shoulders develop more slowly. As for example many organs of boys and girls are different in their development pace. As we know that every individual differ in their rate of progress regarding abilities, intelligences, skills etc. Rote memory for the abstract. We see that the organs of body of a child develop more speedily than the organs of a matured person. So we can find differentially in the process of development.

Now we can say that human development has some basic principles, every development of human being occurs according to these principles. Teacher should understand these principles so that he/she could facilitate the process of growth and development. Teacher should try to make this development process positive and aimful so that students could develop their all over virtues and organs.

Q3. What do you mean by development? What are its various stages? [June-07, Q1][June-05, Q1]

Ans. The term development in its most general psychological sense refers to certain changes that occur in human beings (or animals) between conception and death. The term is not applied to all changes, but rather to those that appear in orderly ways and remain for a reasonably long period of time. A temporary change caused by a brief illness, for example, is not considered a part of development. Psychologists also make a value judgment in determining which changes qualify as development. The changes, at least those that occur early in life, are generally assumed to be for the better and to result in behavior that is more adaptive, more organized, more effective, and more complex (Mussen, Conger, & Kagan, 1984).

Stages of Development

Age groups	Stages of Development	Schooling stage
Birth to 2 yrs.	Infancy	
2 yrs. to 6 yrs.	Early childhood	Per-primary
6 yrs. to 12 yrs.	Later childhood	Primary
12 yrs. to 18 yrs.	Adolescence	Secondary and Senior secondary.
18 yrs. to 40 yrs.	Young adulthood	
40 yrs. to 65 yrs.	Mature adulthood	
Over 65 yrs.	Aged adulthood	

Each and every stage of development is characterized by a set of unique, coherent and distinguishing features.

Each period in life has its own problems of adjustment. Throughout the life span people develop techniques of handling each of their difficulties. All children progress in a definite order through these stages and they all follow similar basic patterns. These stages alongwith their corresponding ages have been identified by development psychologists as follows :

Stage	Time frame
Prenatal	(Before birth)
Infancy	0 to 1 years
Early childhood	1-3 years
Preschool	3 - 6 years
School childhood	6 - 12 years
Adolescence	12 - 20 years
Young adulthood	20 - 30 years
Adulthood	30 - 50 years
Mature adult	50 - 65 years
Aging adult	65+

A brief description of these ages is as under :

1. Prenatal Period (Before birth) - Life begins at the time of conception. When the child is in the mother's womb the particular period spent there is known as prenatal period. All important external and internal feeling start to develop at this stage.

2. Infancy (0 to 3 years) - From birth up to the third of life rapidly in size during their first three years. The acquisition of motor skills link holding things, crawling, walking proceeds from simple to complex.

3. Pre-school childhood (3-6 years) - The growth of height is not so rapid during this stage as is in infancy. Childhood improve eye, hand and small muscle coordination. For example they can draw a circle, pour into a bowl, button and unbutton the clothes, language development is rapid.

4. School childhood (6-12 years) - Primary school years)-School children between the age of 6 to 12 years look much taller and thinner. Children keep getting stronger and faster. They achieve new motor skills. Their competence in all areas of development becomes more pronounced.

5. Adolescence (12-20 years) - It is the span of year between childhood and adulthood which begins at puberty.

This is the period of rapid physiological growth. There are a number of psychological changes which also take place. They jump rope, bicycle, ride horse, dance and indulge in all possible games. Cognitively also they more agile. Social relationships become important, but the hallmark of this stage is the reach for identity. There are a number of psychological changes which also take place.

6. Adulthood (20-65 years) - For better understanding adulthood can be divided into three stages. Thee are :

(a) Young adulthood (20-50 years)

(b) Mature adulthood or the Middle years (50-65 years)

(c) Aging adulthood (65+years)

Strength and energy characterize this time of life from the twenties when most bodily functions are fully developed, until about the age of 50. Thereafter there is gradual decline in energy level.

Q4. (i) Indicate 'G' for 'growth' and 'D' for 'development' for each of the following statements.

a) An infant begins to focus its eyes on an object dangling before it.

Ans. D

b) A six month old baby shows signs of teething.

Ans. G

c) A thirteen year old boy begins to have hair on his face.

Ans. G

d) A three month old baby begins to turn over and lie on its stomach.
Ans. G

(ii) Write 'T' for 'true' and 'F' for 'false' for the following statements.
a) A child talking full sentences is part of development.
Ans. T
b) The difference in height between two children is due to the different rates of their development.
Ans. F

(iii) What is a neonate?
a) An irritable baby
b) An unloved baby
c) A newborn baby
d) An abnormal baby.
Ans. c) A newborn baby is a neonate.

Q5. Adolescence is a period of storm and stress. Discuss [Dec-07, Q3(i)]
Ans. Meaning of Adolescence
The term 'Adolescence' is derived from the Latin word 'Adolescence' meaning 'to grow', 'to mature'. It covers a period of seven or eight years, normally from 12 to 18 or 20 with large variations in many cases.

According to A.T. TERSILD
Adolescence is that span of years during which boys and girls move from childhood to adulthood mentally, emotionally, socially and physically.

WHO defines
Adolescence both in terms of age (between 10 & 19 years) and in terms of a phase of life marked by special attributes. These attributes includes:
1) Rapid physical growth and development- Change in voice, change in weight, height and strength.
2) Physical, Social and psychological maturity, but not all at the same time- physiological change means change in the internal system of the body. Some of them gain weight, height later. So, they feel inferior.
3) Sexual maturity and the onset of sexual activity
4) Experimentation
5) Development of adult mental processes and adult identity.

General Characteristics of Adolescence

According to Piaget the final period of intellectual development is the period of formal operations, which begins at about the age of 11 and is consolidated during Adolescence. At the formal operational stage adolescent develop the capacity for abstract, scientific thinking. Formal operational adolescents can 'operate on operations'. The following are the major characteristics of this stage :

(1) The adolescent's System of Mental operations has reached a high degree of Equilibrium – Adolescence thought is flexible and effective. He can deal efficiently with the complex problems of reasoning. He can imagine the many possibilities of solving a problem.

(2) The Adolescent is able to Apply logical thoughts to all classes of problems – The fact that the adolescent is logical in his approach does not mean that he no larger thinks illogically. Rather, it is a fact that the adolescent shows further advancement in his intellectual development with increasing ages. But, he cannot differentiate between logic and reality. He cannot distinguish between what is real and what is logical.

(3) The Adolescent is able to use Abstract Rules to solve a whole class of problems – For example, consider the problem 'what number is 30 less than 3 times itself? The adolescent has Learned a higher order operation and may set the equation X+30 = 3X and quickly finds the answer of 15.

(4) Formal thought is Relational and Systematic – The adolescent deals with propositions, not objects. He plans the tests adequately or designs the experiments properly. He observes the results accurately. He draws proper logical conclusions from his observation. Thus, Adolescent thought is rational and systematic.

(5) Adolescent becomes concerned with the Hypothetic-Deductive Reasoning – Formal operational thinkers can form hypotheses, set up mental experiments to test them, and isolate or control variables in order to complete a valid test of the Hypothesis.

(6) Adolescent becomes concerned with Analogical Reasoning and Reflexive Ability – The child can explain 'why' and 'how' the Analogy works. They are able to systematically generate all possible solution to a problem or engage in combinational reasoning.

According to ERICKSON'S PSYCHOSOCIAL THEORY OF DEVELOPMENT, the Adolescence comes under the stage of IDENTITY vs ROLE CONFUSION

(12-18 yrs). The Adolescence marks the first time that a conscious effort is made to answer the question "Who am" the conflict defining this stage is identity vs role confusion. Identity refers to the organization of the individuals, drives, abilities, briefs and history into a consistent image of self. It involves deliberate choices and decisions, particularly about vocation, sexual orientation and a philosophy of life. If adolescent fail to integrate all these aspects and choices or if they feel unable to choose at all, role confusion threatens.

According to KOHLBERG'S STAGE THEORY OF MORAL REASONING, Adolescence comes under the stage of 'conventional moral reasoning' (10-20) yrs. Judgement here is based on the loyalty to the established social order, to the expectations of the family, social group, country. The individuals now make moral decisions by considering factors of less concrete and a more social nature such as approval of others, family locality, opinions to the law and order.

1) Interpersonal Harmony – Good behaviour is that which pleases or helps other, based on family and cultural code. Intentions, not just effect, become significant. Approval of others becomes significant.
2) Authority and social order/law and order – The child respects authority by doing what is required and protecting social and religious codes because they are there. As development continues, the individual moves from concerns of pleasing other to a more generalized orientation to follow societal rules and law.

Emotional Development – The term 'Emotion' is derived from the Latin term, 'emovere' which means 'to stir', 'to agitate', 'to move' or 'to excite'. Emotional development is one of the major aspects of adolescence growth and development. Not only Adolescent's physical growth and development is linked with his emotional make-up but his aesthetic, intellectual, moral and social development is also controlled by his emotional development. Adolescent must be trained to control their emotions and achieve a mental balance and stability which will lead to individual happiness and social efficiency.

How Emotions work – All of us observes a large number of persons and objects in this world. We have some feeling for them in our mental make-up. Sometimes our feelings become strong either in favour or against the object or individual or an occasion. This disturbs our mental balance. This disturbance is known as Emotion. It not only disturbs our mind, but the entire organism. It is expressed in various movements and expressions of body and it tries to adjust to face the situation.

Factors in school environment which disturb the Emotional Development of the Adolescents.

- Lack of security
- Economic disparities
- Fearful atmosphere in school.
- Faulty methods of teaching.
- Emotionally unbalanced teacher.
- Traditional concept of discipline.
- Disregard of individual differences.
- Lack of co-curricular actives.
- Lack of sex education.
- Faulty examination system.
- Faulty curriculum.

Following are the role of the school and the teacher in satisfying the needs of the Emotional Development of the Adolescent : -

1) Providing equal treatment irrespective of considerations of wealth status or gender of the Adolescents.

2) He should give an opportunity for development of creating abilities i.e. through music, art, drama, sport etc.

3) Love and affection on the part of the teacher to be made the basis of work.

4) Teacher should also solve the curiosity of the students and a class as a whole.

5) He should use dynamic and progressive methods of teaching-learning.

6) Teacher should give due regard to individual differences of the Adolescents.

7) Classes related to sex education should also be formed.

8) Teacher should also provide a conducive environment.

9) Physical energy is maximum during this period. So, teacher should utilise it to the maximum.

10) Teacher should give students opportunities to solve problem and reason scientifically.

11) Teacher should provide Healthy physical conditions in the schools.

12) Proper orientation should be there.

Q6. List out the main points of physical development in adolescents and discuss their educational implications.

Ans. Physical Development in Adolescence – The growth curves of height and weight from infancy to adulthood, is rapid in infancy, goes down in middle childhood, and shoots up in adolescence. The adolescent not only increases in size or weight but all of his or her body alters; for example, there are changes in the internal organs and body processes and subtle alterations in the composition of the tissues. In males there is the deepening of voice, the growth of the beard and the ability to produce semen. In girls there is the development of breasts changes in the uterine and the pelvic areas and the menarche. For both sexes we have the growth of the body hair particularly in the public and under arm areas, changes in contours of face and body, and the eruption of new teeth. Most children exhibit pre-pubescent growth spurt and a marked increase in height and weight, especially during the month prior to menarche in the girls and the growth of public hair and the first ejaculation of seminal fluid in boys.

There are Changes in Proportions of the Body and in Organs and Tissues– For example, the legs grow relatively longer upto 15 years and then stem length increases slowly. In the childhood the whole body becomes slender but in the adolescence it begins to broaden again. The bones increase not only in size but also in number. The nose becomes so prominent that it perplexes the sensitive boy. The chemical composition of the bones also changes. Sexual maturing, which is the most complicated process of growth and change at this stage of development, is the most prominent feature of adolescence. From 14 to 20 years of age there is a tremendous change in genital types, tests, ovary, epididymis, uterine tube, prostatic urethra and seminal vesicles.

One of the Chief Characteristics of Physical Growth and Development of Adolescents in their Variability – For example, you will find in a certain class 50% of the girls having entered the puberty-cycle whereas the remaining 50% has not done so. A girl at 13 looks practically a young woman but the other of the same age looks still a child. Such variability in the maturation rate is a striking feature of both sexes.

Effects of Early and Late Maturing on Behaviour of Adolescents – The early maturing boy, as we have said earlier, gets a good position among his associates. Since he is tall for his age, he becomes the leader of the group, and the teacher also assigns him a position of responsibilities. This fact creates many problems which he is not yet able to handle. Just at a time when he is trying to an enlarged physical structure he finds more disadvantages than advantages. The only advantage that he gets out of early maturing is that he gets a chance to learn adult roles earlier. The late maturing boy is decidedly at a disadvantage, because he is ignored or slighted both by girls and boys. As he is small in size and weak in body, he cannot take an active part in games and sports with other boys of the same age. The result is that feelings of inferiority begin to develop in him. He becomes submissive and withdraws himself from competition. Some late maturing boys and girls become noisy, and mischievous to attract the attention of their teachers in the classroom. Such a behaviour is not liked by the elders, and the age-mates also tend to become hostile to them. Like many other persons, who for some reason or other, are rejected by their group, the late maturers suffer from criticism hostility of their associates. Psychological differences are thus regarded as the main causes of behavioural differences in the early and late maturers.

Educational Implications of Physical Development in Adolescence – The understanding of physical growth and change throughout the school years is basic for an adequate understanding of the development of personality. Most schools tend to pay no attention to this psychologically important aspect of growth and development. To the adolescent his growth, now in this part of the body and now in that part of the body, may as awkward and puzzling, and often causing stress and strain. But if the parents and teacher do not recognise and realize the problems raised by physical growth and development, it becomes difficult to understand the whole conduct or behaviour of the grown-up boy or girl. The study of the physical growth of the adolescents is of very great importance to understand the psychological problems faced by them. For a boy or girl to be constantly growing and changing is indeed an experience often puzzling and presenting problems in rapid succession. The youngsters of both sexes are faced with manifold anxieties and embarrassments. In a boy's world, especially the physical size and strength, are so important that his slow or rapid growth, late or early maturing in comparison with that of his class boy's mates or associates may determine his position and prestige among them. The grown-up man or woman, when he or she recollects the changes in puberty in his or her adolescent years, he or she is torn by unpleasant recollections of the adolescent years. Therefore, education should give due importance of this stage of development.

Q7. Discuss the role of a teacher in helping adolescence to develop a balanced personality. [June-07, Q3(ii)]

Ans. The period of transition from childhood to adulthood is called adolescence.

Adolescence is very critical stage of development. All type of changes: biological, social cognitive etc. take place during the adolescence stage. Teacher can do a lot of help to adolescents to develop a balanced personality. Teacher should have responsibility of guiding the development of adolescent personality. Here we shall discuss how a teacher can help adolescents a balanced personality.

Following are the ways in which a teacher can help adolescence in developing his balanced personality : -

1. Teacher should understand their problems and help to solve them

Today the problems and anxieties of adolescents are growing larger day by day. They cannot solve these problems without help of others. Teacher should play a role of friend, philosopher and a guide to provide help to adolescents. As a friend teacher should present him/herself to adolescents as a role model as a person. As a guide, teacher should provide them information's which parents refuse to give and which in society is not easily available to him. Specifically it means providing sex education and career education.

Teacher can build interest club, hobby club, subject club or activity club according to the needs of the students. Students should be put according to their interests. As for example, If some students have gardening as a hobby then we can make a hobby club of those students who link gardening as a hobby. Teacher should play a role of guide in these clubs.

2. Teacher should be an ideal person for them.

As we know that every student want to imitate the actions of his/her teacher. So a teacher should present an example of ideal person to their students. As for adolescents, they face the changes of childhood to adulthood. At this time many physical changes are found in them. During this period their growth spurt. A rapid increase in height and weight can be seen at this time. They suddenly catch up with adults in physical size and strength. These changes are the rapid development of the reproductive organs that signal sexual maturity. All the biological changes of physical maturity bring a new interest in sexuality. At this time they can attract towards opposite sex due to their changes feeling. Here teacher should present his ideal life so that students could learn from the life of his/her teacher.

Teacher should behave positively and affectionately to them and teacher should show the practical use of human values in his/her own life. If teacher only speaks verbally about human values and does not follow them in his/her own life he/she cannot expect from adolescents to acquire them in their lives so teacher should present and make his personality balanced first and then try to develop a balanced personality in adolescents.

3. Teacher's help in cognitive development

Many important cognitive developments occur during this time. We see the capacity and style of though broadness, awareness, imagination, judgement in insight in adolescents. Teacher should provide them a range of issue and problem of different kinds that could complicate and enrich the adolescent's life. Adolescents also show an increasing ability to plan and think ahead. Adolescents begin to challenge everything, to reject old boundaries and categories. They become more creative and thinkers.

Teacher should not force his/her own views or old principles on them. Teacher should provide them opportunity to judge the reality of views. Teacher should provide them a chance to think broadly at different problem. Teacher should try to encourage their creativity. Teacher should understand the nature and needs of adolescents and then try to provide opportunity to them to develop their personality positively and aimfully. Teacher should provide them chance where they could express their views fluently as debate competitions, seminars, symposia, brainstorming, etc.

In the end we can say that teacher should play a role of friend, guide, philosopher, facilitator and ideal person to provide help to adolescents in developing a balanced personality. Teacher's responsibility in this regard is very important.

Q8. Discuss the role of the teacher in facilitating growth and development. [June-07, Q1]

Ans. Teacher's role in facilitating growth and development : -

A teacher, should know what to expect from the child (student) and what he needs physically, socially and emotionally.

(1) An Active role. We should not limit our knowledge about student to a formal teacher-taught relationship especially at the time when he (the student) is found to be a member of a drug sub-culture group or is heading in a socially undesirable direction. The routine teacher taught relationship would benefit him only when we deal with him empathetically as a social being, as an individual self and as a biological organism.

(2) Making Student Realise the Various Changes. We should make our students accept the reality of physical and biological changes. If it is done, the transition takes a smooth course without causing any psychological disadvantage.

(3) Condition for Co-ordination. We should create such challenging conditions which may lead to the effective coordination of physical, mental and other functions in order to ensure adequate adjustment to probable life situations.

(4) Effective Responses. We should secure effective and desirable responses, and prevent or eliminate ineffective or undesirable ones. We should arrange conditions in a way that make desirable responses satisfying and not annoying.

(5) Proper Punishment. Punishment should be administered judiciously otherwise it would generate negative reactions.

(6) Positive Training. Positive training in self-direction and self-control should be given to students. Some of the following points can be kept in mind while imparting guidance :-

(i) Avoidance of Punishment. Student should not be punished otherwise it would interfere with his developing leadership.

(ii) Internal Control. Control and guidance must come to the student himself under the teacher's supervision.

(iii) Proper Guidance. One should apply judiciously proper guidance, rational shifts of treatment, and principles of autonomy to ensure smooth passage through the turbulent period of students.

(iv) Avoidance of Harsh Control. Harsh, strict and unsympathetic control and prescription of every detail of conduct leaving no place for self-direction would hinder students mental health and adjustment to life's events.

For Adolescence

When a student has become an adolescent, he reaches the higher levels of his school education. It is necessary to receive adequate knowledge and skills with due preparedness in order to handle their emotional and social needs. As teacher we have great responsibilities as under:

(1) We should appreciate the fact that students at this stage are prone to revolt against established norms, rules and authority. Hence we should be in a position and values which our students would question.

(2) Students at this time need proper guidance to decide on the right course of action. We have to provide them with it.

(3) They are in need of supportive judgements to do things which provide them self-confidence and self-assurance. We should provide them with it.

(4) The range of individual differences in mental ability among adolescents is wide. We should use some plan of classification to secure homogeneous groups in respect of significant abilities and achievements that we may be able to meet curricular and instructional needs.

(5) It is found that in certain tasks a student's performance would improve when others (teachers) are around. This phenomenon is called 'social facilitation' we have to keep it in our mind.

(6) Some studies have shown that when a student is first trying to learn something new, the presence of others is detrimental. In such a situation as a teacher we must assess the situation (considering the class as a social unit) and the personality traits of the students and accordingly facilitate their growth and development.

Q9. Outline the physical development of a child from birth to year age. What can a school do to produce able bodied citizens?

Ans. Physical development is studied horizontally and longitudinally. Horizontal studies gives us data regarding growth patterns of children at specific stages of development. Such studies do not give us information about individual growth patterns. Longitudinal studies are progressive studies of an individual and can be used to compare him with himself at various stages.

Different stages that a child passes through from birth to 16 years of age are the infancy (on the average, from birth to 5 or 6 years of age, during which the sensory channels begin to function and the child learns to creep, to walk and speak), the childhood (on the average from 5 to 12 years during which permanent teeth appear, and the child learns to read, write and care for himself), the adolescence on the average from 12 years to 18 (in some cases to 20 or 25 during which the development of sex organs bring about the appearance of physical sex characteristics.

The specific growth changes from birth to adolescence occur with regard to height and weight, body proportions and growth of internal organs.

During infancy a normal child tends to follow certain definite patterns of growth. Height and weight increase tremendously. The infant boy grows on the average 7 by the age of 9 months and the infant girl grows to 6 ¾'/by that age in height. Weight is doubled during the first 6 months. During childhood and adolescence the height goes on increasing. Hereditary background and environmental factors combined determine height-weight ratio for a particular child. For example, children of short and stocky parents are generally short and stocky; those of the tall and slender are tall and slender.

Different component parts of the skeleton do not grow at a regular rate. When the child is born, the size of bones of arms and legs is smaller than that of the skull. As he grows, the head and torso become proportionally shorter than before and arms and legs become longer. At birth there are no teeth. But as the child grows he gets baby teeth and then a second set of teeth which serve him all his life.

From birth to adolescence all the body systems have different rates of growth. At birth the nervous system is developed sufficiently well. The circulatory system has a balanced functioning too. But with growing years, the heart grows in size and volume. The lymphatic system becomes active at birth and increases rapidly after 12 years of age. The genital system develops slowly during the childhood but grows rapidly from 11 to 12 years of age onwards. Environment plays a significant role in physical growth and development. Favourable environmental conditions, planned recreation and rest, proper diet, well-ventilated living quarters, freedom from care and anxiety are beneficial for proper physical growth. Better nutrition, better shelter, more adequate life necessities are conducive to better health. Behaviour problems in our children spring up because of malnutrition, unhealthy home environment, lack of rest and recreation anxiety and trouble at home.

The individual is first and foremost a physical being. Therefore, any programme of his education revolves round his physical growth and development. The primary aim of education would then be the development of excellent body, good health, active neuromuscular system.

The knowledge of characteristics of physical growth and development is very essential to the teacher. He should not only be conversant with subject he teaches but he should also study the growth characteristics. The learning equipment, the curriculum, the techniques of teaching have to be geared to the proper growth of the child. He has to be careful of the normal physical growth of the child as he has to be careful of his normal intellectual growth. The child who seems to be growing beyond his years as well as the child who seems to be growing shortly, need his special attention. Even a slight physical abnormality during the childhood creates trouble to the individual. Attitudes, interests and emotional behaviour grow out of physical status. Above-normal height or weight or uneven physical growth rate, produce emotional strain and stress in the child. The teacher has to help such a child in solving emotional difficulties and problems.

Many children come from poor homes. Their parents are illiterate and do not know how to take care of them. Children are either mal-or undernourished. They lack adequate shelter. Living conditions are far from satisfactory in villages and in some urban areas too. Proper attention has to be given to the nutrition of the average school child. A midday meal or some other programme with state or public aid may be launched and the problem of malnutrition can be solved.

Every school has a responsibility for preparing able-bodied youths to serve the nation. Sanitary conditions of school premises, a provision of well-ventilated school rooms, sufficient and well-planned programme of sports and games, periodical medical examination and dental care, are a must for a good school.

Q10. Discuss the socio-emotional development of upper primary school children and secondary and senior secondary school children.

[June-05, Q3(i)]

Ans. Socio-Emotional development : Children are not link machines with gradually developing abilities. The development of various aspects link physical, social, emotional, intellectual, etc. take place together. Their development is inter-dependent. It is also inter-related with the development of cognitive skills, self-concepts, ways of interacting with others besides social attitudes and values.

Upper Primary School children

A child's social development during the primary grades is shaped by three major influences:

(1) The parents and the family.

(2) The peer group.

(3) The school experience.

During this stage children try their best to prove that they are really grown up. This is the "I can do it myself" stage.

(1) Children's powers of concentration grow.

(2) Children can spend more time on chosen tasks.

(3) Children often take pleasure in completing them.

This stage also includes :

(1) The growth of independent action by children.

(2) Their co-operation with groups.

(3) Their performance in socially acceptable ways.

(4) A concern for airplay.

By the sixth grade, student often form groups that include both boys and girls. The peer groups serve important purposes to shape their social behaviour:

(a) The children compare their abilities and skills with those of other children.

(b) Members of peer groups also exchange notes with one another about their different worlds.

(c) The membership of groups tends to promote feeling of self-worth.

(d) Not being accepted by the group may result in serious emotional problems.

(e) It leads to the pre-adolescent's changing relationship with parents.

(f) Their friends become more important than ever and will continue to be throughout adolescence

(g) The adolescents want that their parents should treat them differently.

Nine to twelve years old children still depend heavily on their families. They generally affirm that they love their parents. However, they feel their parents do not understand them.

According to thorn Burg (1979), the parents (and teachers) of pre-adolescents should remember two facts as under:

1. Radical Change : When these changes occur, pre-teens break up the well-defined, predictable behaviours and attitudes of childhood. They grow up and change the ways they do things.

2. Need for Guidance : When changes occur, pre-teens need additional guidance. Parents must remember that their direction and reassurance are important to their normal growth.

The school has to assume a wide responsibility in developing in its pupils social consciousness. It is the only institution, second to family, which is charged with the responsibility of socializing the child and the youth. It is the teacher who has no shoulder the responsibility of becoming parent substitute as soon as the child enters the school.

It is the sympathetic and skilled teacher who encourages the development of socially desirable behaviour. It is he who gives him a sense of self-esteem and feeling of security. It is he who provides opportunities to children for organised group living. It is he who leads the retiring child to assert himself and the aggressive child to learn the art of submission.

Television as a Socialising Agent

Television is an important socialising agent that influences children's behaviour and hence their development. Its role is as under:

1. Children learn both aggressive and pro-social behaviour from television.

2. Children also acquire knowledge about social relationships and social behaviour from television programmes.

Emotional Development

Though pre-adolescents are generally happy and optimistic, they also have many fears. Some of them are as under:

(a) Not being accepted into a peer group.

(b) Not doing well at school.

(c) Not having a best friend.

(d) Being punished by their parents.

(e) Getting hurt.

Other emotions in this age group include anger and fear of being unable to control it besides guilt, frustration, and jealously. It is our task to help pre-adolescents in realising that these emotions are not fearful things instead they are a natural part of their growth.

(1) Many children have unrealistic fear. They should be encouraged to discuss those fears.

(2) Feelings of guilt often come in them when a conflict takes place between children's actions, which are based on the values of the peer group and their parents values.

(3) At this stage anger is displayed with more intensity than many other emotions. The parents often tell their children that they should not have any fears. Likewise they should often tell them, they should not get angry.

Emotional Characteristics

Other emotional characteristics of upper primary children are as under:

(a) They desire attention and recognition for their personal effort and achievements.

(b) The have a wide range of behaviours and their moods can swing from one extreme to the other.

(c) They want freedom, yet they fear the loss of security.

(d) They are anxious, doubtful and confused about their physical and intellectual development.

(e) They are very sensitive to criticism of their personal short-comings.

(f) They seek adults approval and acceptance. According to Harlocks following are the characteristic of this age group.

(1) Emotions are intense - It is observed that young children respond with equal intensity to a trivial event and to serious situation.

(2) Emotions appear frequently - Children display their emotions frequently. As they discover that disapproval or punishment often follows an emotional outburst, they learn to adjust to emotion arousing situations.

(3) Emotions are transitory - Young children shift from laughter to tears, from anger to smiles or from jealously to affection. Thus, their emotions have no stability.

(4) Responses reflect individuality - In all new borns, the pattern of response is similar. By the lapse of time as the influences of learning and environment are felt, the behaviour accompanying the different emotions becomes individualised.

(5) Emotions change in strength - Emotions that are very strong at certain ages are found wanning in strength as the child grows older, while others formerly weak, become stronger.

(6) Emotions can be detected by behaviour symptoms - Children may show emotional reactions indirectly by restlessness, day-dreaming, crying, speech difficulties and nervous mannerisms such as mail-biting and thumb sucking.

Secondary and Senior Secondary School Students

An adolescent has the tendency to think about what is going on in one's own mind and to study oneself. He looks more closely at himself and defines himself differently.

The adolescents realise that these are differences between what they think and feel and, how they behave. They are dissatisfied with themselves. They critically examine their personal characteristics and compare themselves to others. This process goes on.

Adolescents try to think whether other people see and think about the world in the same way as they themselves do. They learn that other people cannot know fully what they think and feel. Thus they consider themselves knowing better than others.

1. Identity : The adolescents have cognitive ability to relate the past to the present. They think about the future. This characteristic presents the young adolescents with the problem of understanding the continuity of experience across time and projecting that continuity into the future. To accomplish the adolescents depend on several activities, some of the important activities are as under:

(i) The adolescents pay great attention on how other people view them. This is the reason why they listen carefully to their peers, parents, teachers and other adults for any information that indicates how these people view them.

(ii) The adolescents search the past and often want to know about their ancestors, family tree, their own infancy and childhood experiences.

(iii) The adolescents act on their feelings and express their beliefs and opinions accordingly. They place a high value on being honest and behave in the ways that are true to oneself.

(iv) The adolescents try to find out what kind of persons they are. For this purpose they adopt different ways. They adopt the characteristic of other people to see if those characteristic fit in them. It is found that they take on and quickly cast off the traits of peers, teachers and other acquaintances.

Erikson has given the name identity diffusion to the experience of not having sense of one's identity. This is the unpleasant awareness of continual change in oneself and of the difference between one's self-concept and how others see one to escape this troubling situation.

2. Autonomy : Adolescents have an increase in demands for autonomy that is, for self-determination. As adolescents, awareness of their increasing similarity to adults grow. It becomes increasingly difficult for them to accept adult directions. It is well known to the adolescents that they will have to take responsibility for actions as adults and they need to practice that responsibility in more and more arenas.

It is often observed that those adults who work with adolescents happen to give more advice than is necessary. It should be kept in mind that the sensitivity to the need of adolescents to maintain their autonomy is a valuable characteristic for teachers to keep in mind while dealing with them. The adolescents should be given proper guidance sometimes even firmly, without stopping them for exercising their choice. By allowing choices a teacher, can help the adolescents to develop both responsibility and independence. A teacher can prepare them for adulthood by expecting them to gradually take on more responsibility and to face the consequences of their choices.

3. Conformity : At the time when adolescents seek autonomy from their parents and other adults, they often seek to conform to their group. To gain peers acceptance the adolescents copy one another's style of dress, language and behaviour. Sometimes adolescents are seen forming a group that excludes all those who do not wear similar clothes and use similar languages.

4. Interpersonal development : Peers are the focus of adolescence. Various activities link friendship popularity, conflict with peers, dating and sexual relationships all take a tremendous amount of the adolescents time and energy. Adolescents who have similar interests and values form groups. The friendship made in adolescence may endure through life.

5. Intimacy : In early adolescence, two new needs arise as under:

(i) The need for intimacy, for a relationship with a person to share their feelings and thoughts.

(ii) The need for sexual gratification. Intimacy is first felt and needed by adolescents. There should be someone with whom they can share their feelings and emotions. They try to have intimacy first with peers, usually drown from the same sex, classmates, etc.

To communicate intimacy needs learning to talk about one's feeling and thoughts in an appealing way. Such communication needs trust in the partner's goodwill and tolerance. Learning to develop intimate communication with peers of the other sex is one of their major interpersonal attributes. They find that intimacy with the same sex is easier to achieve because they go through similar changes and are more familiar. This is the reason why the other sex is less familiar for most adolescents. The adolescents who manage to develop relationship with the other sex successfully are those ones who can separate their needs for intimacy and for sexual gratification. They give priority to developing friendship with peers of both sexes. They have great control over themselves and do not confuse sexual intimacies with intimacy that does not include sex.

Q11. (i) Which of the following statements about adolescents are true? Tick mark the correct statements.

a) Although the age at which individual children begin to mature varies, the time required for pubertal changes is quite uniform.

b) Girls typically start their pubertal growth spurt more than a year before boys.

c) During adolescence people begin feeling the need for both intimacy and sexual gratification.

Ans. b) Girls typically start their pubertal growth spurt more than a year before boys.

(ii) Which of the following teaching strategies should be used by a teacher to help students to develop a sense of industry?

a) Maintain a classroom environment that can be described as "unidimensional."

b) Avoid applying labels to students such as "good", "bad", or "above average", "below average".

c) Praise only ability, not effort.

d) Demonstrate to students that there are many paths to success.

e) All of the above can be used.

Ans. b) Avoid applying labels to students such as "good", "bad", or "above average", "below average" and

d) Demonstrate to students that there are many paths to success.

(iii) Teachers who want to help adolescents to develop a healthy sense of

identity should do which of the following?

a) State expectations from the students clearly and also set out the consequences of achieving or falling to meet the expectations.

b) Expose students to various career opportunities.

c) Given students responsibilities.

d) Accept that adolescents will sometimes confront parents, teachers and other authority figures.

e) Teachers should do all of the above.

Ans. e) Teachers should do all of the above.

(iv) Which is the best place for a student to acquire socially desirable habits and attitudes? Tick mark the correct statements.

a) School

b) Home

c) Playground

d) Groups

e) Clubs

f) Camps

Ans. a) School

Q12. Discuss about the normal development of a student.

Ans. The children or students are often told socially behaviour. By doing so we want to make them aware of socially desired behaviour.

Generally, students at the middle and secondary school stage get confused when they find that people sometimes break the rules and the rules apply to some are not always applied to others. For example, we tell children not to tear pages from their exercise books. But many a time we take out one or two blank pages from their exercise books. Similarly we teach them a lie for petty things. Such experiences probably change the children's concept of rules.

Piaget's Views on Moral Development

Piaget (1932) used the interview method to find out the various stages of moral development of the child. According to him, there are four stages of child's moral development-

1. Anomy - The first five years.
2. Heteronomy - Authority (5-8 years).
3. Heteronomy - Reciprocity (9-13 years).
4. Autonomy - Adolescence (13-18 years).

Each stage of moral development is discussed as under:

1. Anomy (The first five years) - This is the stage without the law. At this stage the behaviour of the child is neither moral nor immoral but non-moral or amoral. His behaviour is not guided by moral standard. The regulators of behaviour are pain and pleasure not morality or immorality.

2. Heteronomy- Authority (5-8 years) - Moral development at this stage is controlled by external authority. Rewards and punishments are the things that regulate moral development.

3. Heteronomy- Reciprocity (9-13 years) - At this stage, there is the morality of co-operation with peers or equals.

4. Autonomy- Adolescence (13-18 years) - This stage is called the equity stage also. While reciprocity demands strict equality, autonomy demands equity. The individual at this stage is fully responsible for his behaviour.

Kohlberg focused his attention on the development of moral judgement in children. He treated the child as a moral philosopher. Kohlberg investigated how children and adults reason about rules that govern their behaviour in certain situations. He secured their responses to a series of structured situations or moral dilemmas.

These are kohlberg's stages of moral growth

A. Pre-conventional level - In this level, the rules are set down by others to be followed by the children. There are two stages in this level.

1. Stage one - In this stage physical consequences of an action determine whether it is good or bad.

2. Stage two - Satisfaction of one's needs and sometimes the needs of other determine what is right

B. Conventional level - At this level the individual adopts rules and sometimes subordinates his needs to this level we can see two stages

1. Stage three - At this stage every student wants to be good boy or girl. Good behaviour is what pleases others and is approved by them. Student wants to perform these kind of behaviours.

2. Stage four - Every student performs one's own duty, properly, shows respect for authority and maintains the given social order for own sake.

C. Post-conventional level - At this stage people define their own values in terms of ethical principles, they have chosen to follow. This level also has two stages

1. Stage five - At this stage laws are not frozen, they can be changed for the good of society.

2. Stage six - Self chosen ethical principles define what is right. These principles are abstract and ethical not specific moral prescriptions.

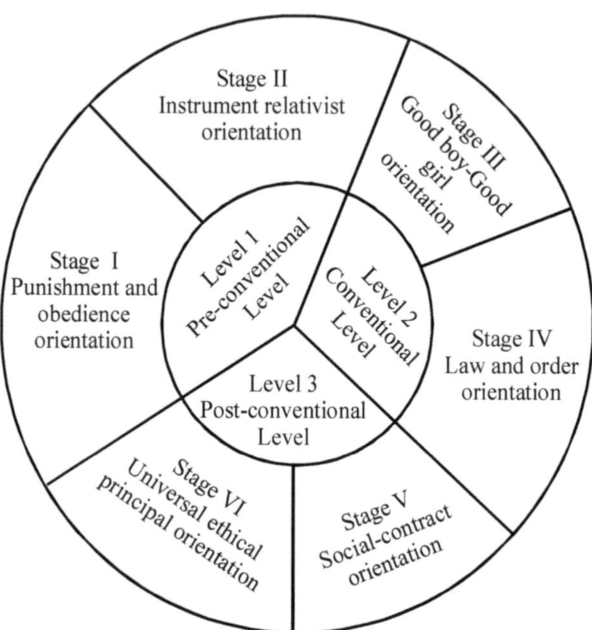

Kohlberg's stages of moral growth.

Q13. Discuss about the role of a teacher in facilitating development of children.

Ans. Role of teacher in Facilitating Development

The teacher or the school has a major role in facilitating the overall development of children once they are enrolled in the school.

Educational Implications of Physical Development

The bodily or physical health of children is indispensable for their success and efficiency in all fields of life. The psychologists have reiterated that this aspect of development should be paid the attention by all those persons who deal with the education and welfare of the children. For this purpose, the school must have a regular programme of health education. Adequate facilities for liberal participation in sport and games and other physical exercises appropriate to the level of growth should be provided to the students. We should give them practical information concerning physical growth, personal hygiene, food habits, etc. It is hoped that a brief, interesting and easily understandable task, introducing them to various development stages, would certainly help them to form a correct picture in their own minds regarding their own changing selves and their roles in life. This may also serve as safeguard against the possibility of their developing irrational worries regarding abrupt development taking place in their bodies. A teacher, can successfully accomplish this task if he has a sound knowledge of the physical development of children.

With the increased rate of physical change consequent to the transition from one phase of development to another, their behaviour and attitudes are also bound to change. We realise the varying treatment, suitable to the physical growth level, is needed by children. It is found that the upper primary, secondary and senior secondary students are very tender physically. This is the reason why they need affection and tender treatment in the classroom. Developing children must not be rashly stuffed with bookish learning. Instead of it, their educational programmes should include a combination of varied activities in and out of the classroom. Adolescents are in need of sympathetic understanding and friendliness. They are often found clumsy, awkward, aggressive and often violent.

It must be remembered that physical health is the basis of all development. The all-round and healthy development of children is exceedingly dependent upon healthy physical growth. Children who have a feeling that they are physically fit are favourably affected by this internal picturing of themselves. They are most likely to develop confidence and a will to improve further. On the other hand, children suffering from a feeling that there is something wrong somewhere in their bodies have less chance to approach life confidently and to make any substantial achievement. A teacher should therefore make efforts to promote a sense of well-being in the children by developing an interest among them in the physical culture programmers of the school. He should promote the development of positive and healthy feelings in children regarding the present state of their physical health. Taking care of physical health of the children at the school leave is the first and foremost function of the physical health instructor and the gymnastics and sports teacher.

Educational Implications of Social Development

(a) Social growth : The social growth of children is a significant process.

This growth is too important to be ignored by the teacher and the parents. Children's social development affects their whole life, including their scholastic achievement. Hence the school should try to provide adequate opportunities that are deemed to be favourable to the social growth of the children. It should create a healthy atmosphere in and outside the classroom. The children will feel it convenient and desirable to develop satisfying social relations with others.

(b) Feeling of security : A class teacher should aim at promoting a feeling of security in the minds of children. Each student should be helped to develop healthy and desirable relations with classmates. He should be inspired to participate in group activities in and out of the classroom.

(c) Knowledge full of utility : Education should develop in the student useful knowledge, skills, habits for successful and effective social living. It is desirable for the teacher to import knowledge in an interesting and stimulating manner.

(d) Form of knowledge : Merely bookish stuff is not enough. Instead of it, the teacher should bring out the social and cultural implications of the various subjects taught in the classroom.

(e) Training : In the same way the training of a student in a particular field is also socially essential. Students must be motivated to take interest in a practical scientific mechanical as technical subject. Consequently they will develop a taste for mastering useful skills in a particular practical subject. Such a mastery and the allied technical skills are economically paying and socially very helpful. It helps a student in making and maintaining desirable social relations throughout adult life. A teacher should keep in mind this fact.

(f) Inculcation of Habits : In a school, a student is able to acquire socially desirable habits and attitudes. It is observed that different children react differently to the same classroom situation. Individual attention should be paid to guide children effectively.

(i) The aggressive children must be taught the art of submission.

(ii) The sky children be given opportunities for self-assertion.

(iii) The delinquent child should be introduced to the desirability of respecting the law.

If the above said opportunities are forthcoming the child will have chance to develop into a socially healthy adult.

(g) Activities : There should be adequate provision of wider socio-cultural activities. Teachers should stimulate children to develop a keen interest in hobbies and in indoor and outdoor recreation. In this connection it is found that group play and other organized recreational activities play a vital role in the child's development. Through these recreational activities the child's makes contacts with other children, student learns to abide by the rules of the game. He is trained in the art getting along with others cheerfully. The students should be given the kinds of cultural and recreational programmes which are best suited to their development level.

(h) Organisations : The clubs, camps, group and societies should be organized for maintaining the social health of children. There should be provision of small literary and social groups, screening of educational films, drama, clubs, boy scout groups, girl guide groups, camp fires, etc. These things gave wholesome social diet for school children.

(i) Guidance : However activities of these organisations should not be entirely in the hands of children themselves. Instead there should be judicious guidance, advice and direction of the programmes by the teacher. However sufficient liberty and freedom should be given to children to manage these group organisations. It will give them great pleasure and satisfy their desire to direct their own affairs.

Q14. List out the method for helping in maintaining emotional balance.

Ans. Educational implications of emotional development : Usually children express many emotions link anger, fear, jealousy, affection, joy, pleasure, etc. Positive emotions help the child to develop a positive outlook about life. The following methods are offered to help children in maintaining emotional balance.

1) Fatigue : Tired children are difficult to handle. Therefore, efforts may be made not to cause undue fatigue to them.

2) Poor health : Children in poor health are irritable. Hence the health of children should be properly looked after.

3) Association with emotional people : Children imitate the behaviour of their elders parents, teachers and other adults and peer groups. Suitable examples should be presented by the elders.

4) Thwarted desires : The more restrictions are imposed on the child, the more revolting he becomes. This means that a suitable disciplinary mechanism should be evolved.

5) Unpreparedness : A child shows emotional outbursts when he is faced with a strange situation or for which he is not prepared. Proper training to face such situations needs to be given gradually.

6) Expression of feelings : Children should be helped to express their emotions in a natural way. They should be helped to develop a realistic understanding of situations that arouse unpleasantness.

7) Self-control : Children should be helped to learn how to control their feelings which may offend others. They should be gradually directed to exercise more of self-control.

8) Counselling : Counselling may be useful in cases of a highly disturbed emotional state of the mind.

Q15. What are the educational implication of moral development?

Ans. Educational implications of moral development : School should have an activity- oriented programme for the moral development of children.

A list of some suggested activities for the moral development of students is given below:

• Organising group projected camps, social service programmes and games
• Organising school panchayats
• Addressing daily morning school assembly
• Celebrating festivals including national days
• Showing appropriate films, stage dramas and plays
• Highlighting them to teaching of saints and seers
• Encouraging them to clean the school campus, playgrounds, public places etc.
• Looking after the school garden
• Organising girl guide and boy scout groups
• Celebrating festivals of different communities religions
• Organising educational excursions and trips
• Domesticating and rearing animal pets
• Visiting backward and slum areas and rendering some sort of service to the people living in such areas
• Arranging community and school get-togethers
• Organising a comprehensive programme of guidance and counseling for brining about moral changes.

Q16. What is the concept of cognitive development? Describe the piaget's concept of cognitive development. [June-05, Q1]

Ans. Cognitive Development - Development is the process of quantitative and qualitative growth of the child and the emergence and differentiation of capabilities over time. It is the function of maturity besides interaction with the environment.

Meaning of Cognitive and Cognitive Development

Cognitive can be interpreted as to perceiver, comprehend, conceive or simply to know. Cognitive development means the growth and capability of knowing, comprehending, or understanding over time, facilitated both by maturity and interaction with its environment. If cognition can be included, the ability to construct mental images involving thought, reasoning, memory and language. A person constructs mental images as the world around is observed, understood and internalized as a mental process. Thus every individual has a unique model based on a unique process of observation.

Process : According to Burner, cognitive development occurs in three phases:
1. Enactive (doing)
2. Ikonic (object models of pictures)
3. Symbolic (signs and symbols)

For instance, for a young child cognizing what an orange means would do as under:
(1) Touching or holding or tasting it (enactive model)
(2) Later seeing pictures of it as model of it (ikonic model)
(3) Still later gradually deciphering the word "orange" (symbolic mode)

First theory of cognitive development we will consider was developed by a biologist turned psychologist, Jean Piaget.

Piaget's Theory of cognitive Development

During the past half-century, the Swiss psychologist Jean Piaget devised a model describing how humans go about making sense of their world by gathering and organizing information.

According to Piaget (1954), certain ways of thinking that are quite simple for an adult are not so simple for a child.

Four Stages of Cognitive Development

Piaget's four stages of cognitive development are called sensorimotor, preoperational, concrete operational, and formal operational. Piaget believed that all people pass through the same four stages in exactly the same

Stage	Approximate Age	Characteristics
Sensorimotor	0-2 years	Begins to make use of imitation, memory, and thought. Begins to recognize that objects do not cease to exist when they are hidden. Moves from reflex actions to goal-directed activity.
Preoperational	2-7 years	Gradually develops use of language and ability to think in symbolic form. Able to think operations through logically in one direction. Has difficulties seeing another person's point of view.
Concrete operational	7-11 years	Able to solve concrete (hands-on) problems in logical fashion. Understands laws of conservation and is able to classify and seriate. Understands reversibility.
Formal operational	11-adult	Able to solve abstract problems in logical fashion. Becomes more scientific in thinking. Develops concerns about social issues, identity.

Infancy : The Sensorimotor Stage.

The earliest period is called the sensorimotor stage, tasting, and so on. During this period, the infant develops object permanence, the understanding that objects in the environment exist whether the baby perceives them or not.

A second major accomplishment in the sensorimotor period is the beginning of logical, goal-directed actions.

The child is soon able to reverse this action by refilling the container. Learning to reverse actions is a basic accomplishment of the sensorimotor stage.

Early childhood to the Early Elementary Years: The Preoperational Stage. By the end of the sensorimotor stage, the child can use many action schemes. Called operations, or actions that are carried out and reversed mentally rather than physically. The stage after sensorimotor is called preoperational, because the child has not yet mastered these mental operations but is moving toward mastery. The first step from action to thinking is the internalization of action, performing an action mentally rather than physically. Between the ages of 2 and 4, most children enlarge their vocabulary from about 200 to 2,000 words. Piaget, are very egocentric: they tend to see the world and the experiences of other from their own viewpoint. Egocentric, as Piaget intended it, does not mean selfish; it simply means children often assume that everyone else shares their feeling, reactions, and perspectives.

Later Elementary to the Middle School Years : The Concrete-Operational Stage. Piaget coined the term concrete operations to describe this stage of "hands-on" thinking. The basic characteristics of the stage are the recognition of the logical stability of the physical word, the realization that elements can be changed or transformed and still conserve many of their original characteristics, and the understanding that these changes can be reversed. According to Piaget, a student's ability to solve conservation problems depends on an understanding of three basic aspects of reasoning: identity, compensation, and reversibility. The student can mentally cancel out the change that has been made. Another important operation mastered at this stage is classification. Classification depends on a student's abilities to focus on a single characteristic of objects in a set and group the objects according to that characteristic. Link conservation, classification, and seriation, the student at the concrete-operational stage has finally developed a complete and very logical system of thinking. This system of thinking, however, is still tied to physical reality. The logic is based on concrete situations that can be organized, classified, or manipulated. Thus, children at this stage can imagine several different arrangements for the furniture in their rooms before they act. They do not have to solve the problem strictly though trial and error by actually making the arrangements. But the concrete-operational child is not yet able to reason about hypothetical, abstract problems that involve the coordination of many factors at once.

Junior and Senior High : Formal Operations. Some students remain at the concrete-operational stage throughout their school years, even throughout life. However, new experience, usually those that take place in school, eventually present most students with problems that they cannot solve using concrete operations. What happens when a number of variables interact, as in a laboratory experiment? Then a mental system for controlling sets of variables and working through a set of possibilities is needed. These are the abilities Piaget called formal operations. At the level of formal operations, all the earlier operations and abilities continue in force; that is, formal thinking is reversible, internal, and organized in a system of interdependent elements. The focus of thinking shifts, however, from what is to what might be. The adolescent who has mastered formal operations can contrary-to-fact questions. In answer, the adolescent demonstrates the hallmark of formal operations-hypothetico-deductive reasoning. The formal thinker can consider a hypothetical situation (people do not sleep) and reason deductively (from the general assumption to specific implications, such as longer workdays, more money spent on lighting, or new entertainment industries). Formal operations also include inductive reasoning, or using specific observations to identify general principles. For example, the economist observes many specific changes in the stock market and attempts to identify general principles about economic cycles. Formal-operational thinkers can form hypotheses, set up mental experiments to test them, and isolate or control variables in order to complete a valid test of the hypotheses.

Q17. What is the method of studying cognitive development?

Ans. Methods of studying cognitive by Piaget, is a one-to-one verbal interactive, inquiry-oriented method. It is known as the clinical method. Certain mental-operation task, in accordance with age and stage of development with supporting material, are prepared. To illustrate a typical Piaget task on probabilistic reasoning for a 14 year old student is as under:

Purpose of the task : Assessment of the child's comprehension of probability.

Materials : 95 one-inch wooden blocks of 4 different colours (35 red, 36 blue, 20 yellow and 4 green) a paper bag, a box.

Procedure : First separate four colour. There after divide each colour group into half. Give one half to the child instructing him to put them in the paper bag or box. Keep the other half in front of the child as a reference set.

The teacher says to the student "I will put out two blocks out of the bag without looking at them. Could you guess the colour that will come out?"

The procedure is continued till all the blocks are pulled out. The teacher keeps asking the child. "Why do you think it will be red?" and so on. It is done for the assessment of the reasoning of the child. Note the justifications given and also note the strategy the child uses for predicting. In between, the teacher uses counter suggestions such as, "transfer of tasks related to probabilistic reasoning are taken up in case the teacher thinks it certain the existence of cognition based on logic.

Criteria for Assessment

For the assessment of a specific level of reasoning, the student should be able to do the following-

1. To make the correct judgement.

2. To justify logically that judgement.

3. To resist successfully a counter-suggestion.

4. To provide a successful performance on a related task (Strauss 1972).

Factors Facilitating Cognitive Development

Factors facilitating cognitive are as under:

1. Internal readiness.

2. Environmental experiences.

3. Social experience.

4. Equilibration.

Piaget and other cognitivists such as wads worth, Flavell, Sullivan etc. put emphases on interactions and equilibration. The key to cognitive development as it relates to educational practice, is the activity of the students, their actions on objects, events and other people. Social interaction relates to cognition through interactive modes with people. Here a person learns about relationship, concepts e.g. competition, co-operation.

Cultural mores and practices, etc. Language in the medium of social experience. The language may be verbal non-verbal.

Q18. What is divergent thinking? Make list a list of dimensions of creativity. How could you identity a creative child?

Ans. Divergent Thinking – Divergent thinking or lateral thinking is the essence of cognitive development. For example some one ask what is the opposite of the word dark. Bright is an acceptable answer. Consider another situation, what is the opposite of a cupboard? Or what ideas come to your mind when you think of sunset? The answer to these questions are not straight jacketed. They may be unlimited, with varying degrees of acceptability. This is the essence of divergent or lateral thinking which means to think in unusual, novel and unique ways.

Concept of Divergent Thinking – In divergent thinking, we think in different directions, sometimes searching what, and sometimes seeking variety. Lateral thinking is another expression used for divergent thinking, it means an original line of enquiry. Creativity or divergent thinking can be identified with openness in expressing feeling, receptivity to ideas, concern for others, desire to grow as a person and actualize one's potentials. Hence creativity is the playful exploration of thoughts by a person who is open, curious and imaginative.

Dimensions of Creativity – Creativity is related to divergent thinking. Therefore, creativity is a multi-dimensional concept. A child with the following characteristic dimensions gives more evidence of divergent or creative thinking than others:

1) Fluency : Ability to mange successfully when a number of ideas are sought.

It is the total number of relevant responses given by an individual to a given stimulus.
Example : In how many ways can you use a stick, a toothbrush etc.?
Scoring : Count the number of ideas produced in each case; their total is your fluency score.

2) Flexibility : The ability to shift your reference and think of various alternatives. It shows the capacity of an individual to use different approaches in responding to a stimulus.
Example : Make a list of five different factors which you would bear in mind in mind when you opt for a career.
Scoring : Each new multiple criterion gets a score. The more the alternative criteria, the more the flexibility score.

3) Originality : The production of novel, usual ideas which are also useful, relevant and apt. It is your capacity to give original responses to a stimulus.
Example : Form a figure using these lines or use the words rough, smooth, fault, and vault and make a poem.
Scoring : A novel, unique and relevant idea gets a score.

4) Elaboration : The ability to generate various alternatives (details) that implement or spell out an idea.
Example : Sarah put her foot on the 10 foot long snake.
Scoring : Varied details that have facilitated or elaborated get a score.

Identification of a Creative Child

More or less every child has the capacity behaviour but some have specific creativity in some areas such as science, artistic contribution etc. It is however, a difficult task to identify a creative child. The following are the major characteristics you may link to look for in your students:

(1) Original thought, expression, action and behaviour
(2) Ask uncomfortable questions at times
(3) Persists/argues for his or her point of view
(4) Proposes alternatives to solutions
(5) Displays a high degree of risk-taking behaviour
(6) Self-concept is high, tends to be more anxious and possesses a greater degree of need for achievement
(7) More tolerant of ambiguity, and

(8) Curiosity/independent and exhibits more autonomy.

Implication for Classroom Teacher

To increase the fluency, flexibility. Originality and exploration of the students thinking/behaviour, the teacher can provide certain conditions.

(1) Pose open-ended, divergent questions with the focus on alternative responses and novelty, and not on right or wrong.

(2) Excessive discipline, reliance on text books, emphasis on rote learning or criticising students for wrong answer reduce their creative potential.

(3) Encourage children to experiment, innovate, discover, hypothesis or imagine possible solutions to any pressing issue.

(4) Develop a spirit of inquiry, tolerate uncertainty; help to speculate, cultivate a deliberate pace of thinking, etc.

(5) Adopt a multi-disciplinary approach to teaching.

(6) Create a supportive environment.

(7) Appreciate student's creative efforts.

(8) Assign/suggest activities of an inter-disciplinary nature.

(9) Use teaching aids that stimulate imagination.

(10) Resist from premature evaluation.

Q19. Discuss the language development of a child at secondary school level.

Ans. Experiential Basis – A study of the development of our language results in a discovery that it is abstraction of a high order. To use the system (words) intelligently requires that one not know the meanings of the respective symbols but that he know the relationships existing among the various combinations. English Language. To the person trained in another tongue the English language seems to lack any logical sequence: it is not regular and leads to much confusion. If the listener does not have the experimental background, a series of words (a sentence) may sound) link a drawn-out hum when uttered in rapid fashion. A man mumbles his lunch order to a waitress. She may not fully hear, yet never misses because those combinations have come to mean but one thing to her.

Language Development – Language is a part of our social heritage and has become more and more complicated with the ages. Some systematization has taken place. We give attention to word endings to label a particular person. Such as mortgage, teacher, realtor, etc. These forms did not just happen, they grew up very definite ways and were adopted through usage. They were accepted just as any word is labeled and becomes dignified today "Chiseler" is a word at point, put into good usage by one of our Presidents and given a very limited and definite connotation.

Contemporary Trends – These familiar endings together with the prefixes and suffixes enable the student to get from new words something of value. At one time an attempt was made to analyze the words completely; that procedure gave way to the use of words as expressed though sentences or parts of sentence. Today, largely due to the emphasis that is being given to good speech, there is gradually growing up a tendency toward the dissecting process.

Effect on Personality. Speech is one of the forms of behaviour which plays an important role in the personality of the individual. The teacher, at all times, should plan his procedure so as to promote the proper mental attitude in the student before calling upon him to recite. Getting the proper start in oral expression will often spell the difference between a good and a poor recitation.

Voice. If a student's voice is satisfying to himself it gives him that confidence which is helpful to clear thinking and especially helpful to continue fluency. It is quite possible to talk well for a long time if there is no undue emotional disturbance, the breathing will then function normally, thereby assisting rather than fluent speech.

Form of Expression – Language as a form of expression is essentially social and useful in communication. It results from a need that has arisen to make another to do one's bidding. It is essential to all the mental process. If we are conscious of something which, if expressed, must be made known though some form of language. The functioning of language and the thought processes cannot be separated. We are rhythmic in nature and the motor processes of language are likewise rhythmical. This rhythm varies among people and accounts for many of the links and dislikes of expressions made by others-either oral or written.

Emphasis on Large Units – Psychology recognizes that words should be taught rather than letters. There is a tendency towards unit reaction. The entire body mechanism responds to stimulus, be it a word or a sentence. So long as a unit idea is present, performance is satisfying. Hence, sentences rather than words should be taught, especially when they serve as a completed unit. An intensive study of formal grammar can be deferred perhaps to the college period. If more attention is given to the usage of units and more practice devoted to their correct form, the time may come when many of the dissecting processes can be completely discarded. The five year old either uses good English or he does not.

Environment. This will depend upon his immediate environment. He is concerned with expression and formulates his ideas in units. He has no need for the disturbing labels which are given to the parts of the unit which he already so ably manipulates. We do not reach the various parts of a machine to all automobile drivers before we train them to be expert operators. If the driver encounters difficulties on the way he can call the expert, the service man. Likewise the pupil can call the expert to guide him in expression and with this guidance he, too, can become proficient.

Appreciation and Expression – The teacher must not only recognize that appreciation is both intellectual and emotional, but he should make possible for each pupil to have a chance to respond to appreciation-arousing situations. In this the teacher should keep in mind the differences in emotional reaction, and the differences in interest which prevail among pupils.

Extent of appreciation – The extent of the appreciation will depend largely upon the number of emotion-arousing elements present as compared with the number of intellectual factors inherent in the situation for any particular student. Literature should be taught for appreciation and for art of expression.

Responsibility of a teacher – The high school teacher of literature has a far reaching responsibility. In high school is determined the attitude which the student will take in his adulthood towards all the mass of books with which he will be stimulated. If the high school student is compelled to analyze to the point of boredom the masterpieces of literature he will be driven form the good to the frothy. The literary studied in high school should be so treated that they will become the companions of the high school student, urging him on the further delightful hours with other selections of their kind.

Q20. What are the functions of language? Write down the main problems of language development and how can teachers help student to solve them?

Ans. Language performs a number of functions based on the purpose of its use. Some of its functions are as under:

1. Instrumental : The way an individual satisfies the need by asking for something (May I take your pen?).

2. Regulatory : Controlling another's behaviour (e.g. teacher asks the student "sit quiet, please").

3. Interactional : Used for maintaining interpersonal (e.g. wishing a friend a happy birthday).

4. Personal : Where one talks about oneself (e.g. I am feeling very depressed today)

5. Heuristic : To find out about the world in general (e.g. Is there any drug to cure AIDS?)

6. Imaginative : Where one talks about one's imagination (e.g. write an essay on the topic "You are on the clouds").

7. Informational : To seek and give varied types of information (e.g. What is the current rate of population growth in over country?)

Language and Culture

Language and culture are related as under:

1. Language helps children to learn habits, traditions, religions and customs of their culture.

2. Language is a carrier of one's culture.

3. Every culture defines what to say, when and to whom, just as it dictates pronunciation, syntax and vocabulary.

4. In culture where politeness is valued, for example, children at a very early age.

5. Sometimes children have to cope with the demands of two different cultures at the same time.

Problems of Language Development

Children develop language skills through socialisation. But it is evident that all children are not equal in their language ability. Some children face problem in this regard. The main problems of language development faced by children are presented as under :

1. Lack of initial listening and speaking opportunities.

2. Poor concept development.

3. Over emphasis on writing prematurely.

4. Inadequate cognition of word meanings.

5. Inability to express through the spoken or written medium.

6. Blocks due to genetic impairment of emotional problems of an impoverished environment.

7. Ambiguities in comprehension such as phonological, lexical or deep structural ambiguities etc.

Implications for Teachers

In this reference, the teacher has a great responsibility. The teacher should be aware of the problems face by students in the classroom. He should create a homely environment in his class. The students should feel free to express and share their feelings, opinions and viewpoints with their teacher.

The teacher has to keep the following in his viewpoint:

1. Language is learned and developed in a social context for functional purposes.

2. Older children should be provided with ample scope to develop listening, speaking, reading and writing skills.

3. Setting where language may be used for various purposes should be created.

4. One should be cognizant of multilingual interferences, identify them and provided remedies.

5. Students creative efforts should be encouraged.

6. Excessive writing or rote repetition should be de-emphasised, a relaxed environment for free expression of ideas, thoughts and feelings should be provided.

7. Students should be helped to develop early reading habits and enable them to do book reviews.

Q21. Briefly define the concept of personality. [Dec-07, Q1]

Ans. Personality: Concepts and Meaning : Personality is the most abstract word used in English language. Its connotative significance is very broad but denotative significance, negligible. Scarcely any word is more versatile. There is no single definition which may be regarded as correct. Some of the definitions are psychological, some are not. The first task is to distinguish between them and the second task is to select from among available psychological definitions one that best fits the phenomenon one wants to assess.

The word personality has been derived from the word 'persona' which means theatrical mask. 'Persona' has four distinct meanings:

(a) What one appears to others and not what one really is.

(b) The part one plays in life.

(c) The sum total of qualities.

(d) Distinction and dignity as in style of writing.

According to the first meaning personality may be thought as external appearance and not the true self. The second meaning of persona regards personality as a role which the player assumes. The third involves distinctive personal qualities in the personality and the last derivative has significance of prestige and dignity.

Q22. Discuss the main approaches to personality. [Dec-05, Q2]

Ans. The field of personality has been approached in various ways. Certainly, any theory of personality would require to explain both, its structure and its dynamics: The explanation is as under:

1. Explanation of structure

(i) Bio-physical approach.

(ii) Bio-social approach

2. Explanation of the dynamics

(i) Psychoanalytical

(ii) Psychosocial

(iii) Social learning

(iv) Personological

(v) Spiritual

(vi) Some concepts of significance

Within each of these approaches, different theorists have forwarded different explanations.

1. Bio-Physical Approaches

It is assumed by the bio-approaches to personality that an individual's personality is determined by his biological and constitutional characteristics. This is done by popular wisdom. Popular wisdom relates joviality with fat people and impulsive anger with the lean and thin. Three propositions gathered from the literature are as under:

(1) Hippocratus Galen's Proposition : According to this proposition personality is determined by "humours" (secretions of glands) blood (red, sanguine), phlegm, yellow (choleric) bile and blank (melancholic) bike.

(2) Kretschmer's Proposition : According to the proposition personality can be explained by reference to the body-build of the individual, short and think (pyknik), slender and weak (asthenic) and balanced physique (athletic).

(3) Sheldon's Proposition : Personality is determined by the nature of embryonic development which results in and is identified by over-development of the stomach (endomorph), or of the muscles (mesomorph) or of the head (ectomorph).

2. Bio-social Approaches

It is assumed by bio-social approaches that personality is formed by the interplay between the individual's biological dispositions and the social-cultural forces impinging upon him. The psychologists who supported this approach studied personal characteristics and/or personality ratings of large samples of persons and subjected the data to statistical analysis.

Eyesenck was interested in a classificatory structure. He derived a 2*2 structure formed by two polarities. Cattell was interested in an elaborate description of structure. He derived a set of 16 factors, called "source-traits." Their propositions can be stated as below:

(1) Eyesenck's Proposition : He explained individual's personality. Two independent polarities, namely, extroversion-introversion and neuroticism stability. They generate by their interactions the four types in the bio-physical Hippocratus Galen's proposition as figured below:

(2) Catell's Proposition : He explained individual's personality structure by psychograph or profile in which he showed his position on bipolar "source tracts" or "primary factors". These are 16 in adults, 14 in adolescents, 12 in children, each shaped by the interplay of heredity and environment differently. An individual's psychographs or 16 PE profiles constructed on different occasions may vary on account of change in mental state or social role.

3. Psychoanalytical Approaches : It was Freud who posited the psychoanalytical approach to diagnose and treat the root psychic causes of pathological behaviours as psychomic patient. Freud looked at the past history of the patient and propounded a theory as follows:

(i) Role of Long Forgotten Memories : We can study an individual's personality by digging up the long forgotten memories of childhood, especially pertaining to breast weaning, toilet-training and relationship with the parent of the opposite sex and the parent of the same sex.

(ii) Id versus Super-ego : We can explain personality-formation by reference to the battle between the natural "id" of pleasure-seeking impulses and the individual's "superego" formed by internalization of the external social-moral demands.

(iii) Role of Defence Mechanism : An individual personality is determined by the furnishing of his "ego" (reality-self) trying to resolve the conflicts between the id and the super-ego by using a variety of techniques called "defence-mechanisms."

4. Psycho-social Approaches : Psycho-social approaches are an outgrowth of the psychoanalytical approach. Adler started as a co-worker with Freud but shortly afterwards come to differ with him. He asserted that human life is not a battle between the id and supper-ego. Instead it was a conscious struggle to achieve superiority which can be facilitated by social factors. Later on, Erikson forwarded this theory of psycho-social development through the entire life-span development through the entire life-span.

Erikson's Propositions : The development of personality can be explained by reference to a series of crises emerging in the eight development stages of life. Each stage prepares for the next in anticipation.

5. Social Learning Approaches : Social learning approaches of personality is rooted in the behaviouristic stimulus response (S-R) psychology. It asserts that man learns, to make responses to stimuli present or constructed in the environment. According to them the interpretations based on "psyche" are not empirical but fabricated only. Two propositions of this type are presented as under:

(i) Cooley's Proposition : He tried to explain personality by reference to the "looking glass self of the individual, his/her self-concept that develops or the basic of how other people of significance in the environmental define him.

(ii) Skinner's Proposition : In his opinion an individual's personality is shaped by manipulation of stimuli in small steps and provision of appropriate reinforcements.

6. Personological Approaches : Personological approaches believe that the human being is an active creator of his or her personality, imbid with a "force for growth" within him or her. This characteristic makes human being different from the rest of the animal kingdom. Rogers and Maslow are the best known in this group. A brief description of them is as under:

(i) Roger's Proposition : The human personality is determined by the efforts of the person to define maintain and enhance his own growing "self" which maintains itself by the use of Freudian defence mechanisms.

(ii) Maslow's Proposition : Individual's personality can be explained by making a reference to the fulfillment of his or her basic deficiency needs (D-needs) and meta-needs (B-needs) of the growth of his being as under:

(a) Basic deficiency needs (D-needs)

(a) Physiological needs
(b) Safety needs
(c) Esteem needs
(d) Love and belongingness needs

(b) Meta-needs (B-needs)

(a) Needs for self-actualisation
(b) Aesthetic needs
(c) Desire to know and understand

7. Spiritual Approaches : The spiritual development of an individual has been the typical philosophic theme of Indian culture. The spiritual development of personality is referred to in terms of "self-realisation" which should be distinguished from "self-realisation." Self-actualisation is the ideal of realism which postulates that an individual possesses. A self. This self is waiting to become actuality. On the other hand self-realisation is the ultimate goal of the spiritual philosophy of idealism. It holds that the real-self of an individual is the divine or spiritual self. It always waits to be discovered and realised. Indian thought has described the ultimate spirit as "sacchindananda" comprising "sat" (existence), "chit" (consciousness) and "ananda" (bliss).

This divine spirit exists in man covered under fine Kosha (sheaths), namely matter (annamya), vital (pranamaya), psyche (manomaya), intellect (vijnanamaya) and bliss (anandamaya)

There are three model paths to realize the spirit (atman). These paths are the intellectual (jnana yoga), the emotional (bhakti yoga) and the actional (harma yoga). Center has identified, for example, ananda yoga (akin to bhakti yoga) in Tagore Karma yoga in Sri Aurobindo. Their propositions are stated below:

(i) Tagore's Proposition. We can explain human personality by reference to the development of the "physical man" into a "personal man" through sub-conscious experiencing of rhythm and harmony between man and nature (universe). As a result, there is the expression of "surplus" energy in man, his limitless potentiality.

(ii) Gandhi's Proposition. According to Gandhiji personality can be explained by reference to the efforts of man in search of truth and "ahinsa" (universal love and concern) through actions which are characterised by selflessness and attachment (anasakti).

(iii) Sir Aurobindo's Proposition. According to him the individual's personality can be explained by reference to his or her "evolution" from the biogenic matter-state to the supermind state which is achievable through integral yoga.

Some Concepts of Significance

Some concepts having significant relationship with personality are as under:

(1) Achievement Motivation - Individuals can be differentiated as high and low on achievement motivation (n-ach). Individuals differ in terms of

(a) Degree or achievement motivation.

(b) Fear of failure (FF).

(c) The value they attach to their achievements.

Locus of Control. Individuals can be differentiated as "externals" or "internals" on locus of control.

(a) Externals believe that life situations are controlled by chance, luck of authorities.

(b) Internals believe that situations are within the control of the person and tend to become independent.

(2) Cognitive Style - Individuals can be differentiated as "field independent" and "field dependent" in their cognitive style.

(a) Field-independents perceive easily the part and the whole separately and are found to be independent.

(b) Field-dependents fail to perceive parts hidden in the whole and became prone to social influences, what others say.

(3) Sensation seeking - Individuals can be differentiated as high or low sensation seekers (SS). Their description is as under:

(a) High SS seek adventure, thrill, unusual experiences (may be musical or drugs) and dislike routine.

(b) Low SS prefer simplicity and quietude.

Q23. Write down the main factors affecting the growing personality of an individual. [June-07, Q1]

Ans. As personality is a complex concept we have an interaction of a number of factors that go to shape the personality of an individual. Some of the general factors are:

1. Genetic factors.

2. Physique.

3. Environmental factors.

4. Personal response.

Both the inherited factors and the environment determine what a child would be. The environmental factors that include parental circumstances, infantile, experiences, home conditions, parent-child relationships, school and society, cultural and sub-cultural influences exerted by school, church and community, all play an effective role in the shaping of personality characteristics.

Genetic Factors : The effect of genetic factors on personality is not direct as there is little evidence that there is a causal relationship between inherited factors and personality traits, such as co-operativeness, aggressiveness and honesty. Hereditary factors exert their effect upon the organism through the constitution make-up. The organism responds to the external world with his psychological mechanisms which the hereditary factors control. Heredity affects the endocrine gland structure which in turn affects the behavioural traits of an individual. Hereditary plays an important role in endocrine structure and its functioning. The endocrines such as thyroid, pituitary, pancreas, gonads and adrenals pour hormones directly into blood stream.

Effect of Body-build on Personality : The laymen believes that the big muscular boy is dominant and aggressive, the fat girl is jolly and easy going and that the lean and thin person is serious and tense. Some psychologists have tried to relate body structure to personality traits.

Body build has a relationship with personality trait, but it should be remembered that in most cases the relationship between physique and behaviour is a result of social behaviour; for example, a child who is suffering from some physical handicap is rebuffed by his peers and is considered loss worthy than the normal one. No direct causal relationship can be assumed to exist between body structure and personality traits.

Environmental Factors : The environmental factors that play a significant role in shaping the personality of an individual are his home, his socio-economic status, community's educational institutions, government, community, religious institutions, local customs and mores.

Home is the most important environmental factor that shapes the personality traits of children.

Socio-economic status of children and youths affects their personality traits through different social goals, ideals and attitudes.

The School can also improve the home conditions by giving parents proper guidance as regards in improvement in nutritional standards and beautification of homes and other sanitary conditions.

Society : The neighbourhood, sub-culture and general culture have also a potent influence upon what a child will be.

Sibling relations : Brothers and sisters are called sibling.

(a) It is seen that a sibling-less only child tends to become overprotected and self-centered unless the parents deal with the child differently.

(b) The eldest child happens to be an only child till the second is born when the first is "dethroned" from the function of solitary affection. It generally develops jealousy in him or her.

(c) Children in intermediate positions have mixed experiences they may tend to suffer more from inferiority feelings generated by comparison. The youngest child is never deprived of the affections of parents and may turn into a spoilt if "babied" child.

Mass-media : The mass media radio, television, the newspaper and the magazine or the comic, etc. communicate to the child the styles of the various sub-cultures in the total culture. Certainly the variety makes the child aware of other forms, objects and styles and creative tensions in him.

Thus we see that the personality development is a resultant of two main factors:

(i) What we are (heritage)

(ii) What we have (environment)

But there is also another factor which should not be lost sight of. It is the individual's response. Two persons perceive the same stimuli but they react to them in quite different ways. One's response is an outcome of one's potential (heritage) as acted upon by environment. Thus, one's personality is the resultant of three forces; what one is, what one has, and what one does.

Q24. Critically discuss the influence of environmental factors on personality development of child.

Ans. Environmental factors play a significant role in the personality development of children. These are the influences of environmental factors on personality development of children.

1. Rearing patterns – Interactions between the infant and mother for satisfaction of biological needs play a significant role in personality development. Care develop a sense of security. Over indulgence or under indulgence of the mother in breast-feeding would determine the oral personality and severity in toilet-training is the 'anal' personality. A mother can make her child disciplined from his/her childhood by providing him/her positive environment. A mother should give balanced affection to her children to make his/her balanced personality.

2. Regularity – Regularity in feeding practices would develop in the child basic trust in the world. While if mother does not maintain regularity in feeding practice then it can develop mistrust in child for world. Similarly toilet-training severity may cause the child to grow into a doubting and shameful person. So mother should have regularity in feeding and other practices to develop personality of her child positively.

3. Parent-Child interaction – Parents behaviour also influences personality development of a child. If the behaviour of parents is rejective then child can face difficulties in adjustment and feel insecurity, nervousness and shyness while dominating parents can make their child dependable shy, polite, self conscious, un-cooperative bold and quarrelsome. Submissive parents can also influence on child. They can make him/her careless, disobedient, independent, self confident etc. Parents should have harmonious, well adjusted behaviour so that they could make their child calm, happy, cooperative, superior in adjustment and independent. Child accepted behaviour make a child socially acceptable and confident. If parents play with their child then he/she feels secure and self reliant. Thus we can say that the parent-child interaction play a significant role in the development process of personality of a child.

4. Social class of the family – Generally, middle class parents tend to develop in their children a sense of self direction, the power of decision-making. Parents in lower class homes do not have experience of building independence and controlling the behaviour of the child. The children of such families develop an attitude that the situations or environment are given and cannot be changed. Thus we can say that the social class of family also influence very much the personality development of a child.

5. Sibling relations – A child's brother and sister also influence his/her personality development. A sibling less only child tends to become overprotected and self centred. The eldest child happens to be an only child till the second is born. The youngest child is never deprived of the affection of parents and may turn into a spoil child. Some studies that the first born children have contributed more geniuses while the last born children tend to contribute some creative, expressive persons. Parents should make positive and balanced behaviour among their children.

6. Neighbourhood – Neighbourhood of child influences his/her personality development very much. A child learns very much from his/her neighbourhood Children see and feel the behaviour of the parents of neighbourhood towards their children and compare to it with their own cases. Children see various family styles and learns how to deal with the variety. If a child finds negative environment in his/her neighbourhood then he can not develop his personality positively.

7. Peer group – A child learns very much from his/her peer group. The child learns to take turns, to suppress his/her wish in favour of the decision of the group. A child moulds his/her behaviour to the standards set by the group which suggests to him continually what would please the group. If a child find acceptable and positive peer group relations, then he/she can build his/her personality positively.

8. School – The school environment makes a child learn punctuality, regularity, and scheduling by conditioning through the bell when to arrive, when to study various subjects, when to play and when to leave for home etc. Although students learn from curriculum of the school but a lot is learn through the school environment in its hidden curriculum. A child can learn rules and regulations to be followed from school environment.

9. Mass-Media – The mass media radio, television, the newspaper and the magazine or the comics etc communicate to the child the styles of the various sub cultures in the total culture. Today T.V., films, etc. are influencing the personality development of a child very much. Now we can say that various environmental factors influence very much the personality development of a child.

Q25. What is the impact of mass media on personality? [June-06, Q3(vii)]

Ans. Films, television, radio, newspapers and magazines are the most prominent forms of the mass media. They influence the behaviour pattern of persons in a different manner.

1. Films : Films create an environment in which one experiences a near real life situation empathically for about two hours and a half. The growing personality of childhood and adolescence figs in the films of their taste the portrayals of reality (which they believe are true). They long for glamour of appearance, role models and villains, and varying patterns and styles of behaviour, how and whom to respect or fight. The impact of films is increasing continuously since the tried of hero-portrayal has shown a shift from the mythological, historical, national and social to a matured individual, to a frustrated post-adolescent and to loving and tormented adolescent.

2. Television : Television creates an entirely different sort of environment. It exerts its influence as under-

(i) Through its serial presentations it encompasses one's thought by continual and prolonged discussion of the role-models and patterns of behaviour.

(ii) It forces a person to tune in on time.

(iii) A person viewing television, gets engrossed it as if all what he is watching is true.

(iv) The viewer realise that by the visual stimuli only time has been spent for nothing.

(v) It turns the constant into a passive person as it permits no time and imagination to express oneself in one's own way.

(vi) The school going children and adolescents start neglecting their education, if parents do not intervene.

(vii) The long arrays of advertisements initiate the child and the adolescent into exploring market products and change or develop food habits, bathing habits, clothing habits and some inferiority complexes.

3. Radio : Prior to the emergence of television, radio was the major mass medium. The impact of radio relates to the social awareness, knowledge and role models and personal upbringing, besides entertainment.

4. Newspaper : The mass medium of newspaper has two basic characteristic:

(i) It is restricted to those who can read and

(ii) It reports and discusses reality.

Each newspaper reflects and builds a particular ideology of thought or reality. It also motivates the development of regularity.

The result is that generally newspaper-reading becomes a habit of the individual. It develops in readers awareness and knowledge of the events across the world.

5. Magazines : The magazines present a collection of reading in a selective area. A magazine creates a selective environment. Consistent and persistent interest in a magazine gradually builds in the individual typical attitudes and values communicated through the magazine. Thus, it becomes evident that mass media play prominent role in affecting and moulding the personality of an individual.

Q26. How will you as a teacher, facilitate social development of your student?

Ans. Social growth or development of children is very important process

which cannot be ignored by the teachers and the parents. Teacher can facilitate social development of his/her students. Teacher should create a healthy social atmosphere in and outside the classroom where students could develop/learn social relations, norms, values etc.

Teacher should provide various group activities for students where students could work participately and co-operatively with their classmates. Teacher should try to develop healthy and desirable social relations among classmates. The aim of education should be to develop in the students useful knowledge, skills, habits and attitudes that are fundamental to successful and effective social living. Teacher should try to make an environment where students would not develop the feeling of being inferior to others. Teacher should not make any difference among his/her students due to their caste, sex, religion, social class etc. The organisation of clubs, camps, group and societies is also very helpful in maintaining the social health of children. Teacher should leave the activities of these organisations entirely in the hands of children themselves. Judicious guidance, advice and direction of the programmes by the teacher are always helpful in getting the maximum social gain out of these group activities. Thus teacher can facilitate social development of students very much.

Understanding the Learner as a Unique Individual

Q1. What are individual differences? Enumerate the important ones with examples. **[June-07, Q1]**

Ans. Individual Differences : Individual differences are the individual's abilities, aptitudes, attainments, interests and attitudes. There are also temperamental and emotional differences.

Abilities. Individuals vary in both the quality and quantity of their intelligence. Three broad categories of intelligence have been identified in school children when they are about to enter secondary schools. These are general intelligence, verbal intelligence (including ability in number) and practical-spatial intelligence.

Memory and ability to reason. In is also possible to distinguish within general intelligence between memory and the ability to reason and find relations. With American pupils Thurstone has identified primary abilities, which include verbal ability, word fluency, numerical ability, memory, spatial ability, reasoning and perception.

Variation in quantity of intelligence. In order to study variations between individuals in the quantity of intelligence we may take the results of applying a verbal intelligence test designed for a 10-11 year old population. Many of the published and unpublished tests contain about one hundred times and the mean scores usually fall within the score range of 40-50 correctly answered items. These items are shown in the following table:

Standardized Score To an I.Q. Basis	Percentage of Children within This Group	Description	Approximately Suitable for Secondary and Higher Education
145 and over	.2	Exceptionally bright	University and higher education.
130-144 115-129	1.8 10	Very bright Bright	Grammar school, technical schools and technical college university
110-114 85-99	38 38	Average	Secondary Modern School
70-84	10	Dull and Backward	Special class in Secondary Modern School
55-69	1.8	Montally Deficient	Schools for educationally subnormal
Below 55	.2	Idiots	Institutions (ineducable in the ordinary sense).

Other Conditions. It does not follow that the exceptionally bright child will become a Newton, Goethe, Shelley, or Galton. Many other conditions have to be fulfilled. The child would need zeal, energy and opportunity. Very brilliant children may tend to become isolated, particularly if they have poor or restricted home backgrounds. Their vocabulary and thought is on different plane from that of their relations and intimates: The ideal conditions for a brilliant child are that his home and surroundings should be cultured and intellectually stimulating. Galton was such a child, that he enjoyed a stimulating and intellectual background at home. Conditions were nearly ideal for him.

Aptitudes. When the psychologist speaks of an aptitude has in mind the potentiality a person has to succeed in an occupation or school attainment. He devises tests to discover in advance whether a person has an aptitude for learning foreign languages or for engineering. The aptitudes which interest us most at the end of the primary school years are those for the different kinds of secondary education. It is primarily a question of aptitudes, on the one hand, for academic, abstract and bookish education and, on the other, for practical, constructive, creative, technical education.

Problem of Variations. Clearly the problem of variations (from individual to individual) in these aptitudes relates to the similar problem of variation in the quality of intelligence, which we have just discussed in the previous section. Are these individual differences so marked as to justify our view that the aptitudes for the two broad field of study really exist? The answer is affirmative on the whole. The tests and other situations designed to measure the aptitudes correlate very significantly with the later measure of attainment in the grammar or technical school subjects.

The Criterion. This measure is called the criterion, and the correlation between aptitude tests and the criterion given the predictive power of the tests. The choice of a criterion, whether of success in a grammar or technical school, presents some difficulty. For instance, we usually make use of examination results, but a child may profit more from a secondary school than his success in school examinations reveals. For all that, success in examinations during and at the end of school ranks very high in the pupils, parents, teachers and employers opinion of what constitutes secondary school progress.

Estimates. Such estimates have to be discussed carefully to avoid unwanted 'halos'. Generally the fuller and richer the criterion the less objective it is. The simple compromise seems to lie in the five or fifteen point scale, preliminary discussion of the scale, and the choice of concrete examples to illustrate the criterion; for the benefit of those required to make the assessments.

Graded scale. The graded scale can also be applied to less tangible features of the secondary pupil's development-his emotional and social reactions to school life, his interests and aptitudes-which form a considerable part of his 'profit' in the secondary school.

Attainments. It is unfortunate that the interest we have shown in the past in attainment in the barest 'core' subjects of the three R's has itself limited the children's opportunity for enriching their experience and making the widest use of their powers. This tendency has been further aggravated by the objective test methods used to evaluate attainment in Arithmetic and English, for these methods tend to be reflected in current teaching practice.

When the pupil passes to the grammar school we assume that the richer the curriculum the better. It is also particularly important to apply this principle fully in the curriculum of the secondary modern school.

Interests. Any topics which interests a child are of significance in his education, but two fields of his interests are of particular value: the school subjects he likes best and the leisure activities with most interest him. Among interests in school subjects, those marking off academic or bookish interests from practical and non-literary interests may be of assistance in the allocation of pupils to secondary schools.

Q2. Define intelligence. **[June-06, Q2][June-05, Q3(iv)]**

Ans. Few problems are more significant to teachers than to understand the nature and nurture of intelligence and a few terms in educational psychology have been so variantly defined as intelligence. Below are given a few definitions of intelligence to explain what intelligence is.

Definitions of Intelligence – Binet who devised an intelligence test for the first time never gave a formal definition of intelligence. His scales originated not from a final theory of intelligence but from a research to discover individual difference. To him intelligence seemed to be the result of a complex interaction of higher mental processes and with this idea in mind he believed that intelligence could be measured by an extensive sampling of many kinds of test items. L.M. Terman, states that intelligence is the ability to do abstract thinking.

Intelligence-Approaches – Intelligence has been investigated from different approaches. Notable among them are psychometric approach and information possessing approach which are as under:

Psychometric approach – This approach (the psychology of dealing with the measurement of differences among people) endeavours to measure differences in intellectual abilities. In its opinion, intelligence is the ability to learn in an abstract manner or to think or adapt to his or her environment. On an analysis of this definition it becomes clear that there is found certain degrees of relationships among learning ability, abstract thought and adaptability. This reflects the close agreement among young psychometricians about intelligence as intellectual ability involving several related mental operations such as abstract thought, learning ability and adaptability shown as under:

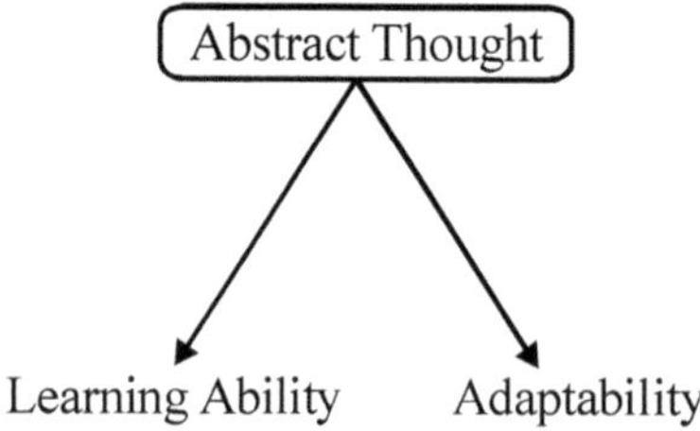

Psychometric Approach – Among the theories of intelligence, there is two-factor theory and the multifactor theory:

1. The two-factor theory of intelligence : It states that all human intellectual abilities have in common a general factor.

Superman's theory is an example. He calls the general factor the 'g' factor. He describes it as the mental energy involved in all mental activities. He adds the specific factor's in intelligence which is specific to a task.

2. The multifactor theory of intelligence : It describes intelligence in terms of separate factor or underlying specific abilities. Thurstone's and Gulford's theories are examples of this type. Their description is as under :

Thurstone's theory of primary mental abilities : This theory states that the under mentioned nine factors make up intelligence and each is involved in several intellectual operations.

1. Numerical factor (ability for mathematical operations)

2. Space factor (ability for manipulating objects in space)

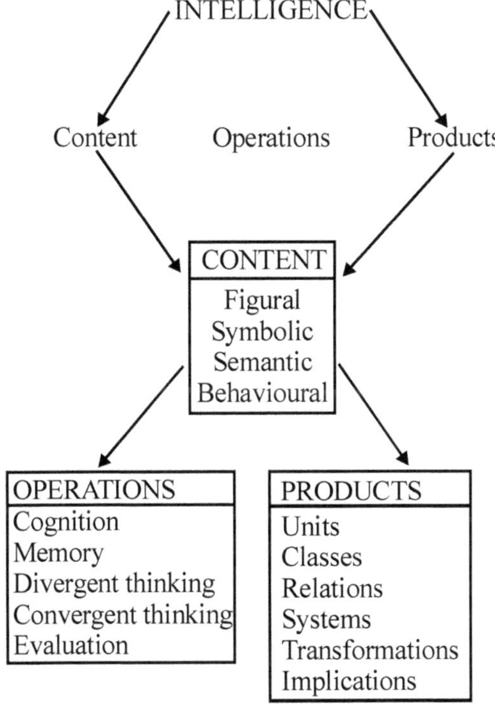

Gullford's Description of Intelligence
Consisting 4×5×6= 120 factors

3. Verbal comprehension factor (ability for verbal comprehension)
4. Word fluency factor (ability to think or to infer rules)
5. Rate memory factor (ability for memorization)
6. General reasoning factor
7. Deduction factor (to deduce from rules and principles to specific)
8. Induction factor (to infer from specific to general) and
9. Perceptual speed factor.

Guilford has described intelligence in terms of three independent dimensions, those of content, operations and products when five forms of operations – cognition, memory, divergent thinking, convergent thinking and evaluation – operate upon four forms of content – figural, symbolic, semantic and behavioural and six forms of products – units, classes, relations, systems, transformations and implications – are produced. These together make up $(4 \times 5 \times 6)$ 120 factors.

In the late nineteen eighties, a fifth content (auditory) has been added making a total of 150 factors.

Information Processing Approach : The psychometricians view intelligence as intellectual abilities. However on the contrary to it the information processing group (psychology that deals with the way the mind processes information and formation of thought processes) goes one step further as it lays emphasis on the cognitive processes underlying the intellectual abilities. Cognitive processes consist of various processes of the mind such as memory, seasoning, visualization, problem solving, etc. For instance, Robert Sternberg's Triarchic Theory to understand the information processing view of intelligence is as under:

1. Performance Component : This component refers to the cognitive process involved in performing a task or solving a problem. For example the student is asked to solve a problem 'Cauliflower is a vegetable as cow is to what?'

The performance components consist of the following:

(a) Encoding : We place the information about the problem (task example) in the memory.

(b) Inferring : It refers to the relations in the problem statement (as cauliflower and cow in the above mentioned example). We infer the relation between cauliflower and cow.

(c) Mapping : This refers to higher order relations. We relate the relations between cauliflower and vegetable to cow and mammal to arrive at the solution.

(d) Response : We state the answer-mammal.

2. Knowledge Acquisition Component : This refers to the meaningful acquisition of new information by relating the information (relation between cauliflower and vegetable or cow and mammal) to the prior knowledge in the mind.

3. Meta Component (Knowledge about one's own thinking) : It refers to how one directs ones own thinking i.e. the way in which one directs one's thinking to understand the problem and choose its solution.

Q3. How are IQ and Mental age related? How will you determine the IQ of a 5 years old child?

Ans. Intelligence is measured by means of mental tests which are samples of various kinds of behaviour. Intelligence of a child is inferred from what he does and what he knows. The units in which intelligence is measured at M.A. and I.Q.: the relation between them being given by the following equation:

$$IQ = \frac{MA}{CA} \times 100 \qquad \text{...(1)}$$

or $$MA = \frac{IQ \times CA}{800} \qquad \text{...(2)}$$

When the child's MA and CA are equal his IQ is 100 and the child is said to be of average intelligence. By average intelligence we mean not that the child has IQ = 100, no more, no less. Even if the IQ of a child is greater than 85 and less than 115 he is said to be of average intelligence. Thus, there is an average trend in intelligence. The growth in MA tends to slow down as growth in height or weight slows down as one reaches maturity. Till the age of 16 we generally indicate the intelligence of children by their MA or IQ but after that age the relative standing of an adolescent is denoted by deciles or percentile ratings. A decile is one of the nine points that divide a ranked distribution into ten parts, each containing one-tenth of all cases. A percentile is one of the 99 points scores that divide a ranked distribution into groups each of which contains $\frac{1}{100}$ of the scores.

The MA unit has not an equal distance as are centimeters on a meter rod. It means that the difference between an MA of 2 years and an MA of 3 years is not the same as that between an MA of 12 years and an MA of 13 years. We have to determine the unit for each year separately. A large number of children of various chronological ages are given an intelligence test which contains a sample of tasks. Tasks that are performed by a majority of 7 year old children on the basis of the average performance are given a mental age value of 7 and so on.

Let us exemplify the above statement. In the third revision of the Binet's test for the age CA = 5, we have the following 6 tasks :

1. Identifying absurdities in pictures.
2. Describing similarities (as between coal and wood).
3. Copying a diamond.
4. Solving a social problem.
5. Recognising appropriate opposites to words.
6. Repeating five digits.

These six tasks can be performed by a majority of 7-year old children in a certain country at a certain time. Each of these items has a credit of 2 months if correctly answered. These six items have 7-years MA value.

For each mental age we have tasks. If the sum of the mental age values equals the chronological age, the child will have an IQ of 100. If the 5-year old child answers all the items on the year V level, 4 of the year VI level, 3 of the year VII level, 1 of the year VIII level and none of the year IX level his total mental age is 76 months (2 month's credit for each answer at these levels).

Number of the Item	M.A. (equivalent months)
upto V year level all,	60
VI ... 4	8
VII ... 3	6
VIII ... 1	2
Total	76

$$IQ = \frac{76}{60} \times 100$$

= 126.6

= 127 nearly.

Thus, child has an IQ on Binet's test as 127. The child will not always get the same IQ if tested on different days because he may feel better on one day than on another or because his motivation or emotions may be different on two days. He will also not earn the same IQ if tested on the Weschsler test instead of on the Binet. IQ differs from test to test for one child.

Q4. Write down the different categories of students based on their intelligence once level. Which instructional strategy will you use for

handling them?

Ans. The different categories of students based on their intelligence level are as under:

(a) Gifted - These students who possess IQs of 130 or above called gifted students. They are superior in intelligence and have high ability to reason. Such students can perform academic activities grasping concepts perceiving, seeing, memorizing relationships, dealing with abstract ideas, generalizing, critical thinking and solving problems more effectively and quickly. Such students take initiative intellectual work and follow complex directions.

(b) Normal - Normal groups have those children whose IQs range from 90 to 110 and they are able to profit from regular school programmes with varying degrees of effort.

(c) Disabled - There are children with disability due to low level of intellectual functioning or specific learning deficits. They are impaired in their ability to learn and to adapt to the demands of society. Mentally retarded children are of different categories as under:

(i) Border line, (IQ ranges 90-70) and educable mentally retarded (IQ ranges 70-50) Such children can perform academic activities but they are slow in their learning. They need special instructional strategies.

(ii) Trainable mentally retarded (IQ ranges 50-35)-Such children are capable of learning only certain sedimentary literacy materials and simple occupational skills. They are able to take care of their personal needs. They require special classes or schools to study in.

(iii) Severely retarded (IQ below35)-Such students are dependent on their families for their personal needs.

Children with specific learning defects are called learning disabled group. They have difficulties in one or more psychological processes, think, speak, read, write, spell or do mathematical calculations. These difficulties are identified as:

1. Aphasia (difficulty in grasping spoken language)
2. Dylesia (difficulty in reading)
3. Hyperlexia (little or no comprehension)
4. Dyscalculia (difficulty in doing arithmetic)
5. Dysgraphia (difficulty in writing)

Strategies for Handling

Some instructional strategies for handling individual differences are as under:

1. Organisation of instruction for the development of cognitive process – Instruction should aim at developing student's cognitive process beyond the attainment of information alone. The focus should be on the development of such cognitive processes as memory, visualization, reasoning and problem-solving.

2. Using existing cognitive level as base – Student's existing cognitive level is the base for further cognitive development. We should observe the reasoning level of our students and identify which operations or activities they can perform and which they cannot. In this connection to see part-whole or cause-effect relationship is an essential indicator of their cognitive level.

3. Strengthening memory – Learning or problem solving often requires retaining fairly large amounts of information including vocabulary, concepts, principle, etc. in the memory system. Mnemonics or aiding the memory helps retain new information in the memory. For example mnemonic, VIBGYOR i.e. Violet, Indigo, Blue, Green, Yellow, Orange and Red is used to help recall the colours of the rainbow. Rehearsal is another strategy for remembering. It means actively repeating the ideas to be learned so that the ideas are registered well in the memory.

4. Formulate level specific instructional strategy – The instructional strategies which are deemed to be the best for one group are not necessarily the best for another. Gifted students require intellectually more demanding (higher order thinking) learning situations. Enriched learning experiences can be provided to them.

5. Use individual meeting – This strategy provides us with insights into a student's learning and cognitive processes, for example, a student has difficulty in comprehending passages. We can give him a series of passages with questions and observe the way the student answers in each passage. In this way we will go in insights into the student's difficulties and will be able to help him to overcome the difficulties.

6. Provide instructions to overcome learning disability – We should design structured instructions to meet the nature and level of learning disability.

Q5. Define aptitude what are the components of aptitude? Do individual differ in aptitude? [June-05, Q3(iv)]

Ans. The set of abilities essential for acquiring knowledge and skills specific to an area of performance is called aptitude. Precisely, it denotes the set of abilities required to perform a specialised activity. For example, when we say aptitude for engineering and aptitude for art, the set of abilities involved in learning performing in engineering is different from that of art. The same is true for medicine will tell us more about these sets of abilities.

Components of aptitude

(1) Intellectual processes – Intellectual processes are a major component of aptitude. It refers to multiple cognitive processes related to thinking such as memory processes, restructuring symbols and ideas, perception of relations and patterns between ideas, spatial comprehension or orientation, reasoning, problem solving, judgement, etc. These cognitive processes are important for recognition of information and for innovation, invention or discovery while performing a task.

(2) Sensory components – Sensory component refers to the abilities related to sensory process such as vision and audition. Vision implies the ability for visual sensitivity (link. Colour sensitivity, etc.). Audition means the ability to hear tones at different pitch levels (link pitch discrimination, loudness discrimination, etc.).

(3) Psychomotor component – Psychomotor component refers to the kind of abilities involved in the gross body movements or its parts-trunk, limbs, hands, etc. The kinds of abilities involved are strength, impulsion, speed, precision and flexibility. Strength means strength of body parts-leg, trunk and hand (e.g. hand grip). Impulsion refers to the rate of initiation of a movement and can be identified using reaction time to light or sound (e.g. time taken to start at the signal in an athletic event). Speed means the rate of movement (e.g. hand or finger or leg speed while performing an act). Precision implies steadiness in performing an act or movements (e.g. putting pins through tiny holes rapidly). Flexibility refers to the looseness of the joints (e.g. touch toes with fingers without bending knees).

It is important to note that when we speak of aptitude, say mechanical aptitude, this is a combination of separate abilities related to cognitive process, sensory and psychomotor for performing mechanical activities such as writing with a pen. The same is true for mathematical, music, graphic art or athletic aptitude. Here you may ask why we discuss psychomotor component under cognitive domain. We need to discuss this psychomotor component when we deal with specific activities may be required for acquiring knowledge and skill for performing routine tasks. For instance, let us take the example of a pilot. While navigating an aircraft the pilot has to perform several complex operations with speed and precision involving specific abilities related to cognitive, sensory and psychomotor components.

Intelligence v/s aptitude – Aptitude is differ from intelligence. While intelligence refers to a set of mental abilities and skills, the term aptitude refers to the set of those abilities which directs individual performance in certain specific areas, such as teaching aptitude, mechanical aptitude, etc. You may like to know the difference between aptitude and academic achievement. Though both are important for determining future learning, academic achievement reflects the effects of learning of a specific subject or a set of subjects during a given period of time. Aptitude reflects the cumulative influence of a combination of a set of abilities and a multiplicity of experiences (including learning subjects) in daily life. For example, a student of your class may be very intelligent but that student may not have an aptitude for public speaking or dancing for that matter.

Individual Differ in Aptitude

Individuals in differ aptitude. An individual may have a mechanical aptitude. Another individual may have an aptitude for mathematics or yet another may have an aptitude for logic. Such differences are due to the differences in the combination of abilities which are related to the cognitive process and the sensory and psychomotor components for instance, mechanical aptitude is connected with ability for spatial relations, ability to acquire information on mechanical matters and ability to comprehend mechanical differences in aptitude using aptitude tests. Aptitude tests for areas such as mechanical skills, science, language, music and graphic art can be used to identify the aptitude of students in each area of performance. The aptitude test, in fact, provides a measure of the candidates promise or teachability in a field of study, say law. In other words, the test would tell whether the candidate possesses the required aptitude or readiness to profit from studies in the concerned field of study.

Instructional Strategy for Handling Individual Differences

The suggested approach for handling individual differences is adaptive instructional system. In this approach at least two alternative instructional treatments are needed to ensure academic success, which is the most appropriate instructional treatment for the student depends upon his or her existing level of aptitude (learning readiness). Students with high aptitude may choose unstructured instructional strategy. With minimum guidance from teacher, they may be encouraged to learn through the discovery oriented approach. You may use the inductive process but instructional treatment is essentially learner-centered.

In contrast, highly structured instructional treatment for low aptitude learners is designed in small units through sequential steps and feedback. Frequent summary and review with simplified illustration, analogy and precise explanation of concepts and principle to be learned will facilitate progressive learning. Periodic achievement and aptitude assessments and comparison of these scores with the aptitude scores obtained at the start of instruction would tell degree to which each learner in the specific treatment group has achieved.

However, for those are unable to profit from either of the alternative treatments presented above, compensatory aptitude training is suggested. This consists of directed reading skills, study habits, self-learning skills, note taking and related activities. The main aim of compensatory aptitude training is to develop readiness for entry into structured treatment. Periodic monitoring should be formulated to identify the students who reach the required level for entry into alternative treatment.

Q6. What is creativity? Do individuals differ in creativity? What are the techniques of attaining creativity among students?

Ans. The ability to create or discover something that is novel and has some value for the society is called creativity. For example, the discovery of penicillin, formulation of the concept of relativity, creation of television, Tagore's work Gitanjali and the link are acts of creativity. The definition of creativity stated that something that is created should be novel and of some value. Novel means the unusual nature of the thing that is created whether it is penicillin, the concept of relativity or Gitanjali. The emphasis is on the production of something new. Equally important is the value which means that products of creativity should be of some value to humanbeings. For instance, the discovery of penicillin, formulation of the concept of relativity and creation of television have been turning points in the development of knowledge as well as for human beings and society. Further, Tagore's writings speak certain basic truths about humanity and seem as powerful now as when he conceived them. Psychologists in general, to name a few, Guilford, Hayes, Taylor, Torrance, Wallach and Kogan, accept the novelty and value aspects of creativity.

Do Individual Differ in Creativity

The major component of creativity is divergent thinking which refers to the thinking process involved in generating alternative ideas or answers to a given problem. Creativity involves a cluster of abilities based on the divergent thinking process. They are as under in a hierarchical order.

1. Ability to sense problems i.e. an awareness of the defects needs and deficiencies in the environment. For example-Sensing the need to improve the telephone.

2. Fluency i.e. the ability to express or generate multiple solutions of a given problem or concept. For example-List the number of uses of the newspaper.

3. Flexibility i.e. the ability to state a variety of solutions or answers to a problem and reflects the ability to change the direction of one's thinking. For example-Variety of uses of the newspaper can be identified as source of news, packing material.

4. Originality i.e. the ability to produce unique or new ideas. Inventions are the most common example of this aspect of creativity. For example-Ability to suggest a new title of a poem.

5. Elaboration i.e. the ability to develop well an idea or insight. For example-The idea that by providing only information to students does not develop their competencies rather the task or activity-based approach would ensure students involvement in learning and development of competencies.

6. Redefinition i.e. the ability to improvise operations in situations where a familiar function is performed with an object which is not normally used to perform such a function. For example-using a bangle or a cold drink can draw circles. Though creativity is essentially based on the ability of divergent thinking, psychologists opine that components such as intelligence, knowledge and motivation are linked to creativity. In fact, intelligence involves, cognition and convergent thinking i.e. form of thinking which is needed in a situation where there is only one acceptable answer.

Psychologists opine that a certain level of intelligence is required for creativity. For instance, Machinnon had studied highly creativity individuals link (biologists, mathematicians, architects and social scientists. These person had IQs ranging from 120 to 177. The study indicates that highly creative individuals had higher than average level of intelligence. Yet they were not brighter than their noncreative colleagues. It means that there is no difference in the IQ scores of say, the highly creative architect and the non-creative architect. Thus, if a person possesses higher than average level of intelligence alone it does not guarantee or give assurance of creativity. It implies that creativity is essentially divergent thinking process but there is a place for cognition and convergent thinking too.

The reality is that creativity is directly linked to knowledge and motivation. A biologists or a musician cannot become creative until he acquires a great deal of knowledge in the field of biology or music. By devoting study over a long period of time one becomes able to gain knowledge in the field. Motivation to produce original work is another factor. Motivational factor, consist of the following.

1. A desire to question.

2. High intellectual persistence.

3. Tendency to put up with frustration of not being able to find solution.

4. Delight in trying with ideas and curiosity.

Thus divergent thinking abilities, intelligence, knowledge and motivation are helpful in understanding creativity and in identifying individual differences in creativity. The fact is that individuals do not possess the same level of divergent thinking abilities, knowledge, intelligence and motivation. Such differences create difference in creativity. Such individuals, besides some other traits link the ability to sense problem fluency, originality, flexibility, elaboration and redefinition, are not found in the equal level in the same individual. Again differences in intelligence, knowledge and motivation strengthen, the difference in creativity. Thus, differences in divergent thinking abilities, intelligence, knowledge and motivation, are responsible for differences in creativity in the field of study or work chosen by individuals.

Techniques of attaining creativity among students – Creative abilities can be enhanced if appropriate, supportive behaviour and classroom practices are provided. Following are the techniques of attaining this.

(1) Encourage unusual or odd questions : As a teacher you should encourage your student's curiosity and accept unusual question. For instance, a student may ask you, how does a cloud form? Using the following activity you may illustrate the answer as follows:

The teacher takes a half-filled beaker with boiling water and closes the top with an ice piece. Students are asked to observe what happens. They notice evaporation and a cloud-link formation in the upper portion of the beaker. In the ensuing discussion they relate water, heat, evaporation, temperature, cloud, and rain all this leads further to the concept of different states of matter.

Your acceptance of the questions encourages the student's curiosity to know. Quite often teachers dismiss such questions by saying, 'you find for yourself'. An indifferent or negative attitude of a teacher damages a student's thinking process and creative effort. Suppose you are asked by a student-why does the moon change shape every night? If you don't know the answer, welcome the question and help him find out an appropriate answer through discussion or using reference materials.

(2) Provide activities to promote creative thinking/abilities : For instance, ask students to list unusual uses they can think of the following:

Ballpen	Paper	Rope
Shoe	Book	Candle

Discuss the answers and help each student to understand his or her fluency, flexibility and originality. Continue the exercise using different items.

(3) Organise brainstorming sessions : This is a strategy where each member of the group generates ideas to find solutions to a given problem. The leader (you, as a teacher) presents the problem to the brainstorming group and directs each member of the group to state one idea at a time. After one rounds. One is encouraged to generate an idea based on another's idea (hitch hiking) but not allowed to criticise another member's idea. Ideas thus generated, are further scrutinized by members for choosing the idea with the most potential to solve the problem.

(4) Use synectics : Synectics is a strategy based on analogies to generate ideas. Analogies provide a structure to generate ideas by connecting a familiar content with a new content, or looking at a familiar content from a new perspective. You can use direct analogy or personal analogy. In direct analogy you compare two objects or ideas. To help students get an insight into the mechanics of a car, for instance, compare it (the mechanics of a car) with the movement of a bird. The students list the connections they see between a car and a bird.

Bird	Car
Brain	engine
Food	petrol
Nervous system	mechanical connections
Sick	breakdown

Now ask students to write a short paragraph indicating the analogical connections. In personal analogy an individual is asked to empathies with an object or an idea to be compared. If the discussion is about air, ask students to imagine themselves to be in the air and express what they feel.

(5) Provider students situations to evaluate their own ideas or thinking : Students who make evaluation of their own thinking are less likely to be inhibited in future questioning.

(6) Extra credit for creative thinking : While evaluating students performance in your subject, look for creative ideas. Students exhibiting creative effort should be recognised and rewarded by extra credit. Well, creativity cannot be fostered unless as a teacher, you display originality in your classroom behaviour.

Q7. What is academic achievement? Are learners different from one

another in their academic achievement?

Ans. Usually academic achievement is the marks secured in a subject or subjects. A critical analysis reveals that these marks are only indicators of the knowledge and capabilities attained by them in that subject. Academic achievement should refer to the knowledge and capabilities acquired by each of them in science. Thus, academic achievement is the acquired potential (knowledge and capabilities) in a subject or subjects.

The question is how students acquire their potentials in subjects. Psychologists address this question using scheme theory.

Scheme means knowledge structure, which is created by the students in their memory. Knowledge structure is the internal representation of external realities. To illustrate, a student forms a knowledge structure of 'bird' (external reality) in terms of shape, wings, feather, flying and living in the nests or branches of trees (internal representation) knowledge structures-different types, characteristics, bending of light, convergence and divergence of light and image. Later on, we can widen the structures by relating the phenomenon of refraction in nature i.e. (rainbow) and functions of optical instruments i.e. (human eye, microscope, telescope) it is stated by schema theory that learning takes place forming appropriate knowledge structures (schema) by relating new information e.g. principles of microscope to the existing knowledge structures e.g. principles of refraction.

The question is how we know that the student has formed the appropriate knowledge structure?

If we ask students why we use convex lens instead of concave lens in microscope, they will be able to answer only if he or she possesses appropriate knowledge structures about the microscope. The answer to the question would indicate the student's knowledge structures of a microscope. In this way, the marks awarded to a student represent his way, the marks awarded to a student represent his or her knowledge.

The knowledge is formed by relating new information to the existing knowledge. It means, that appropriate domain-specific knowledge facilitates acquisition of new knowledge. Domain-specific knowledge means existing knowledge or pre-requisite knowledge which is necessary for learning new information in a subject. The persons who have appropriate pre-requisite knowledge e.g. refraction principle learn more from new information e.g. microscope than from those persons who lack such knowledge in science. This is true of all subjects. In this way, a student makes progress in attainment of knowledge in a subject by relating new information to the existing knowledge. The progressive nature of knowledge attainment suggests the cumulative nature of learning. It is expected that with knowledge the student attains related capabilities. The knowledge discussed above includes comprehension. In other words, after learning, the principles of refraction, a student should not be able to recall, identify and recognize it i.e. (the concept of refraction) but should also be able to demonstrate, differentiate, illustrate and explain it. Knowledge is the base for attaining the related capabilities involved in the following:

1. Application i.e. (ability to apply the principle in a new situation).
2. Analysis i.e. (ability to compare, contrast and differentiate)
3. Synthesis i.e. (ability to derive, formulate, modify, originate) and
4. Evaluation i.e. (appraise, judge, assess).

Difference of academic achievement in learners

The psychologists say that the learners differ their academic achievement.

1. The learners who possess appropriate pre-requisite knowledge learn more effectively than those learners who lack such knowledge. Differences in pre-requisite knowledge possessed by students create differences in the attainment of knowledge.

2. Secondly knowledge is attained progressively. Progressive differences in knowledge attainment lends to cumulative differences in knowledge attainment. This form of differences is called Mathew Effect. It means that academically rich get riches and those who are poor continue to be poor. In this way, differences in pre-requisites and cumulative knowledge lead to differences in the knowledge possessed by the students.

3. Thirdly, the learners differ in their capabilities to manipulate the knowledge in a given situation and the differences are identified in terms of the abilities to apply, analyse, synthesise and evaluate knowledge.

Q8. Which instructional strategy will you adopt for cop up with the differences in academic achievement?

Ans. Instruction should aim at the development of knowledge and capabilities of all children. The major strategies to cope up with the differences in academic achievement are as follows :

1 Provide appropriate pre – Requisites to organise and learn new information : You have seen that new information is learned by linking it to pre-requisite knowledge. So, first ascertain whether the student possesses the appropriate pre-requisites for learning new information and if not, provide the pre-requisites. Advance organiser is a suitable strategy for providing the appropriate pre-requisites. Advance organiser is a general overview of new information presented in advance of processing new information. The student is told in advance what the main point or the main concepts to be covered will be. For instance, prior to learning a lesson on mammals (new information) students can be asked to describe the characteristics of domesticated animals link a cow or sheep. Knowledge of the characteristics of a cow or sheep activates the appropriate pre-requisites to learn about mammals. Advance organiser is effective to focus a student's attention on the key points. Careful application of advance organizers can improve the impact on student learning. An advance organiser may be a statement, a descriptive paragraph, a demonstration or even a video programme. Application of advance organiser is more effective for low-ability learners. More skilled students can invent their own model.

2. Use visual aids – A visual aid creates the mental image of ideas(s) and represents and facilitates students' thinking concretely by reducing the amount of abstraction. Graphics, charts, diagrams, photographs, models and real objects are the various forms of visual aids. For instance, a chart depicting a transport system would facilitate students to attain the conceptual clarity and the characteristics of transport system.

3. Use analogy, example and illustration – Analogy is a productive instructional device and allows students to think and learn. Analogy encourages students to draw parallels between a familiar idea and the idea to be learned. The new idea is taught by referring to the similar features of the familiar idea. For instance, you can introduce the structure of animal cell (idea to the learned) using the analogy of egg (familiar idea). Using a raw egg and a drawing or a model of an animal cell, you can provide a situation to show that the animal cell in some ways resembles the egg. The cell membrane is like the outer skin and shell of an egg. The cytoplasm is like the egg white. The cell nucleus is link the egg yolk and so on. Likewise, use examples and illustrations to explain concepts and principles.

4. Ensure learner's active involvement in learning – Only listening to the teacher's talk will not ensure effective learning. Besides talking, you can provide tasks (manipulatable conditions) for student's active involvement. For instance, you can deal with a lesson on 'environmental protection by formulating a series of tasks for students performance. Tasks consisted of analysing textbook lesson, identifying effect of environment, designing a poster campaign, writing a story, drawing cartoons and formulating strategies for environmental protection. Students are first exposed to the idea in the textbook and subsequently small group can be formed where each group consists of high of the cognitive process are involved in each task and by performing the task students are expected to attain understanding as well as to shape their cognitive processes. If the teacher is dealing with a story mapping technique (how elements of a story are organised) is appropriate to ensure students' involvement. In this situation, activities should be provided for identifying/setting (time place of story), characters, problems or goals (what the characters are trying to attain or to resolve), episode (events that occur), theme (underlying message) and resolution (characters' effort to resolve the problem).

5. Periodic assessment – It provides an opportunity to students to rehearse and remember information. It helps teachers to identify the students' level of attainment and get an insight into their weaknesses. The results would help in identifying those who need remedial instruction or those who can proceed further.

Q9. What is interest? What is the method adopted by a teacher to arouse interest in class work? [June-07, Q3(iii)]

Ans. Interest -The term interest is used to designate a concept pertaining to factors within an individual which attract him to or repel him from various objects, persons and activities within his environment. Interest is viewed in various was as under :

1. Webester defines interest as excitement of feeling accompanying special attention to some object or concern, such as, an interest in Botany.

2. An interest is something with which the child identifies his personal well-being. Interest is a source of motivation which drives people to do what they want to do when they are free to choose. They specify a condition or cause of attention. We read a book, or attend a lecture on religious discourse, because we are interested in them.

3. The term 'interest' is also used to connote the felling of pleasure resulting from giving attention to something.

4. Interest is defined as a feeling of pleasure resulting from attending to something not a cause but a result.

Interests become stable by the time development and growth reaches a level of maturity in an individual. Slow maturers have interests in children while their other agemates develop interests those of adolescents.

Interests are influenced by cultural factors and are emotionally weighted. Interest is weakened by an unpleasant emotion (likewise it is) strengthened by pleasant emotion.

Aspects of Interest

Interest has both subjective and objective aspects as under:

1. Subjective – In the subjective aspect, the emphasis in on the feeling component.

2. Objective – In the objective aspect, the emphasis is on the motor behaviour of the individual.

All interests have cognitive, affective as well as motor aspects. The components that make up the cognitive aspects of interest are based on personal experiences gained from various means of communication at home, at school, and in the country.

Interests give rise to certain activities. The attitude towards these activities is part of the affective domain.

Method to arouse interest :

Identifying Interest : Every teacher wants to make his lesson interesting. He uses such teaching methods as may appeal to children's interests and experiences and tries to set the material to be learnt in the matrix of their needs, concerns and environment. Such methods are likely to be more effective than those that do not appeal to children. Effective teachers start with the interests of children and relate the entire school work to them so closely that their children acquire a very strong desire to learn. Once interests are found out and used, they attract the attention of pupils and also furnish clues to their basic drives. It may be assumed that when such fields of interest are identified and used, effective learning is bound to result.

Helping Children in Developing Desirable Interests : The problem of interest does not end here. It involves far more than making a subject or lesson interesting which usually means rather superficial classroom motivation. This becomes at once clear when we regard interest as a more or less stable goal which tends to direct if not dominate behaviour. Interests are preferences and likes but even more than these, they are goals in which a person find avenues for satisfaction and self-fulfillment. If we recognise what an interest really is, and what it stands for, and how it affects the life of boys and girls we teach, then nothing of greater significance can be done than to help them find and develop desirable and fruitful interests.

Establishing a Self-propelling Interest : Interests are acquired like any other goal by an experience of success. Reading, for example, becomes an interest because one gets satisfaction out of it. A sense of identification or ego involvement becomes attached to it. If properly organised, reading provides a variety of satisfying success experiences. Similarly many other co-curricular subjects may be established as interests. If a teacher wants the material he teaches to have a permanent effect, he should do all he can to establish the material as a self-propelling interest.

Kindling Interest and Sustaining it: Many curricular subjects do not become self-propelling interests because they are not properly organised. Modern Algebra, for example, is not an interesting subject because it is organised in such a way as to deaden interest rather than promote it. Routine procedures have to be mastered and there is nothing in them which can give pride and pleasure to the students. The motivation is negative and we cannot get a positive effect from negative cause. Hence, Algebra becomes dull and un-interesting. One may say that Algebra should be interesting because it is worth studying. But what is worth studying? A subject worth studying is one whose effects are lasting. The effects of Algebra-teaching are not at all lasting. Details of facts and techniques here are always forgotten both in and out of school. Hence, if the teacher of Algebra wants to establish his subject as a self-propelling interest, he should not only kindle interest in it but let the fire go on burning. For this he will have to sacrifice some sacred and cherished conventions like ground – covering and excessive drill on fundamentals.

The function of the teacher is not to cover the ground and follow cherished conventions. The duty of the school is not to take a predetermined body of content and trick it up to make it interesting. Its true function is to organise both content and teaching-learning situation with a view to establishing vital interests. The school and its teachers should do everything to develop significant interests and follow a deliberate policy and intelligent planning to promote them.

Once developed, interests tend to perpetuate themselves and become stronger as time goes on. Once an interest is kindled, it has the same feeding tendency as a forest fire. For example, when a person begins stamp collecting, he finds more and more in it. The self-perpetuating tendency of interests is a tendency only. Hence, teachers should not only develop or arouse interests as may shape and mould the pattern of their children's lives and determine their happiness but should try to perpetuate them so that they may flourish and not wither away as time goes on.

The following suggestions are given to kindle interest in an instructional material:

1. Give a chance to your pupils to observe and experiment.

2. Use playway method of teaching.

3. Proceed from known to unknown; from particular to general.

4. Change subject or topic when your children begin to feel boredom.
5. Take children on educational tours.
6. Let children feel a need to learn a particular subject.
7. Satisfy curiosity.
8. Give proper amount of homework.

Q10. Discuss the nature of attitude. How are they learnt or acquired? What are the reasons of different attitude?

Ans. Personality tract which indicates towards individuals likes or dislikes is called attitude. Attitude influences the way an individual behaves towards an object, institution or a person. Attitude towards a particular object is influenced by parents, teachers, school and society in which the individual lives.

Nature of Attitude

Environment around us consists of all kinds of objects, people, groups and institutions. An individual does not always react, to these experiences a afresh in every encounter. The cognition, feelings and response dispositions that these objects recurrently evoke, get organised into a unified and enduring system. Attitudes predispose the individual to act in particular ways towards these objects, persons, situations or ideas and there is a degree of consistency in his response to these.

According to G.W. Allport, "Attitudes is a mental and neutral state of readiness. Organised through experience, exerting a directive and dynamic influence upon an individual's response to the objects and situations with which it is related." Thus the attitudes of a student are formed due to his experience and interaction with real situations.

Attitudes provide the frame of reference for a person's life. Attitude involves organisation of motivational, emotional, perceptive and cognitive processes. In this way, attitudes are reinforced by information (the cognitive component) and often generate strong felling (the emotional component) that may lead to a particular form of response (i.e. the action-tendency component).

Harrison (1976) has identified three components in attitudes as under:
1. Beliefs
2. Emotions
3. Behaviour

These are explained as under :

1. Beliefs are what one considers desirable and undesirable.
2. Attitudes are accompanied by emotions they influence each other, the resultant

behaviour is always a complete interplay of both.

3. The individual displays his likes as dislikes (attitudes) through his action (behaviour).

Attitudinal information is governed in the following way :

1. On the one hand, by socio-cultural influences operating on the individual.

2. On the other, the nature of experiences that the individual has and the information he is exposed to.

Positive and Negative Attitudes

Many attitudes cannot be neutral so children acquire or learn positive as negative attitude from their parents, peers and schools.

A brief description of them is as under:

1. Negative Attitudes – They lead to avoidance, disagreements, arguments, conflicts or other confrontations. Prejudice is a premature or snap judgement that is made before examining the facts.

2. Positive Attitudes – They can induce an individual to assist other people, to be at peace with his word.

Acquisition of Attitudes and Attitude Change

Initially, all the children imitate the attitude of parents. Later, in school, teachers and peers contribute to the formation of attitudes.

Unchangeable Nature of Attitudes

Attitudes, once formed, are resistant to change. Explanation, unconditioning or rational analysis of errors in perception or fallacies cannot change attitude. Attitudes, whether good or bad, do change. Many attitudinal changes are accompanied by changes in the personality.

Facilitating Learning of Attitude

To facilitate learning of an attitude, it is necessary to identify the attitude to be acquired and clarify the meaning of the attitude. After getting it done a person should share his experiences about attitude building. It would be better if he can arrange appropriate contexts for practice and reinforcement of the attitude. For this one can also use group techniques to facilitate understanding and acceptance of that attitude.

Dealing with Extreme Attitudes

We should not emphasise on agreement upon all attitudes and values. However there must be a sufficiently large core of common attitudes and value for people to live together reasonably well.

Individual Differences in Attitude-Causes

Once can see individual differences in attitudes in students. This is due to variety in maturity levels, planned and random experiences, extent of warmth physical surroundings, exhibited, democracy and indulgence in home environment, schooling, playmates and exposure to media. An object liked by one may be disliked by others and vice-versa. The result would be attitudinal differences among individuals.

An intellectually mature individual can change and modify his attitudes, if he happens to realise that his attitudes are narrow, biased or even wrong. On the other hand, the intellectually immature individual will cling to his attitude even though there is enough evidence to indicate that it is desirable.

A young child is reverent in his attitude towards religion. Adolescence children are reported to be skeptics and agnostics. Adolescents differ in their attitude towards authority (teachers, principals, leaders, and parents) the difference depends on the satisfaction or figures of dissatisfaction which they derived during the course of their interaction with them.

Q11. Define the term values. What values do children team in schools? What are the cause responsible for individual difference?

[Dec-05, Q3(iii)]

Ans. Schools are established by society to preserve and transmit culture and value system i.e. the role of school is perceived to develop human resource in conformity with the norms set out by the society. For instance, in interest and attitude, students differ in their perception about various trait and virtues of the society. Let us study the various components of value system in this section.

Values Meaning and Nature: A value is an orientation towards a whole class of goods which are important in one's life. The value is labelled with the specific goals to be achieved in life. A person may have strong convictions about freedom, good health, close family relationships or success. In good health a person's important values he may believe that people should eat nutritive food, do exercise, take rest and avoid drugs and alcohol.

Growth of values- Basic values are likely to be learned during early years. These values enter into every phase of life. They include attitudes towards success, competition and problem-solving etc. The values also include the virtues of honesty, industry, co-operation, obedience and the like.

Development of Values

Some values are derived through the natural development process. They cannot be traced to specific elements or events that occur along the way. Many satisfying and unsatisfying experiences, learning about the effects of the activities of others. Knowledge of the human organism and its animate and inanimate surroundings, and the adoption of concepts considered useful by others, all contribute to the formation of values. Through introspection, there is internalization of things held dear, warm and friendly by someone with whom the child identifies. Through identification, the child arrives at a status similar to that of the model or ideal. Rules and guides are internalized when the child desires to make them part of his or her own personal life.

Values and the School

Can we teach values? Should we teach them? How can we teach values in classroom? These are some of the questions that are of great importance to you, as a teacher. Whenever teachers teach or come into contact with children, they have an influence upon individual child or upon groups of children. Schools always exhibit the importance of values in their purposes and programmes of study and most deeply desire to nurture those values in their own students. The values held by adults are not, most of the time, handed down to the younger generation.

Educational experiences, undoubtedly, promote certain values and cast others aside. The school curriculum contains innumerable value judgments made by those who have designed and developed it.

A useful technique in teaching values is to survey existing Indian philosophies. Reading about philosophical viewpoints makes you aware of the values of the society you live in. You may also point out values presented in movies, art creations, and social situations that become a part of classroom activity.

Schools are where young people spend most of their time. Therefore, schools are the place for major intervention to help promote healthy child development. School experiences affect the development of the sense of responsibility, honesty, moral courage and friendliness in students.

One of the key factors in value development is the amount and quality of peer interaction. Children learn about justice and fairness through sharing their ideas, feeling or experiences. Yet the process is slow.

Values to be Taught

1. It is essential to teach values related to the conservation of human life.

2. Students should be made aware of the dangers of impulsive action, carelessness, thrill seeking, and other unwanted behaviours.

3. They should be taught to have the feeling of responsibility towards personal and public property. Stealing, willful destruction. Defacing property owned by persons, groups or institutions (as in student violence agitations) are examples of value-oriented behaviour.

4. Laws passed for the protection of individuals should have a rightful place in any system of values.

5. A positive value should be given to a law.

Method

It is observed that special classroom teaching methods can affect the level of student's moral maturity. The dilemma-discussion approach is very affective in making students of all age group aware of values and virtues of the society.

Q12. What is social adjustment? What difficulties are felt in social adjustment? [June-06, Q3(ii)]

Ans. The study of child's social adjustment by parents and teachers is essential for two reasons: First, patterns of behaviour and attitudes formed early are rather persistent. Second, the kind of social adjustment children have contributes to the evolution of their self-concept. The degree with which a student adjusts to other people and the group with which he identifies, given an idea of skills such as the ability to effectively deal both friends and strangers, etc. Socially well-adjusted students generally develop favourable social attitudes towards other members of the society.

Criteria of Social Adjustment

There are various criteria to judge whether a student is socially well adjusted or not. The following are the four main criteria:

(1) Over performance – When children's social behaviour conforms to the standards and expectations of the group they are identified with, they are socially adjusted/accepted members of the group.

(2) Adjustment to different group – Children who can adjust reasonably well with different group of people as well as peer groups are considered socially well adjusted.

(3) Social attitudes – Socially wee-adjusted students exhibit favourable attitudes towards people, social participation, and social group interactions.

(4) Personal satisfaction – To be socially well-adjusted, student should be reasonably satisfied with their social relationships and the roles they play in the social system.

Difficulties in Social Adjustment

Making good social adjustment is difficult. Some difficulties in the way are as under:

1. An unhappy children results in an unhappy and maladjusted adulthood. Children should be taught about factors that contribute to poor adjustment in society.

2. The children with poor social behaviours at home fail to establish good social behaviours outside their home.

3. Children having an authoritarian home climate show resentment against all in authority.

4. Those children who do not find good models to imitate in their family find themselves handicapped outside their family.

5. The children rejected by their parents or those who imitate deviate behaviour of their parents develop aggressive and deviant behaviour patterns.

6. Children feeling dejected, maltreated, tested or bullied by other siblings lack motivation to try to make good social adjustment.

7. Lastly. Lack of necessary or proper guidance and help in making good social adjustment, despite motivation to make it, leaves them trying little to acquire proper social adjustment.

Q13. Define self concept with characteristics. How can self concept be development?

Ans. Self-concept is composite of the beliefs, ideas or perception one has about oneself: one's physical, psychological, social and emotional characteristics, aspirations and achievements. This is what an individual refers to as I or me and is the totality of meanings, attitudes and feelings which the individual has of himself/herself-the complete description one could give of his/her present self. According to hamacheek your opinions of your health, appearance, disposability, influence on others, abilities, and weaknesses are part of your self-concept. If we could place a student in a situation in which he/she felt absolutely free to describe him/herself as accurately as possible, the possible description such as intelligent, hardworking, caring, mature, responsible, insightful, etc., would capture the essence of his/her self-concept. A self-concept is a person's total view of him or herself. The physical self-image is usually formed first and is related to the student's physical appearance. Psychological self-image is based on thoughts, feelings and emotions. They (physical and psychological self-image) consist of the qualities such as courage, honesty, independence, self-confidence, aspiration and abilities of various kinds.

Characteristics of self-concept :

(1) Self-concept is organized – To arrive at a general picture of the self, the individuals collect and organise a great deal of information on which they base their perception.

(2) Self-concept is multifaceted – Self-concept includes areas such as social acceptance, physical attractiveness, academic abilities, etc.

(3) Self-concept is hierarchical on a dimension of generality – the multifaceted characters are in a hierarchy which is developmental in nature. Self-concept becomes increasingly differentiated with increasing age.

(4) Self-concept is stable – Though success/failure or superiority/inferiority in a student may bring change in himself-concept. It however does not change the primary self-concept of the person. It, however, does not mean that self-concept can not be improved through appropriate interventions. There is dispute among researchers over (1) whether self-concept can be improved or not (2) if yes, to what extent.

Development of Self-concept

Self-concept is based on what children believe their parents, teachers and peer think of them. If children believe that these significant people think favourably of them, they think favourably of themselves too. Encouragement, love, praise. Positive comments, sincere caring on the part of parents and others, contribute to the development of positive self-concept or high self-esteem among children. Self-concept is largely learnt over a period of time. With increasing age the self-concept tends to become stable. The individual does not change his attitudes, feelings or ideas about himself.

Children who are constantly and rarely shown affection develop poor self-concept. Children with low self-esteem have less self-confidence and develop feelings of inferiority. They find difficulty in interacting with other children and getting accepted by them. As a result the children with self-concept often develop problem behaviour that attract negative attitudes from peers, teachers and others. Students with positive or high self-concept tend to accept others with ease. They are better achievers as compared to children with low self-concept. They rely on themselves rather than on others and are willing to accept criticism and suggestions. On the other hand, students with low self-concepts are sensitive to criticism and blame themselves whenever things go wrong.

Q14. What is motivation? Distinguish between intrinsic and extrinsic motivation with example. Discuss various theories of motivation.

[June-06, Q3(iv)]

Ans. Motivation refers to the why of behaviour. Hence we question one's motivation, we ask-why does he do what he is doing? This is an attempt to understand the reason behind an action. The reason could be the driving force behind a student to take some challenges or leave them.

The concept of motivation accounts for differences is school achievement beyond those resulting from differences in intelligence or scholastic aptitude. The concept is used to account for differences in behaviour in the same student and also differences between similar types of students.

Motivation is the term used to describe what energises and directs a student and sustains his activity. It is sometimes compared with the engine and steering wheel of an automobile. Energy and direction are at the centre of the concept of motivation to perform an activity.

Intrinsic and Extrinsic Motivation

Intrinsic motivation is satisfied by internal reinforces or factors and this does not depend on external goals while extrinsic motivation depends on needs that are satisfied by external reinforces. If you are intrinsically motivated, you will perform an activity because you enjoy it. An extrinsic motivator supplies an outside reward. If you envoy learning in itself, you are intrinsically motivated. On the other hand if you are studying to earn a course credit, certificate or degree, you are extrinsically motivated. You have both types of motivation in studying. Learning is far more long lasting when it is sustained by intrinsic motivation. Extrinsic motivation, however, may be necessary to get the student to initiate certain actions or to get the learning process started.

Besides enjoying learning, if the student looks forward for a good grade, a well paid job, he qualifies for both intrinsic and extrinsic motivation. Psychologists have found that some behaviour may be internally motivated for some students and externally for other students. Motivation express the reason of the behaviour when student take part in teaching learning process then there is some reason which motivate him/her to take part in process. Here we shall discuss various theories of motivation with the help of suitable examples.

Theories of motivation and their use to motivate student :

1. Need Disposition Theory – According to this theory, an organism behaves in order to reduce its needs. Any person work to complete his/her needs. People are motivated to take action and invest energy in pursuit of three motives (1) Achievement, (2) Affiliation (3) influence. As for example everyone works to achieve some goals. A student learns sentence pattern of English to achieve the performance of expressing his/her views in English. To motivate our students we, as a teacher, should understand the need of the students and then try to organise our teaching learning process in such a manner so that they could achieve their needs after taking part in it.

2. Maslow's theory of motivation – According to this theory every person works to fulfill his/her needs. He maintains that a person will remain at a given need level until those needs are satisfied, then move on to the next. According to this theory there is a sequence or order in the basic needs. People's motivation derives directly from their needs. When person fulfills his/her present needs then he/she moves to the next. In other words these basic needs or their sequence help very much to motivate our students. Maslow postulated seven basic needs in a hierarchical order-

7. Physiological needs-Need for food, drink, sleep etc.

6. Need for safety-Avoidance of danger and anxiety desire for security, protection and family stability.

5. Need for love and belongingness-Need for affection, in family or peer, group affiliation and personal acceptance.

4. Need for self esteem-Need for self respect, a feeling of adequacy, competence, mastery.

3. Need for self actualization-Self fulfillments and achievement of personal goals and ambitions, starving for full use and exploitations of talents, capacities and potentialities to achieve goals.

2. Need to know-Curiosity, a need to learn about the world

1. Aesthetic need-Need to experience and understand beauty for its own sake.

First four needs are 'deficiency needs' and the last three needs are 'being' needs. We can motivate to gratify the being needs when deficiency needs are met. A teacher should understand all these seven needs are their sequence so that he/she could facilitate need fulfillment and could motivate students to wants it.

3. Theory of achievement motivation : This theory is based on the work of Hoppe (1930) sears (1940), McClelland (1958, 1961) and Atkinsou (1958, 66)

A. Hoppe (1930). He described that people raised their level of aspiration after success and lowered them after failure. According to this theory we should have goals at realistic level, achievable and satisfying. If we have high goals then they will not be fulfilled and so students will lower their level of aspiration due to failure in achievements of goals. We should not have goals at very low level. If a student is given a test paper framed at very low level then after giving answer of this paper he/she cannot raise his aspiration. So we should try to set goals at realistic level so that they could achieve them and get motivation for next stage.

B. McClelland (1961, 1971) stated that the need for achievement directly influences academic performance. People with strong needs for achievements use their own skills to improve themselves. For example the students who have strong needs, try to acquire these needs by their great efforts and skills. According to McClelland, need for achievement is related to parents' attitudes. Parents who are high achievers themselves, demand independence and help developing self confidence.

4. Attribution Theory – According to theory we understand how students explain their success and failure and the implications, those explanations have for achievement-oriented behaviour in the future. Students often use one of the seven different forms of explanation for their success or failure. As for example if a student has personal short coming, he explains that he had been bad at that particular subject. Student explains, unreasonable teacher behaviour, as the form that the teacher wanted to fail him.

At the end we can say that every teacher should understand various theories of motivation so that he/she could motivate students with the help of these theories. A teacher should always try to motivate students for taking part in teaching learning process effectively and aimfully.

Q15. Discuss some grounds that are help responsible for differences?

Ans. Differences have been measured in both physiological as well as psychological terms. We often come across the differences in intelligence and the more narrowly defined intellectual processes such as memory, judgement and problem-solving.

(1) Group Differences – The group may be formed on the basis of sex, age, caste socio-economic status and personality. We may like to know about such group differences. The information received may be helpful to us in dealing with such group in day-to-day life.

Equality is a dominant concern of the modern time. It refers to equivalent qualifications, equivalent capabilities, equivalent abilities, same rights and same opportunities of learning and of working. But the very ideology of gender is based on an idea of assumed differences between males and females. The question is whether females differ from males in terms of traits, skills, values and competencies or not. It they are not different, the reasons for discrimination between males and females in various areas or domains have to be studied.

(2) Differences in terms of sex – Many educationists or educational psychologists compared the performance of males and females as the subject of the study. They divided the sample into two separate categories: males and females. Research studies done in this area have shown such differences on both sociological as well as biological bases. The studies aimed at achieving a better understanding of differences between two groups formed on the basis of sex. Many of these studies were conducted to find out not only how much average differences in a particular trait the two sexes had but also what other traits and external factors were correlated with each of these sex groups.

It is observed that as far as general intelligence is concerned, males and females appear to be equal. The differences are either related to specific abilities or specific traits. Males show superiority over females in the ability to reason and to detect similarities and in certain aspects of general information. Girls show some superiority in memory, language and aesthetic comparisons. Males excel in a number of skills and in understanding spatial relations while females excel in verbal aptitude and memory. The female students develop facility in the use of language at an earlier age than the male counterparts. At pre-school stage, girls have larger vocabulary than boys of the same age and have higher scores in reading, sentence completion and the like. But the differences in terms of intelligence are not such as to call for different roles assigned to them by society. Therefore, in educational programmes there should be no discrimination in the treatment given to boys and girls.

(3) Differences in Terms of Age – Age influences individual difference as under :

1. With an increase in age, many differences appear in both boys as well as girls.

2. An individual's ability to adjust to the environment grows with the age.

3. With increasing age the individuals develop ability to deal with more and more different problem solving situations which result in better adjustment with the environment.

4. As a child grows from infancy to maturity, his or her mental powers increase. His or her body, nervous system, brain and its functions mature, there is a maturity and development in the mental capacity.

5. The child grows in experience and this too adds to his or her mental capacity. But as compared to the influence of age in adulthood, we find that its influence during childhood is greater. It means a few years in the age of the child make much more difference than a few years in the life of an adult.

6. Age differences in mental growth of the same child are not the same. During certain periods of growth these changes are rapid while during other periods they are not.

7. Some people believe that the changes occurring due to change in age stop at a specific age i.e. 15 or 16 while others think that intellectual growth ceases at the age of 20 or 25.

8. After maturation mental growth becomes slow, though some individuals continue to grow intellectually. Recent research studies have proved that there is a great scope for developing mental abilities as we use a very small portion of our brain at a given point of time. Many older people continue to learn effectively and often in a new direction.

(4) Differences in Terms of Caste – It is observed that the differences were there in the so called higher mental processes such as reasoning, attention, foresight and judgement. The primitive races excelled in terms of sensory and motor characteristics, keenness of the senses, quickness of response and perception of slight details. In fact it is very difficult to carry out psychological studies on pure races. When we compare two races living in one country the question of classification becomes very difficult. The influence of cultural and social milieu gets mixed up with that of variety of hereditary endowments of various ethnic groups. The psychological tests used for such studies are also not available to study such group differences. Certain groups may have excellence in certain areas which could fruitfully be utilized for peer group learning.

(5) Differences in Terms of Socio-Economic Status – Studies have shown consistent differences between the average ability, achievement and aptitude of individuals belonging to different socio-economic backgrounds.

1. Children with very low mental ability were born to parents of all SES levels but these are much less common amongst those belonging to higher economic status.

2. When scales are used to measure economic status, the correlations between the two come to be about 0.30. It was observed in some studies that when subjects are asked to rank occupational titles on the basis of prestige, these ranking tend to follow the pattern of the differences in intelligence.

3. Knowledge of the meaning of socio-economic class differences are important because such conclusions are significant for social policies in a country tries for equalization of opportunities and has a concern for maximum development of all her citizens. In fact, this is more general hereditary-environment discussion which raises many questions, for example, "Are poor people poor because they are poor?"

Two Opinions – There are two sets of people as under:
(a) One of them believes that present intelligence tests are not really measuring the potential ability of lower class children. So, lower class children are consistently and repeatedly underestimated and discriminated when compared to other higher class children.
(b) The second line of thinking rests on the hypothesis about the importance of early experiences on general intellectual development.
The cultural deprivation results in differences between these children and the children belonging to other groups which widen with increase in the chronological age.
(6) Differences in Terms of Personality – Differences in personality make-up bring about differences in intellectual pursuits and achievement. Individuals, due to intellectual diversity in interest and goals, habits, background, mental abilities, etc. seek general outlets for expression realization.
Some are extroverts and some introverts. Some feel comfortable with one learning method while others go for a different learning method. Some are aggressive others are submissive.

Q16. What is gender issues? Discuss with the help of suitable example the implication of gender issues for teachers.
Ans. The movement for educational development of females had to face multidimensional problems which come in the way of their advancement and progress. Most of these problems are due to differential treatment given to females both in the educational as well as social settings.
Nature of Gender Issues

Nature of gender issues are an under :
1. Society perceives a female child as different from a male child. As such it assigns stereotyped roles to the female child.
2. It is seen that some teachers in the school, while teaching, give examples and use teaching strategies which are biased against girl students. Such teachers opine that girls should have a different type of education which may be helpful for them to develop as a good housewife and a mother.
In fact, girls and boys may to some extent differ in terms of certain abilities and both these sets of individuals excel each other in terms of certain abilities. Therefore we should evolve specific teaching-learning strategies to develop

their inherent abilities to the maximum and also to prove extra opportunity for development of other competencies in which they are weak. We must make some bold efforts for replacing the professional value system by a belief in the equality of sexes. An attempt should be made to recognize the individual differences between girls and boys and make use of these during the teaching-learning process.

Another issue to be discussed is the social attitude towards girls which is reflected not only in the treatment received by girls, but also in the instructional materials meant for them. This becomes more serious in case of girls coming from weaker sections of society i.e. scheduled castes, scheduled tribes. They carry the stigma of belonging to a weaker section. Both these educational and social perceptions come in the way of the development of a girl child in our society. Most parents hesitate in sending their daughters to school for education, because they think that the money which is required for educating girls could be more usefully to spend on their marriage instead of education.

State governments have started a number of welfare schemes for female children and some programmes have been developed to promote their education, yet girls remain the biggest group outside the educational system. The economic educational and social issues related with education of girls are of great importance for the teacher to consider.

In co-education system, teacher has to teach both boys and girls in class. The teacher he or she should not make any different between boys and girls due to their sex. For example, a teacher should not think that a girl should be taught such kind that she could be a good housewife. Teacher should understand their inherent abilities and try to develop these abilities through the use of specific strategies.

As a teacher, we see that mostly parents of lower class families do not want to send their girls in school they think that giving education to girls is totally fruitless and wastage of time and money. They think that the money required for educating girls could be more usefully while spending on their marriage instead of education. Teacher should develop awakening in the society about the need of education of girls. He/she should encourage parents to send their daughters in school. The curriculum and instructional materials should be transacted keeping in view the issues related to gender as well as individual differences. We see that Indian girls are timid and take a lot of time to open up and participate in the learning process. Teacher should encourage them to take part in teaching learning process. Teacher should organise co-curricular activities specially to girls so that they could develop self image. Teacher can do very much to solve these gender related problems.

Q17. What is heredity? What is its role in the building of a person's personality? [June-06, Q3(iii)]

Ans. Heredity – An individual has a specific set of limits which are the result of his biological heredity from parents or fore fathers. This called heredity the term 'heredity' may also be used in another sense, for example, if a child is brought up in a particular social environment say of a tribe, the value of that tribe and the norms of that tribe are inculcated in him through other members of that social group and we call it social heredity. In the same way, a student in a classroom situation brings with him a specific cultural heredity also. Here in this section our discussion will be focused on the influence of only biological heredity on individual differences. Each individual has a specific set of potentials which are developed through the environment. These potentialities and characteristics possessed by the individual are the result of his biological heredity. The influence of heredity is so strong that twins brought up in drastically different environment show very much similarity in terms of their mental abilities and other traits. This shows that even drastically different environments are not capable of overcoming heredity influences.

Genetic Basis of Individual Differences – Generally when we talk about heredity we invariable, mean genes received by the individual from his parents at the time of conception. These combinations of genes are called chromosomes. Similar chromosomes from pairs and very similar to each other in terms of appearance and characteristics. Each human cell contains 23 pairs of chromosomes, which may be seen only with the help of high powered microscopes. Each individual, at the time of conception is in the form of a single cell divided into two daughter cells which again divide themselves. This process of division ultimately results in a matured organism. At the time of division, each cell has two identical sets of chromosomes resulting in identical heredity. Which cell will develop into a skin cell and which one into a bone cell depends upon the cellular environment. Genes of the individual interact with this cellular environment in different ways during the process of specialized development of different cells. A different type of cell division takes place when the individual attains sexual maturity. This process is called meiosis. Meiosis involves two cell division, during which the chromosome number is halved.

Reasons for Difference – Individual difference is the result of a number of possible combinations of genes. In this system even a simple looking and small characteristic is the result of various genes. As is apparent, individual germ cells of each parent and those of two parents i.e. mother and father have a number of possible combinations of genes. As a result, we find individual difference between two siblings. Since identical twins develop from the division of a single fertilized ovum, they are identical in terms of heredity. Physical characteristics are a result of heredity. Various physical characteristics i.e. colour of hair, eye, skin, etc. are the result of various combinations of genes. If an individual receives two genes of albinism from the parents, the person will be an albino. Such an individual will be called homozygous. If the individual gets albinism from one parent and normal colouring from another, he will be called heterozygous. Since normal colouring is dominant such individual will have normal colouring.

Determination of Sex – Likewise the sex of the individual is determined by the pair of chromosomes received from the parents. When the individual receives X chromosome from both the parents, the sex will be female. But if the individual receiver X chromosome from the mother and Y chromosome from the father, the sex will be male. Certain genes received by the individual through X chromosome result in sex-related characteristics.

Diseases – A female receiving one dominant gene of hemophilia i.e. colour blindness from one parent and one normal gene from another parent is not likely to have this disease. The reason is the normal gene will dominate the hemopilis gene. In the case of a male, if a dominant hemophiliacs gene is passed on to the individual by the mother, the individual is likely to have this disease as the Y chromosome of father will not carry this gene at all.

Heredity and Mental Development – Watson claimed to train any healthy child into someone expected or desired. The experiments on animal breeding proved that some kind of mental ability could be inherited. The early experiments on rats were conducted by Tryon (1942) at the University of California and by Heron (1935) at the University of Minnesota. They studied wide differences in maze learning (finding a way to a cheese through a maze) done by various groups of rats. They studied the ability to learn maze over generations after generations and it was found that with each generation the groups drew further apart. Many psychologists interpreted these characteristics of rats as analogous to human intelligence. When these bright and dull rats were exposed to other learning problems, it was found that bright rats were not good at everything.

Searle – Searle (1949), found that rats from each group showed a characteristics pattern of high or low scores which were quite different for each group. It was found that the bright animals were characteristically food drivers, economical of distance, low in motivation of escape from water and timid in response to open spaces. The dull rats were better in water motivation and timid of mechanical apparatus features.

Arthur Jensen – Arthur Jensen of the University of California at Berbely found that white children were genetically superior to black children. This argument claims that I.Q. has an extremely high genetic factor (about 80%) and that there must therefore, be racial differences in intelligence. This study was later on criticized by many researchers. Jensen based his argument on the concept of hereditability. Since I.Q. is the result of heredity, environment and critical period (kaal), the hereditability value for I.Q. lies somewhere between 0 to 1.00. Jensen has argued that the actual value is somewhere near 80. Since the teachers often treat black children as if they were devoid of intellectual resources, the children begin to fulfill his expectation by achieving less and less as the school years go by. One of the reasons for this drop relates to the placement of the least competent teachers in these schools. It is found that black children often do not progress beyond the (viii) or (ix) grade level. Its reason may be that the level of their teacher's (non) competence does not help them beyond that point. One study found that two-thirds of the teachers tested stood lower than junior high school level on a proficiency test.

Heredity and family resemblances in intelligence – For a common person, resemblances among the family members in terms of intelligence is an indicator of the influence of heredity on different abilities of the some family. Psychologists have carried out some systematic studies to see the influence of heredity on behaviour pattern of the members of the family. However, in a family, it becomes difficult to differentiate between the hereditary and environmental influences. If, in a sample of large family groups one notices intragroup similarities, it may be attributed to their heredity while the rest of the influences might have been caused by the environment. These researchers have tried to test the following hypotheses:

1. Correlation to be Higher – If environment is an important factor, correlation between like-sexed siblings should be higher than those between different-sexed siblings. The environment is more closely similar to the two brothers or two sisters than it is for a boy or a girl in the family.

2. Correlation Co-efficient to be Lower, Environment – If environment is an important factor in the production of intellectual traits, correlation coefficients between siblings should be lower for these traits than for physical characteristics like eye colour, height and head measurement, which are thought to be almost entirely hereditary.

3. Correlation Mother and Children – If environment is an important factor, correlations between mothers and children should be higher than those between father and children. The mother is more closely associated with the children during their early formative years.

4. Correlation between Siblings – If environment is an important factor, correlations between siblings should be higher than correlations between parents and children. The fact that they belong to the same generation would operate to make the siblings' environment more similar. Scattered evidences have been cited both for and against each of the hypotheses presented above.

Way for Evaluation

The best way to evaluate the influence of heredity is to take subjects who experienced the same environment but who are known to differ in genetic endowment and compare them with a group in which both heredity and environment are the same. We can do it by comparing the amount of differences between identical twin pairs with the amount of difference between fraternal twins or between siblings. Two terms viz., concordance and discordance are used in such studies.

These can be explained as under :

1. Concordant -If both the twins show certain characteristics, they are called to be concordant.

2. Discordant - If one twin shows it and the other does not, they are called discordant.

Whenever the percentage of concordant pairs is much higher in case of identified twins than fraternal twins, there is a sound basis for concluding that the traits in question have a genetic origin.

Role of Heredity

The role heredity plays in certain kinds of psychiatric difficulties has been established by a large-scale study of New York Psychiatric Institute under the leadership of Kallaman (1950). The study was started with a group of persons with certain diagnosis and then to locate and check up on their blood relatives. In case of individuals who suffered with schizohphrenia (psychoromatic disease), it was found if one of a pair of identical twins has the disease, the chances are that eighty-six times out of a hundred the other twin has it also. The other fourteen who are not frankly schizophreinic have schizoid personalities.

Some Other Research Works

Significant research work has also been done to study neuroanatomical traits in the house mouse and the determination of associated differences in behaviour. Stores (1967) found highly significant and substantial strain differences. Studies on brain weight have given an ample basis for optimism regarding our future ability to manipulate, at least, some of the compound traits which underline it. Roderick et al. (1973), and R. Wimer et al. (1969) show that identifiable genetic control exists for the sizes of some specific portions of the central nervous system. Studies conducted by Terris (1964), C. Wimer and Prater (1966) and Wimer et al. (1969) provided some evidence to support a positive between brain weight and activity in the open field.

Q18. What is environment? How does it cause differences among individuals?

Ans. Environment and Individual Differences

Role of Environment – According to the studies most of us, except identical twins, get fifty percent of our genes from our parent. We are likely to develop hereditary characteristics quite different from that parent. Foster homes provide different environment to study its effect on Identical twins under controlled conditions. By doing careful analysis of the results it can be easily found out how much difference the environment makes in shaping personality. Newman, Freeman and Halzinger (1937) found that the pairs reared apart show mere differences in I.Q. But Woodworth (1941) pointed out a factor called error of measurement that is always involved in intelligence testing. Woodworth concluded that environmental differences do operate to produce I.Q. differences in persons with exactly the same hereditary potentialities.

Wood Worth's Opinion – The special component of environment influences intellectual development of an individual. Woodworth showed that educational influences can produce I.Q. differences in persons having the same heredity but it is the large rather than the minor environmental discrepancies that are important. Newman, Freeman and Holzinger (1937) tried to identify the factors present in the environment which produce personality differences in separated identical twins. Two main conclusions drawn from the studies of identical twins are as follow :

(1) Marked educational differences are able to produce substantial differences in measured intelligence.

(2) Intellectual differences in the population as a whole are so large that they can not be accounted for in terms of environmental differences alone.

A teacher should know about the impact of a good educational system on the individual. It means it is quite possible that the intelligence level of the population as a whole can be moderately increased. But it can not be accepted that individuals with low intelligence can be brought to the level of the bright ones through a good system of education.

Children in Foster Homes and Institutions

A number of research studies have been carried on children adopted by others and brought up in good homes. However, the shortcoming is that the studies are not carried out in two situations i.e. before and after adoption and in this situation it becomes difficult to pinpoint the effect of environment on the development of the child. Again, while selecting a foster home for a child, the concerned agencies try to locate homes where the child with his intellectual abilities and personality could be adjusted. This factor is called selective placement.

In one of the earlier studies, attempts were made to find out how successful adopted children were in their life. 77 percent of the subjects were found to be capable, only 10 percent were delinquents or vicious. Burks (1928) found that a superior home can result in a moderate increase in a child's tested intelligence, but can not bring him to the level of individuals who have both superior heredity and superior environment. Leahy's (1935) study was also much closer to Burks study in terms of its findings. All these studies agreed in their findings and led us to believe that the average intelligence of adopted children was somewhat higher than that of children in homes of the educational level from which they come.

Some Other Research Findings

The studies conducted at the University of Iowa showed that the environment exerts a large influence. In one of the studies it was found that the older the children were, when they entered the orphanage, the lower their I.Qs were. It compares the results on the increasing retardation with age of isolated groups. Another study of the University of Iowa showed that children placed in the superior adoptive homes turned out higher on the average than those placed in the less superior environments.

Some of environment inputs that appear to affect an individual's personality and intelligence are as under:

(1) Nutrition – One of the environment factors is nutrition. Gross deficiency of diet can adversely affect I.Q. and even produce mental retardation.

(2) Kwashiorkar – An illness resulting from a protein-deficient diet has been found to be extremely damaging the intellectual development.

(3) Khesari pulse's effect – A specific variety of pulse (khesari) available in certain area of Madhya Pradesh in India results in crippled individuals.

Recent Studies

Recent studies have led to some speculation that inadequate protein intake prevents full development of the brain especially those areas which are involved in memory storage.

Bloom (1964) has emphasised that an abundant early environment is the key to the full development of intelligence. David krech has shown that without stimulus heterogeneity animals are less able to learn and their brains develop fully.

Variables

The three crucial environment variables listed by Bloom (1964) are as under:

1. The stimulation that the children receive for verbal development.

2. The affection and reward that the children receive from verbal reasoning accomplishments, and

3. The encouragement which the children receive for active interaction with problems, exploration of the environment for learning of new skills.

Murlidharan and Srivastava (1995) examined the impact of temple ecology on cognitive development of children. Children associated with temples emerged to be more cognitively competent than children from nontemple areas.

DESH AND KAAL (PLACE AND TIME) Exert influence on the total personality of the individual. The place and its environment influences attitudes, interests and over all development of the individual. Same individual placed in different environments at various time is likely to exhibit different behavioural pattern. Again, a child shows different behaviour in different subject periods or at different places viz. play ground, home and school.

So far as kaal or time is concerned, as age increases intellectual development increases less. Initially the speed is faster but it becomes slower and slower with age. Bloom feels that the differences between a beneficial and a stuffing environment during these early childhood years can produce I.Q. differences of 20 points.

Q19. Discuss the interaction and misconceptions regarding heredity and environment. [Dec-07, Q3(iv)]

Ans. Interaction of Heredity and Environment : A large number of individual differences are caused by the interactive process of heredity and environment. To each child heredity provides a potential and the dynamic forces of environment act upon that a potential in a different way. Let us illustrate how the interactive forces of heredity and environment produce differences in individuals. We may have for the sake of illustration one trait (intelligence) and at one end of the diagram we place the rod measuring the rate of mental maturity (I.Q.).

There are three children of the same percentage X and Y each. The hereditary potential for these children A, B, C or for P, Q, R is the same being represented by the equality of height of the cones. But as environmental factors influence members' sets differently, the hereditary potential is realised in different amounts or degrees. With least stimulating environments only a part of the potential is realised (A, P) and with very stimulating environments we have full realisation of the potential (C, R). The differences between the six children are due to interaction of hereditary potential and the environment.

Misconception regarding heredity and environment.

We have many misconceptions regarding heredity and environment due to lake of proper knowledge. People uses two terms in born and heredity interchangeably. It is usually believed that whatever is in inborn in heredity. Some think that taking birth is the end of the heredity. We should not consider birth as the end or beginning of one type of influence as it is only a stage of development. We should understand that heredity does not necessarily results in resemblance of offsprings to their parents. Heredity does not refer to any transmission as these skills or behaviours are consciously learned by the parents and do not fall within the purview of heredity. We have many other misconceptions too. It is believed that if a heredity origin is identified under a given condition, nothing or very little can be done to improve it. Really this is not true. Many heredity diseases are curable. Some people think that all heredity characteristics cannot be changed but it is not totally true. There are very few heredity characteristics that be changed by any known environmental factors.

Q20. Discuss the implications for the teacher regarding heredity and environment.

Ans. A teacher should know about the implications of hereditary and environmental backgrounds for the teaching-learning process. The measured intelligence of individuals or groups of individuals is related to some extent to their educational experiences. There are intellectual differences in terms of the amount of formal education, even in cases of siblings who initially look alike. Again, many individuals who were originally labeled as feeble minded or mentally retarded become able to function as normal persons in their communities after they have received the right kind of education or training. This indicates the positive impact of a stimulating environment on the development of the individual. Therefore, a favourable stimulating and supportive educational atmosphere should be provided to children coming to the school. Following suggestions are given :

1. Teaching Strategies – The curriculum development, teaching strategies or guidance, knowledge of one's heredity and environment backgrounds, and their impact on an individual's personality is very handy to teachers and curriculum developers. Educationists attach great importance to the selection of proper teaching methods to suit the need of the students.

2. Selection of Children –The selection and placement of children in various groups should be done on the basis of their qualities, skills and talents.

3. Educational Guidance – Students need educational guidance to either select a suitable course of study or to improve the level of their achievements.

4. Counselling for Adjustment – Guidance also involves counselling for adjustment to educational, emotional or social situations.

5. Reduction of Educational Variability – The purpose of individualized instruction is to reduce the educational variability among individuals by catering to their specific needs arising out of individual differences.

6. Helping Every Child – Individualized instruction aims at helping every child according to his capabilities. The individualized instruction is not meant to impart instruction to each child separately. A group of students similar to each other in terms of intelligence, interest, personality, etc. can be taught together.

7. Utilization of Information – We can utilize information about every child's personality and cognitive development for the purpose of selection and placement in a suitable vocation.

8. Group Formation – Children with specific skills, whether obtained through heredity or acquired through environment, may be put in suitable groups or advised to go to a particular stream of education.

9. Essentiality of Counselling – Counselling should be an integral part of educational guidance in our system. The guidance aims at making the individual aware of his own interests and abilities and to guide him in the proper direction.

10. Corrective Measures – We should observe each student for the initial period carefully and find out details about him. On the basis of our observation we can develop specific corrective measures to take care of his deficiencies so that he could be brought at par with other students. This will also ascertain the quality of education for each student.

Understanding the Learning Process

Q1. What is learning? What are its main characteristics?[June-05, Q2]

Ans. Learning according to Crow and Crow is acquisition of habits, knowledge and attitudes. 'The process of acquiring new knowledge and new responses is the process of learning', says Woodworth. Such formal definitions of learning are at best, incomplete attempts to explain briefly an exceedingly complex affair. Learning is not only getting knowledge of subject-matter or skill in art by study, by experience or by being taught, it is also an acquisition of habits, attitudes, perceptions, preferences, interests, social adjustments, values and ideals.

Psychologists' Views

The Psychologists' 'Views on learning' are as under :

1. Munn – Munn defined learning as to process of being modified more or less permanently, by what happens in the world around us by what we do, or by what we observe.

2. Hunder and Hilgard – According to Hunder and Hilgard, 'learning' is the process by which behaviour (in the broader sense) is originated or changed through training procedures (whether in the natural environment or in the laboratory.)

3. Boaz – To Boaz learning is a process by which the individual that are necessary to meet the demand of life in general.

4. Geoch – According to Geoch, 'learning as we measure it is more or less a permanent change in behaviour which occurs under the motivational conditions of practice.'

5. Commins and Fagin – Commins and Fagin have described 'learning as a sequence of mental events or conditions leading to changes in the learner'. Sequence of Mental Events.

They have elaborated the sequence of mental event as follows :

1. The learner has needs and is therefore in a state of readiness to respond.

2. The learner meets a problem (or learning situations) by solving which his need(s) is (are) likely to be satisfied. But for solving it a new interpretations required because previously learned responses are inadequate for reaching the goal (or solution) and satisfying his need(s).

3. So he interprets the situation with reference to his goals, and tries response(s) which seems to satisfy his need(s).

4. If his response leads to the achievement of his goal, he will tend to interpret and respond to similar situations in future in the same way. Otherwise he keeps on trying and re-interpreting the problem until satisfying consequences or results are achieved.

Analysis – On analysis the above and similar other explanations and definitions of learning we can easily infer that :

1. There are certain general characteristics of learning and

2. There are factors which influence learning.

These are the characteristics of learning

1. Learning is goal directed or purposive – Learning becomes meaningful and purposive when we want to achieve some goals from it. Every human being wants to achieve some goals in his life. Always, learning is found goal directed of purposive. There cannot be found goalless learning.

2. Learning is an active process – Learning is an activity. The greater the activeness or effort in the part of the learner the better will he/she learn. A passive learner cannot learn anything.

3. Learning is individual – The rate of learning differs from person to person. In a class every student is a unique person and he has his own problems, needs, purpose, aspirations, interests, likes and dislikes. So their learning process also are differ from other. So learning is individual process.

4. Learning is the outcome of the interaction of the individual with the total situation – A student learns by responding to the total learning situation and not in the context of some single stimulus. So a good teacher should set the environment carefully for framing a learning situation.

5. Learning is creative – Learning is a creative process which combines the knowledge and experiences of the teacher. According to Crow and Crow, critical thinking involves direction, interpretation, selection, insight, creation and criticism.

6. Learning is transferable – As we know that we can use learnt material in other situation to solve problems. We can apply our rules, theories in other situation so learning is transferable also.

Q2. Discuss the principles of learning. How will you use these principles in your classrooms?

Ans. The process of learning continues throughout life. All human being learns any kind of behaviour in their whole life. There is not any existence of life without the process of learning. There are various learning processes through which we acquire beliefs attitudes and skills. Here we shall discuss the principles of learning and their use in our classroom.

Principles of learning and their use in classroom

1. Law of effect – When a modifiable connection between a situation and response is made and is accompanied or followed by a satisfying state of affairs, the strength of the link with that situation is increased. Here satisfying state means that students would satisfy through the learning process. We should organise teaching learning process by such kind that students would get satisfaction. They should be involved in some kind of game or action which gives them pleasure and satisfaction. If we try to organise their learning process in which their usual movements and interest are restricted then their learning is delayed. We can use this principle in our class too. We should organise our teaching-learning process with the actions and games in which students take part happily. They should be according to the interests, age level and needs of the students. We should organise play-way method and learning by doing method.

2. Law of intensity – We should offer a quick reward or response on the positive behaviour of the students regarding their teaching-learning process. According to this principle the greater the reward the more it facilitates learning. On the other side the more the reward the stronger is the motivation and stronger the motivation the faster and surer is the learning. This is called the law of intensity. We should offer reward speedily after the positive response of the students. If we have gap between the response and rewards than we cannot motivate the learners effectively. The shorter the time between response and reward, the stronger is the learning. So the teacher should understand principle and should use in his/her teaching learning process to make it more effective and aimful. We should use the skills of reinforcement in it. As we find negative response of learner then we should not give punishment to learners but should try to make correct it through affection and consideration of the reason of mistake.

3. Law of practice – As we know that practice makes a man perfect. If a worker practices daily to complete a job then he/she can gain mastery and skillful control over it. If the things learnt are repeated time and again they gain permanence in the learners' memory so a teacher should use various kinds of exercise in his/her teaching learning process. If we teach a theory or principle in our teaching learning process then we should try to organise a practice related activity in which students could apply these rules on their daily live's problem to solve them.

Teacher should organise necessary practices to make his teaching effective. If the learner does not make use of his learning, he forgets it due course of time. As for example, we should make students to repeat the mathematical tables again and again or write a miss-spelled word correctly a number of times. After teaching a structure of new sentence pattern, we should organise a test exercise containing that kind of structure and we should provide much time to students to make practice of it. By practice they can learn that structure effectively and permanently.

4. Law of readiness – According to this law we should make our students ready first then we should organise our teaching learning process. Without a will to learn there cannot be true learning. The will to learn is, the prepareness or readiness of mind. If a student is forced to learn then we cannot organise a true or real teaching learning process. First we should try to motivate students for learning. If a student is forced to do a thing when he is not ready to it, we cannot expect good results from him. So we as a teacher should know the needs and interests of learning and then try to motivate or make him ready for learning. As for example before organising a teaching learning process related an English topic we should make ready students through a recitation of Rhyme. A teacher should connect his teaching-learning process with his/her pre-knowledge and interests. We should connect our teaching-learning process related daily lives of students. We should make students ready for learning besides forcing him for it.

In the end we can say that a teacher should understand the various principles of learning thoroughly and then try to use these principles in his teaching learning process to make learning process more effective, participative and aimful. We should use various learning principles to make students ready to learn, to motivate them for learning, to make practices of learnt matter.

Q3. What are the conditions affecting learning?

Ans. Conditions Affecting Learning – Learning is in the context (learning material) when we say that a student is learning our answer is not complete, we just give an incomplete statement. We should say a student is learning what? And the answer to this 'what' indicates towards the content a student is expected to learn or the objectives he is going to achieve. Besides, learner and content, in a conventional classroom, there is a teacher who through the act of his teaching helps the students learn. Thus there are three categories of conditions which affect learning namely.

1. The conditions related to the content.

2. The teacher.

3. The learner.

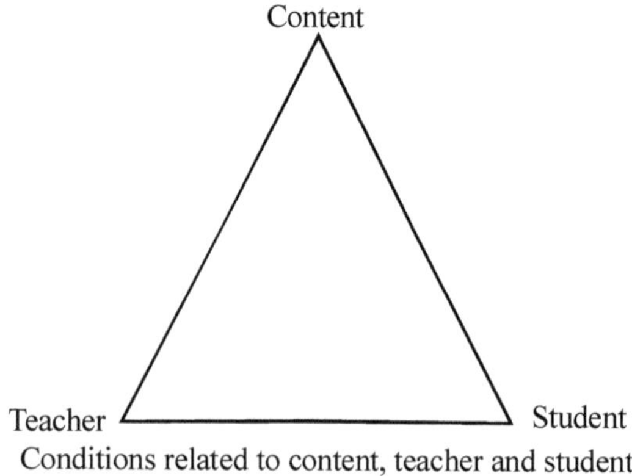

Conditions related to content, teacher and student

Unless a teacher knows 'What to teach' and the student knows 'What to learn' it will be impossible to carry on the process of learning. The answers to these two questions specify the content or the curriculum. The activities, the objectives and the organisation of the curriculum determine the nature of the learning process.

The conditions related to student are perhaps the most important in facilitating efficient learning. So educationists on providing a favourable learning environment to the students, whether in school or at home the student should be given a calm, clean lighted and well ventilated space for his study and related activities.

The physical and mental health of the student also affect his learning. Only a physically and mentally alert student can learn properly.

Reasons for Deficiency – Sometimes, students show deficiency in learning. There may be so many reasons-some are as under:

1. Type may not be properly motivated.

2. They may not be interested in what is being taught to them.

3. The teacher might have used defective method of teaching or the activities he has chosen are beyond their maturity level.

4. The student may be over-burdened due to heavy home assignment given to him in one or more academic subjects. Such a practice creates unnecessary tension in the mind of the student. So the student feels tired and bored in his study.

Q4. Discuss the relationship between maturity and learning give suitable example? [Dec-05, Q3(vii)]

Ans. Learning And Maturation/Maturity

Maturation is an important factor which influences learning. Maturation is a natural process. For maturation an external stimulus is not necessary and its sequence is biologically predetermined. On the other hand, learning is a change in the individual. It is a process which takes place as a result of 'stimuli' from 'without'.

The behaviour is said to have matured if a behaviour sequence develops through regular stages (irrespective of intervening practices or training) In case training procedures do not modify or speed up the behaviour. Such procedures are not important. The changes are not classified as learning.

The swimming of tadpoles and the flying of birds can be attributed to primarily to maturation. But in the case of human beings, it is not easy to decide whether the activities result from maturation of learning. The child learns to talk only when he reaches a certain stage or age in maturation. Again he does not learn the language just because he attains that age. The language which he learns is that which he hears. Thus the two processes maturation and learning are closely related to each-other. Maturation facilitates the process of learning. Learning becomes effective when appropriate maturity has been attained. Learning takes place only if the stage for that type of learning has been achieved through a process of maturation.

A teacher, should know how to differentiate between maturation development with that of changes due to learning. For example-Our typical human brain develops with age. It is a maturation process. But our knowledge, our habits are acquired though stimulus-response activities or in at her words learning. Maturation is important for learning. Before we learn anything, our sensory, motor and nervous structures should attain a certain level of maturity. For example, we cannot make an infant run simply because he has not acquired the appropriate maturity. So until a certain level of maturation is acquired by the child, training (or learning) may be of no avail. We should bear in mind that during the early development period of the child, greater level of maturity brings more efficient learning, and learning of complex skills requires a higher level of maturity.

Q5. What is verbal learning? Discuss the process and implication of verbal learning for class room practice. [Dec-07, Q3(v)]

Ans. Verbal learning is considered by most modern cognitive psychologists as either inadequate or ineffective in ensuring learning in students. For verbal learning is often considered a passive learning experience as the action is completely undertaken by the teacher. The students are therefore, looked upon as inactive or passive recipients of knowledge.

The Nature of Verbal Learning

According to Ausubel (1963 ; 1977) learning is equivalent to subsumption which is the inclusion of new information into an existing cognitive structure. Thus entails the following process:

• Recognising (of the verbal information),

• Relating (new information to what already exists in the cognitive structure), and

• Meaningful learning (as a result of the above).

For example, if you want to teach students about 'moths'. The pattern according to Ausubel would include, the recognition of the organism as an 'insect' or 'small winged creature' i.e. placing the new information in some existing category of child's cognitive structure. The second step would then be to relate this information with what already exists in his structure. This is done in terms of comparing the new information 'moth' to what is already known about insects, in terms of similarities and differences. This results in meaningful learning for the child.

According to Ausubel organising and explaining relationship both old and new, is the task of the teacher, and not of the student. Bruner help that the task of organising information should be undertaken by the students. Only then will learning become meaningful. The advantage of verbal learning over discovery learning is that verbal learning would-

1. Include a larger body of information.

2. Require less resources, and

3. Be economical in terms of time.

Process of Verbal Learning

Ausubel explains the process of meaningful verbal learning with the help of the following key concepts:

Subsumer – The subsumer is akin to Piaget's concept of schema. It is a conceptual framework, wherein higher level concepts include (subsume) other ideas. Subsuming involves incorporating new material meaningfully, within this conceptual framework.

Subsumption – The process of building the cognitive structure (subsumer) by subsuming new information into it takes place in two vital ways:

1) Derivative subsumption – When the new information is derived from the already existing structure, the process of derivative subsumption takes place. For instance, if a general category of 'mammals' is already present in the cognitive structure, the specific example of a horse, elephant, etc., even when presented as new information is derived easily and therefore is easily learned.

2) Correlative subsumption – When the new information requires that the existing structure be altered, correlative subsumption takes place. In the earlier example, if the new information was 'whale'. The existing structure will have to change to accommodate the new kind of mammal. This kind of learning is more challenging, yet when acquired, is better remembered. This is comparable to Piaget's concept of accommodation.

Dissociative subsumption – Remembering is dissociative subsumption i.e., it requires the ability to separate new learning from the old. Ausubel holds that recall is facilitated or enhanced, according to the dissociability of the new information. Information which is similar to what already exists, will be learned faster yet paradoxically because of the similarity with the existing structures, learning is low in dissociability and therefore difficult to recall. When information is unique or different, the reverse occurs.

Implication for Classroom Practice

Ausubel subscribes to the notion that new ideas are best introduced from the general (abstract) to the specific (concrete). This implies that students must be provided with a conceptual framework on which they can anchor new ideas being elaborated later. The advanced organiser, serves this very purpose. It introduces the main ideas and makes all the relationship between these ideas explicit.

Advanced Organisers

There are two types of advanced organisers as under:

(i) Comparative advanced organisers – It is based on derivative subsumption and involves direct comparisons. For example, comparing the respiratory system of animals and human being before introducing the human respiratory system.

(ii) Expository advanced organisers – This type of the advance organise is based on oblique and not on direct comparisons. For example, when two system, such as the circulatory and the respiratory are compared; a new subsumer is sought to be established as an offshoot of an existing one. Other implications of verbal learning are as under:

(a) The lecture method is neither ineffective, nor passive if it is organised or based on theory of verbal learning.

(b) Since learning is facilitated when new information is similar to the existing one, points of similarity must be established.

(c) Since recall is facilitated when differences are distinct, differences between new and existing knowledge must also be highlighted.

(d) It is necessary for the teacher to assess the child's existing cognitive structure before introducing new information.

Q6. Discuss critically various modes of learning support four answer with example. [June-07, Q4]

Ans. Learning is a continuous process which exists from birth to death. An individual learns various facts things, concepts, events through various medium. These means or medium through which we learn anything can be defined as modes of learning.

Modes of learning

1. Learning by observation – This is the first and foremost mode of learning. Every human being learns various things through observation. Here by observation, we do not mean only seeing a thing rather it refers to the act of perceiving or observing the stimulus. In observation process, we do not take help only eyes as in seeing but we take help of other organs also for listening, smelling tasting and touching. A person observes an event, thing etc. when he is interested in these. So we should first try to make interested the child in these things and then he can observe them aimfully. This interest is aroused as a result of the impulse evoked by instincts. The greater the impulse the more is the amount of interest attached to it. And the greater the interest the more the attention paid to the object.

We as a teacher should provide opportunity to students to observe new things according to their interests. We should provide a chance to students to grasp the meaning of the demonstration of an action. We should try to fix images of how the model looks in each step of the demonstration. Teacher should provide them verbal directions also while students are observing the action or things. We can teach various parts of human body by giving a chance to students to observe the model of human body.

2. Learning by imitation – Students can learn very much by copying the actions. Imitation is the tendency to repeat the observed actions of others. In the beginning, the child learns his movements, actions, and gestures by imitation. As we know that students take very much interest in copying the actions of others. The capacity of imitating is very much prominent in children and we must have observed that they take delight in imitation. We as a teacher can use this mode of learning in our teaching-learning process. Students can recite poems with actions of parts of body by imitating the recitation of his/her teacher. A science teacher can teach about experiments through the mode of imitation. This imitation should be willingly and deliberate. Students should imitate the actions of the teacher consciously. Teacher should try to arise interests in students about the action and then provide the chance of imitating to students. A child learns very much from his birth to primary education level through imitation. We should use this mode of learning in our teaching learning process also.

3. Learning by Trial and Error – As we know that every human being learns from his/her own errors. Like this students can learn from their own errors. Students try to solve any problem and they do not succeed due to some errors. Teacher should provide them feedback about their errors, and reasons of the errors. When students know the errors and their reasons then they make another trial avoiding from the errors which they have made in their pre trial. Here the role of the teacher is very important. Teacher should provide feedback about the errors after every trial and then provide them treatment of these errors so that they could avoid from these errors in next trial. Some of the laws underlying trial errors learning are law of readiness law of effect and law exercise. As for example if students are trying to make a experiment of composition of carbon dioxide, they try to compose it but they do not succeed in first trial due to some errors. Teacher should provide them feedback about their errors and their reasons after it students will try again to compose it without using these errors. At last they will succeed in composition of carbon-di-oxide gas.

4. Learning by insight – If an individual reaches the solution all of a sudden while solving a problem, we say that he has learned by insight. In fact the person reaches the solution by understanding the relation between different aspects of the problematic situation. In daily life of every student he/she comes across to many problems and he/she solve them. In this solving process, they learn many principles, processes, facts and theories. These learning can be said learning by insight. In the mode of learning by insight, student analyses the various aspects of the situation and tries to establish a meaningful relationship among them. On the basis of this new perception, he defines the situation. This process goes on till he solves the problematic situation all of a sudden. That is what we mean when we say that a learner suddenly gets an insight into the solution. This may be call learning by insight.

In the end we can say that a learner does not learn from any specific mode of learning but he/she can use any mode from these modes according to his/her needs. So teacher should provide positive situations to learners so that they could learn through these modes according to their ability, needs and interests.

Q7. What is transfer of learning? How many type it has? What teaching methods facilitate the occurrence of transfer?

Ans. Transfer of learning is a phenomenon of learning being facilitated in situation B by virtue of common elements, ideals, or generalizations that have been learnt in situation A. Learning in one situation A has an effect on learning in situation B. It has an adaptation to the second situation. In other words, if in classroom situation certain habits, skills, ideas or ideals are acquired, learning other habits, skills, ideas or ideals in another situation met in daily life is facilitated or inhibited. The effect is either that of facilitation or inhibition. For example, learning the methods of solving problems in arithmetic, may facilitate learning the method of solving problems in algebra. "Transfer is the application or carry-over of knowledge, skills, habits, attitudes or other responses from a situation in which they are initially acquired to some other situation" says Kolesnik.

Types of Transfer of learning

Transfer of learning may take place in three ways.

1) Positive transfer – Positive transfer occurs when the acquisition of one type of performance facilitates learning of another type. In the positive transfer, learning of one activity makes learning of another activity easier. For instance, school children that memorised poems, mathematical tables and other verbal material show better learning of the similar new material as compared to the children who did not get previous training in memorization. It is also a common experience that learning of pedalling of tricycles makes the pedalling of bicycles easier. In all these examples we have noticed that previous learning of a related skill benefits the learner in subsequent learning.

2) Negative transfer – Negative transfer occurs when the previous performance puts hindrances in the performance of the subsequent task. The contents, techniques, or principles which make for negative transfer are opposed to those required by the new situation. For instance, after the end of a year, most of us continue to write the previous year on our cheques for sometime. If the telephone number of our friend changes, we often continue dialing their former number. When we switch over from riding a bicycle to driving a scooter we often pull the clutch level for stopping the vehicle instead of using the foot brake. These types of habits interference are examples of negative transfer of learning.

3) Zero transfer – The zero transfer refers to the fact that previous learning has no effect on the subsequent learning. For example, a cricketer who improves his bowling skills is not expected to transfer this skill to improve his batting skill.

The following are the instructional techniques that facilitate occurrence of transfer:

(1) establishing a clear-cut goals

(2) encouraging understanding of principles, processes, relationships

(3) encouraging over learning

(4) challenging students to formulate their own principles

(5) emphasizing ideals and attitudes.

Establishing Clear-Cut Goals : The leaning in the first situation can facilitate learning in the second situation only when the previous learning has been effective. For previous learning to be effective it is necessary to have clear-cut goals before the learner. He should know where he is going. The teacher also should know where he is leading the learner. Stated simply, your objectives may be development of knowledge, habits and attitudes. Every teacher wants to give knowledge and every learner wants to gain new knowledge, but he should be led to develop a desire to gain new knowledge every day. He should feel that he is worthy and able. He should develop confidence in himself. There are some of the desirable attitudes the teacher may aim at developing. Similarly, he may develop in the learner good work habits which include system, thoroughness, perseverance and determination. So, for effective learning and consequent transfer both the teacher and the taught should have clearly defined aims.

Understanding of Principles, Processes and Relationships : The teacher has to adopt such instructional techniques in his day-to-day teaching that encourage the understanding among pupils. 'Learning by doing' is a teaching method which develops understanding. So learning by doing has a greater transfer value than learning by drill. If the teacher wants that his pupils should learn the role of citizenship in human life, he should encourage them to participate actively in student government.

Activity projects, field trips and T.V. lessons are ways to check mere verbalization and improve understanding. But their use in teaching can be justified only when the method of presenting subject matter facilitates transfer. Common elements in Solving problems in Arithmetic and in actual life situations, for example, may be found not and indicated.

The pupil should be encouraged to understand the principles, processes and relationships well. A principle is a statement which compresses many factors and conditions. For example, the Principle of Conservation of Energy states that energy can neither be created nor destroyed. It is not sufficient to simply state it, memorize it or read it from a Text Book on Higher Secondary Physics. It is necessary for the student to understand the many factors and instances that have gone into its formulation.

Understanding processes is also very important for effective-learning. It is not enough that a child should be able to solve a mathematical sum or give an answer to a question. Teachers should ask their students to explain why and how they got a certain solution. They must be able to discuss the steps they have taken in getting a certain answer.

Understanding of relationships is also very useful. A teacher teaching a modern

Indian language, for instance, should try to indicate relationships between the vocabulary of that language and Sanskrit from which it might have descended. The teacher of mathematics or science should relate these subjects to everyday life.

Encouraging Over learning: By overlearning we mean seeing what has been learnt in many situations. A teacher should conduct thorough instruction, i.e. he should cite many examples, relate older knowledge to new knowledge, as often as possible. Thorough learning or thorough instruction is sure to give maximum transfer. Thorough instruction is only possible through drill, review, discussion and presentation of various examples.

Do not cover the ground. But elaborate on the materials covered. Not only will this method enhance learning but will increase the amount of retention as well as facilitate further learning.

Encouraging Self-Study: Giving principles, processes, facts, and skills readymade to pupils is not enough. Let them try to give their own version to a principle. Let them try to search out a process. Let them study facts themselves. Let them discover something for themselves. It has been experimentally found that self-discovery shows more transfer than instruction in which the teacher gives the facts, principles or skills himself.

Q8. Discuss the behaviouristic approach to learning.

Ans. Behaviouristic Approach –The behaviouristic approach describes learning as a connection between stimulus and response. This approach to learning emphasises that behaviour begins with reflexes i.e., natural responses and new behaviours result from the acquisition of new bonds of stimulus and response through experiences.

The major tenets of the behaviouristic approach are as under:

1. Learning brings about changes in behaviour.

2. Learning takes place if environmental conditions are arranged appropriately to generate changes.

3. The resultant behavioural changes are objectively observable.

The important behaviouristic approach to learning is postulated by B.F. Skinner.

Concept of behaviouristic approach to learning

Behaviourists were greatly influenced by the work of the Russian Psychologist named Ivan Paulov. They believed that overt behaviour was determined by a complex system of independent stimulus-response connection, mode more complex through learning. Thorndike, Watson and Skinner, gave more emphasis on objectivity in behaviour.

Characteristics of Behaviour approach to learning

The behaviouristic approach has the following characteristics:

1. It believes in the objective study of behaviour animal and human being both (objectively observable behaviour).

2. This approach considers environment more important than heredity in the determination of behaviour.

3. The chief method of learning is conditioning.

4. Conditioning is the key to the understanding of behaviours, which is composed of stimulus and response links.

5. According to it, one unit of knowledge gets associated with a new unit of knowledge by virtue of similarity, contrast or contiguity.

Skinner's Operant Conditioning

According to Skinner Psychology aims at predicting and controlling the behaviour of organisms. Behaviour refers to an activity of an organism that can be observed and measured by another person or organism or by the experimenter. Skinner used the operant conditioning approach to the study of learning (operant is the response made by an organism to the surrounding environment). When a dog, for example, is taught a trick, it is rewarded by food or by patting after it makes the appropriate behaviour. Operant behaviour can be evoked by a wide range or stimuli. Operant conditioning is also known as reinforcement conditioning. Here the reinforcement is correlated with the response rather than with the stimuli.

Skinner opines that the basic law underlying this type of conditioning is that in case the occurrence of an operant is followed by a reinforcing stimulus, the conditioning is strengthened. Skinner put a hungry rat in a box' (known as Skinner box). When the rat after fretting about, presses a box level by chance food is released. Every time rat does this, and gets food. After several repetitions the rat learns that if in case it is hungry, it can get food after pressing the lever. So, it goes straight to the lever, presses it and gets food. Thus food reinforces the rat's activity of pressing the lever. Here behaviour and appropriate response are important factors. If reward is withheld again, the behaviour extinguishes.

Educational Implications

1. Shaping behaviour -The behaviouristic approach throws light on habit formation, habit breaking and the role of incentives in learning. This approach helps in shaping the behaviour of students in the desired direction.

2. Increase in the vocabulary -The approach helps the teacher in increasing the vocabulary of his students.

3. Introduction of Teaching Machines -The most significant contribution of this theory in educational practice is the concept of programmed learning and introduction of teaching machines in teaching learning as under-

Programmed Instruction

1. In this system of teaching-learning pre-established subject matter is broken down into small discrete steps.

2. These are carefully organized into a logical sequence.

3. They can be rapidly learned by the students.

4. Each step builds upon the previous one.

5. Reinforcement is given after each step.

6. There is a provision of checking the progress.

If the response is correct, the students can go ahead. If not, he can proceed to the next step after registering the correct response.

Programmed instruction is highly individualized instructional strategy and is an effective innovation in the teaching-learning process.

Teaching Machine –Teaching machines present in an essentially predetermined sequence. They permit the students to respond and give them immediate feedback. Teaching machines present a question or other stimulus to a stimulus, provide a means of response, and then inform him of the correctness of his response immediately after he had responded.

According to Skinner's theory, the following procedure is applied to ensure effective learning in the students:

1. Learning objectives should be defined very specially in terms of behaviour.

2. For developing motivation among the students, there should be use of the classroom reinforcers like praise, blames and grades, etc.

3. Objectives should be arranged in order of simple to complex.

4. In the classroom the principle of immediacy of reinforcement is very important.

5. There should be proper use of positive and negative gestures.

6. Reinforcers should be used periodically. It will enable the possibility of extinction of the desired behaviour to be resisted.

Limitations of Behaviouristic

The behaviouristic to learning has certain limitations as under:

1. This approach explains emotions, thoughts and actions entirely by reference to only his overt behaviour.

2. The theory that the human being is a machine which may not be true.

3. It has ignored the structural and hereditary factors which are very important in the development of psychological process of language.

4. It does not adequately take into account the element of creativity, curiosity and spontaneity in the human beings.
5. The view that all human behaviour is acquired during the lifetime of the individual gives no place to the importance of genetic inheritance.

Q9. What do you mean by humanistic approach to learning. Critically discuss its educational implications. [June-05, Q3(ii)]
Ans. Humanistic approach to learning means a process that is inevitable and unique for every individual. Humanistic approach considers human being as the central part of learning by humanistic approach. Learning should be as the way in which the individual develops his unique way of controlling his environment and attaining his best potential. The humanistic approach makes use of creativity, belongingness, self-development, co-existence mental health, values etc. humanistic approach is concerned with the welfare of all human beings. This approach believes in co-existence. This approach emphasises on learning in natural environment of human love, peace, co-operation, freedom, and equality. It believes that learning should be need-based and experience-based. According to humanistic approach to learning, self motivation can result better learning. In this approach every individual develops his natural own way of learning thus student takes more responsibility for determining what they are learning. Humanistic approach believes in co-existence. It is a new approach to learning teacher should understand it and use it according to needs of the situation time to time.

Educational implications of humanistic approach to learning
1. Place of the child in teaching-learning – According to this approach student plays a central role in whole teaching-learning process. This approach believes in child-centred-education. This approach, considers that we should first understand the needs, interests, abilities, age level, attitudes, aptitude of students then try to organise teaching learning process according to these. It emphasises on reach, touch and teach the child according to his nature, and interests. All teaching material, its process must be related to individual characteristics of students. So we standard of students.
2. Emphasis on individuality – According to this approach every individual has his own individuality. Teacher should respect and develop this individuality through education. Individual differences should be respected and internal virtues of individual be developed. Teacher should understand this individuality and organise his/her teaching-learning process according to this individuality.

3. Understanding the child – According to this approach, we should understand the child first of all, and then teach him. We, as a teacher, should know our students, their interest, personality, capabilities and background environment and use teaching methods and content accordingly. Because this approach believes in student centred education so before teaching, a teacher should understand students thoroughly.

4. Method of teaching – In this approach teacher should use methods of teaching which are based on psychological principles. Teacher should not use teacher centred and traditional methods of teaching in it. Teacher should emphasise on active learning which could consider the learner. Teacher should use the methods which could teach according to needs, interests, abilities and attitudes of learners. Learner's readiness, mental set and motivation are considered as basis for deciding the method of teaching to be used. So teacher should use learner centred innovative methods of teaching.

5. Discipline – Teacher should not force student to be disciplined. He/she should encourage self discipline and self-control among students. Students should be given the responsibility of to be disciplined.

6. Place and role of the teacher – According to this approach student plays a central role in teaching learning process. Teacher acts as a guide, friend or helper of the students. Students should freedom to develop and make progress according to their own pace, needs and interests. Teacher should be considered as the milestone in the journey of total development of the child. Teacher should not force his own methods and views on students but he should be only a guide in this development process.

7. It is a democratic approach – According to this approach students should be taught in democratic environment. He/she should provide a rich environment with a view to have their around development.

In the end we can say that this is a new innovative approach to teaching which advocates child at the centre of teaching learning process. A teacher should understand the individuality of the learner and then organise his/her teaching learning process according to needs, interests and abilities of the learner. He/she should be as a guide only and students should be given chance to develop according to their own pace.

Q10. Discuss Jean Piaget's cognitive approach to learning and its educational implication. [June-07, Q3(i)]

Ans. Jean Piaget's Approach – Piaget studied the growth and development of the child. The main objective of Piaget has described the process of human thinking from infancy to adulthood.

Jean Piaget has redefined intelligence, knowledge and the relationship of the learner to the environment. Intelligence like a biological system is a continuing process that creates structures. In continuing interactions with the environment, he needs intelligence. In the same way, knowledge is an interactive process between the learner and the environment. Knowledge is highly subjective in infancy and early childhood. It becomes more objective in early adulthood.

According to him, learning is a function of certain processes. They are assimilation accommodation, adoption and equilibration.

Brief description of these processes is as under :

1. Assimilation – It is an incorporating new objects and experiences into the existing schemata. In this context, schemata refers to well-defined sequences of actions. The observation of surroundings and process leads to assimilation in the early stages of learning. Thus, assimilation accounts for the children's ability to act on and understand something new in terms of what is already familiar. Assimilation is followed by accommodation.

2. Accommodation – Accommodation is the adjustment of internal structures to the particular characteristics of situations. For example, biological structures accommodate to the type and quantity of food at the same time that the food is being assimilated. Similarly in cognitive functioning, internal structures adjust to the particular characteristics of new objects and events. Accommodation also refers to the modification of the individuals internal cognitive structures. As the child continues to confront experiences in the environment, he has either to combine his previous schemata and arrive at new schemata known as accommodation.

3. Equilibration – In cognitive development, equilibration is the continuing self-regulation that permits the individual to grow, develop and change while maintaining stability. Equilibration is not a balances of forces but it is a dynamic process that continuously regulates behaviour. It indicates the balance between assimilation and accommodation.

4. Adaptation –The accommodation helps in combining or expanding or changing the new schemata based on his new experiences. Thus, the individual is helped in adjusting to his new environment. This adjustment to a new environment is given the name 'adaption'. Adaption is not permanent one because he develops many new or modified schemata as he alters or extends his range of action. Adaption results from the interactionist processes between the organism and environment. Piaget has mapped out, in detail, the stages by which particular cognitive functions develop and the times at which given concepts may be expected to appear.

Piaget has propounded the stages as under :

(1) Sensory-motor stage -This extends roughly from birth to age. As the name implies, the schemata that develop during this stage are those involving the child's perception of the world and the coordinations by which he deals with the world. During this period the child does as under :

1. The child forms his most basis conceptions about the nature of the material world.

2. The child learns that an object that has disappeared can reappear.

3. The child learns that some object even though it looks very different when seen from different angles or in different illuminations.

4. He relates the appearance, sound to touch of the object to one another.

(2) Preoperational stage - It is known as the second stage extends roughly from about age 2 to 7.

1. The child has internal representations of objects before he has words to express them. These internal representations give the child greater flexibility for dealing adaptively with the world, and attaching words to them, gives him much greater power of communication.

2. The child begins to exhibit the effects of having learned language.

3. He is able to represent objects and events symbolically.

(3) Concrete operations stage - The third stage extends from 7 to 11 years. The sort of operations include classifying, combining and comparing. The child in the stage of concrete operations, can deal with the relationships among hierarchies of terms, such as robin, bird and creature. He is aware, as the preoperational child is not, of the reversibility of operations.

(4) Formal operations stage - The fourth and final stage around age 11 years. It includes improvements in abstract thinking. Two characteristics are visible at this stage:

1. Now the person can view the issues abstractly.

2. The person can judge the validity of logical argument in terms of their formal structure, independent of content.

3. He can explore different ways of formulating a problem and see what their logical consequences are.

4. He is atleast ready to think in terms of a realm of abstract propositions that fit in varying degrees in the real world that he observes.

Characteristics of Formal Operational Stage - The important characteristics of the formal operation period or stage are as under:

1. Learners survey many possibilities.

2. Learners design a system of what is hypothetically possible is structured and followed by empirical verification.

3. Learners become critical of their own standards and look objectively at the assumptions in hand.

4. The learners can conceive of an imaginary world.

5. The learners generate hypotheses, discuss and proceed them to test.

6. The learners become conscious of their own thinking and provide rational justification for their thinking, judgement and actions.

7. Their thinking goes beyond the immediate present and attempts are made by them to establish as many vertical relationships as possible.

8. The learners go even to the extent of finding empirical and mathematical proofs for their observations.

9. Learners, notions, ideas and concepts are formal which belong to the present and future.

Educational Implications of Paige's cognitive approach to learning

The direct or indirect educational Implications of Piaget's approach to cognitive development are as under:

1. Piaget's description of cognition indicates that cognitive development is a continuous process from birth to adulthood. So, the teacher should try to determine the level or stages of development of learners and accordingly he should plan his instruction or teaching.

2. It is accepted that childhood is a necessary and important phase in the development of logical thinking.

3. It is accepted that the relationship, between the educational system and the child is unilateral and reciprocal one.

4. Active methods that require the students to rediscover or reconstruct to be learned should be used.

5. Experimental procedures and free activity through training should be introduced for liberal arts and science students.

6. Science and mathematics are taught with actions and operations.

7. The classroom should be a centre of real activities carried out in common so that logical intelligence may be elaborated through action and social change.

8. Give-and-take can be developed in the group.

9. Audio-visual aids can be utilized as accessories in the student's personal investigations of truth.

10. Students must be allowed to make their own mistakes and to correct these errors themselves.

11. The process of experimentation by students at all ages is important. Only learner can acquire the skills that are necessary for formal operational thought.

12. The cognitive activity, generated by experimentation, is essential. A child can be mentally active without physical manipulation, just as he can be mentally passive while actually manipulating, objects.

13. Various activities in pre-school curricula can provide opportunities for cognitive development: e.g.: Block painting, finger painting, cooking, dramatic plays, etc.

14. Classroom activities should maximize the child opportunities to construct and coordinate many relationships.

15. The classroom should provide situations to children in constructing their own knowledge. As such, the children can comprehend the world in new ways at different cognitive levels.

16. The implications for educational practice are important:

(a) A variety of activities, games and experiences should be provided.

(b) Individualized mathematics laboratories that utilize a variety of materials, for measurement and experimentation. Examples should be used for blocks, dried pears, matchboxes, drinking straws, pipe cleaners and so on.

17. At the pre-school level, it is found that the child has greater interest in the observable effects of his or her actions than in relating the result to an organized cognitive structure.

18. Games and activities that can provide experience with classification and serration are also needed.

19. Drill and practice should be given in the classroom to make teaching learning effective.

Limitations of Piaget's Approach

Piaget's approach to learning has some limitations as under:

1. His terminology is not very clear to its readers.

2. It is forgotten that the children may lose confidence in their ability to figure out things.

3. A child cannot engage in abstract thought and cannot perform any useful scientific activity.

4. He is too preoccupied with numerous epistemological considerations.

5. Piaget's whole work lacks scientific methodology as conventionally understood.

6. Piaget's emphasis is on concepts of relationship. He does not investigate nominal concepts.

7. This approach is lengthy and time consuming.

8. In this approach no direct teaching is involved.

9. Mathematics and science cannot be applied in early childhood.

10. Tailoring narrow exercises for individual children has neither practicability nor necessity.

11. The child does not notice the contradiction in his or her own explanation.

Q11. What do you mean by domains of learning? Discuss cognitive domain. [Dec-05, Q3(ii)]

Ans. Domain of Learning – Human behaviour has a dynamic quality that keeps changing in response to various stimuli which it receives from the environment. From infancy we are continually learning new skills gaining information about the environment around us and developing contain beliefs and attitudes. These in a way form the domains or areas of learning. These domains are not mutually exclusive. Rather they overlap each other. Therefore learning is not considered to belong to any particular domain. In other works, for example psychomotor development requires proper knowledge or understanding i.e. cognitive development on the part of the students.

Cognitive Domain – The word cognitive originate from the word cognition which means to know. In educational processes learning mainly focuses upon the cognitive domain. Learning processes in the cognitive domain are associated with those mental operations which are used to manipulate information from the environment. In this way, cognitive domain involves a number of activities varying from exposure to information to its organisation or processing in the learner's mind. This information can include visual forms which involve seeing as it could be verbal i.e. hearing or listening. Various psychologists and educationists like Bhoom, Grulund Meger, etc. have tried to analyse the learning of the cognitive domain.

(a) Knowledge - Possession of knowledge or information is the foundation from which all higher thinking grows. Data facts concepts or principles are memorised at this level of learning.

(b) Comprehension - The second level of learning is comprehension. At this level those mental operations which help in understanding of facts, concepts, principles and generalizations are included. In other words, the meaningful processing of information takes place after the recognition or identification of kind of information.

1. Translation-Here the student transforms known concept or definition into his own words or phrases.

2. Interpretation-Here the student tries to find out interrelations among the various recognizable components of any information (like data. Facts, concept, principles, generalization theory etc.).

3. Extrapolation-This involves some kind of predictions or drawing conclusions keeping in mind the situations which are beyond those given to the student.

(c) Application - Information becomes meaningful when it is applied to a new situation. The mental operations at this level involve the use of concepts, principles or theories in real or concrete situations.

(d) Analysis - When information gathered is broken down into its constituent elements or arts, such that the relationship among parts becomes clear. We say that the information is being analysed.

(e) Synthesis - It involves arranging and combining the various parts in such a way as to form a pattern or structure which might not have been clearly perceptible earlier.

(f) Evaluation - The mental operations at this level involve making of judgement which may be based either on the criteria of consistency or logic as may involve some comparison with standard or norms.

All the six levels of mental operations have been taken up (in increasing order of complexity) in the hierarchy of levels in learning. Thus any cognitive level should involve the earlier ones. Again, knowledge comprehension and application are more clearly liked in the hierarchy than the three other levels in the cognitive domain.

Q12. Discuss affective domain.

Ans. In learning, the student as a person/individual is wholly involved in intellectual abilities. Some students have more interest or aptitude for a particular subject as compared to others. Besides this observation, it is also true that educational objectives also deliberate upon development of desirable beliefs, values, attitudes, etc., along with seeking knowledge. Therefore, learning in the affective domain includes changes in interest, attitudes, values and feelings. All these behaviours ultimately lead to better adjustments abilities in student in the society.

The main organizing principle in the affective domain is the degree of internalization, that is, the extent to which the feelings or emotions are incorporated by the students as a part of his or her personality. The main organizing principles in the affective domain are :

a) Receiving: This means the sensitivity of a student to certain stimulus patterns of stimuli (phenomena) and his willingness to receive or attend to them. Receiving consists of (i) awareness of the stimuli, (ii) willingness to receive, and (iii) selected attention.

b) Responding: This level of learning goes beyond the receiving level. After giving attention or perceiving the stimulus or object, the student actively responds to the object.

c) Valuing: This level of the affective domain implies perceiving a concept as having worth and consequently revealing a consistent preference or commitment in behaviour towards it.

d) Organization: For situations where more than one value is relevant, the student organizes the values into a system and also determines the inter-relationships among them.

e) Characteristics: After the values have been organized in the individual's mind, they control his/her behaviour to some extent. This is the stage of internalization the degree of internalization depends upon the consistency of the internal organization of the student.

Learning in the affective domain does not seem to lend itself to such exact assessment as it could in the cognitive domain.

Q13. Describe psychomotor domain of learning.

Ans. Psychomotor Domain: This domain pertains to the manipulative or psychomotor skills which can be developed under the supervision or guidance of an expert or skilled person. For example, the skill of driving a car can be acquired effectively under the direct supervision of a skilled instructor. Learning psychomotor skills has three characteristics. They are:

1. Responsive chains : Learning of skills involve a chain of motor responses i.e., one muscular movement leads to another muscular movement.

2. Coordination : The coordination of perception and motor acts is essential in skill learning. For example, a person who learns the skill of driving a car has to coordinate movements of various parts of his body.

3. Response patterns : Skill learning involves organization of stimulus and response patterns. For example, a child with mastery on riding a bicycle commits minimum errors while riding a bicycle. The skill becomes a habit.

Dave (1969) attempted to classify learning situations in the psychomotor domain into five categories. They are: initiation, manipulation, precision, articulation, and naturalization (mechanization and internalization).

The first three categories are quite clear. Here articulation emphasizes the coordination of a series of acts which are performed appropriately in terms of time, speed and ease. Naturalization refers to the highest level of proficiency or skill whereby an act becomes a routine to be performed with natural ease by a person.

Another classification (Kibler, 1970) has child developmental psychology as its frame of reference :

• **Gross body movements :** This class of skills includes movements of limbs in isolation or in coordination with other parts of the body.

• **Finally coordinated movements :** This class of skills includes coordinated movements of the various parts of the body, such as hand-finger, hand-eye, hand-ear, hand-eye-foot, hand-eye-foot-ear combinations, etc.

• **Non-verbal communication behaviours :** This class of skills includes facial expressions, gestures, body movements, etc., to convey messages.

• **Speech behaviours :** This class of skills includes sound production, sound-gesture coordination, etc.

Harrow (1972) operationally defined 'psychomotor' and developed a classification which also deals with sub-categories of psychomotor behaviour and along with concrete examples. This classification is more useful to teachers of physical education. Thus the psychomotor domain covers any observable movement of one's body that belongs to the domain of learning. Learning of skills, at times, is a component of cognitive and effective learning too. As compared to the affective domain, learning in the psychomotor domain can be assessed with much more precision.

There are five stages of psychomotor learning: perception set, guided response, mechanisms and complex overt response.

• **Perception** is the process of becoming aware of objects, qualities or relations by way of sense of organs.

• **Set** is a preparatory adjustment of readiness for a particular kind of action.

• **Guided response** is the early step in the development of skills. It is the overt behavioural act of a learner under the guidance of a teacher. Readiness is a prerequisite for this kind of response.

• **Mechanism** means that learned response has become habitual. At this level, the learner has achieved a certain confidence and the degree of skill to mean that learned response has become habitual. At this level, the learner has achieved a certain confidence and the degree of skill to perform an act which is part of his repertoire of possible responses to stimuli.

• **Complex overt response** will show that the learner can perform a complex motor act, as he has attained a higher skill.

Q14. Discuss Learning Outcomes.

Ans. Learning Outcomes : The outcomes of learning means the terminal behaviour in terms of performance or achievement by the student. Learning outcome should be and interpreted in terms of different categories of leaning capability. Learning outcomes constitute the objectives of teaching learning experience. The expected learning outcomes have to be based on the level of learning in the three domains. If we consider in a broader perspective, learning outcomes, are derived from the curriculum *i.e.* a sum total of teaching learning experience. It is derived from the broader aims of education. In this way, intended or expected learning outcome are specific objectives which signify the levels of learning in any of the three domains *i.e.* cognitive, affective and psychomotor.

Formulation of specific objectives helps us in distinguishing various aspects of learning such as affective cognitive and psychomotor. It also helps in making learning more articulative at various levels. These levels are cognitive, affective and psychomotor. They also help in the following fields :

1. Planning proper learning situations.

2. Identifying specific learning problems of student as they facilitate specific assessment of learning.

Specific objectives are formulated in the beginning of instructional planning statement with specific objectives should have the following characteristics:

1. The kind of behavioural outcomes expected

(a) as a result of learning, and

(b) the content to be covered.

2. An objective should be stated in terms of student behaviour or learning outcomes.

3. A behavioural objective should clearly indicate (with respect to the learner) as under:

(a) Specific action verb i.e. performance.

(b) Conditions under performance to be shown.

(c) The extent to which performance to be shown i.e. minimum standards.

Q15. Discuss, with examples, implications of domains of learning (cognitive, affective and psychomotor) for the teaching process.

[June-07, Q3(iv)]

Ans. As we know that education is development of body mind and spirit. If we try to correlate physical, intellectual emotional and spiritual development with the domains of learning, we find that development of intellect falls in the cognitive domain, while emotional and spiritual development is concerned with the affective domain and physical development is through skills which comprise of the psychomotor domain.

Whole teaching-learning process is directed by instructional objectives which are found as the form of behavioural terms. We want to get these pre-determined objectives after teaching learning process. These objectives are formulated through different domains. Identification of learning at various levels in the different domains and then formulation of specific behavioural objectives as learning outcomes, will help in designing or planning instruction and also evaluation. These domain related objectives serve as guidelines in learning instruction and evaluation. These domain gives specificity and clarity in formulating instructional objectives. Through these instructional objectives, we can get a direction to educational activities. They provide a clear direction for choosing various programmes of curricular and co-curricular activities. So we can say that these domains of learning has very much implications for the whole teaching learning process.

Q16. What are the learner associated or personal factor that influences learning? [Dec-05, Q3(i)]

Ans. Factors Affecting Learning : Learning, as you have studied, can be defined as a process of bringing relatively permanent changes in the behaviour of the learner through experience or practice. An examination of this definition may reveal that learning process is centered on three elements:

1. The learner whose behaviour is to be changed or modified.

2. The type of experience or training required for modification in the learner's behaviour.

3. The men and material resources needed for providing desired experiences and training.

Therefore the success or failure in the task of learning in terms of introducing desired modification in the behaviour of a learner will automatically depend upon the quality as well as control and management of the factors associated with the above cited main elements. Let us discuss briefly these factors.

Factors Associated with Learner : Learner is the key figure in any learning task. He has to learn or bring desired modification in his behaviour. How he will learn or what he will achieve, through a particular learning act depends heavily upon his own characteristics and ways of learning. Such things or factors associated with this can be described as follows:

1. Learner's physical and mental health – Learning is greatly affected by the learner's physical and mental health maintained by him particularly, at the time of learning. A simple headache or a stomachache can play havoc with the process and products of learning. A child who does not maintain satisfactory physical health, have to suffer adversely in terms of gains in learning. Similarly, the mental state and the health of a learner at the time of learning become potent factors in deciding the out come of his learning. A tense, emotionally and mentally disturbed learner cannot show satisfactory results in learning.

2. The basic potential of the learner – The results achieved by the learner through a process of learning depend heavily upon his basic potential to undergo such learning. Such potential may consist of the things given ahead:

(a) Learner's innate abilities and capacities for learning a thing.

(b) Learner's basic potential in terms of general intelligence and specific knowledge, understanding and skills related to a particular learning area.

(c) Learner's basic interests, aptitudes and attitudes related to the learning of a particular thing or area.

3. The level of aspiration and achievement motivation – Learning is greatly influenced by the level of aspiration and nature of achievement motivation possessed by a learner. How can we expect learner to achieve a thing for which he has no aspiration?

Also, too much of aspirations make it impossible for an individual to achieve this. A person has to maintain the level of his aspiration and achievement motivation at a reasonable level. That is to say, his aspirations should be neither too high which will result in non-achievement of any of his goals, nor too low as not to try to achieve goals which he is quite capable.

4. Goals of life – The philosophy of immediate as well as ultimate goals of one's life affect the process and product of learning. His mode and ways of looking towards things, his inclination towards learning a particular subject and patience and persistence in pursuing his learning despite the heavy odds – all depend up on his goals and philosophy of life.

5. Readiness and will power – A learner's readiness and power to learn is a great deciding factor of his results in learning. No power on earth can help a learner if he is not ready to learn. Certainly, if he has a will to learn a thing, then automatically, he will himself find ways for effective learning.

Q17. What is motivation? Discuss.

Ans. Motivation has been defined as impulsion to do something to satisfy a need. The stronger the need, the stronger the impulsion and stronger the motivation. Till the need is not satisfied the person remains in the state of tension. This state of tension forces him to do something to satisfy the need and reduce his tension. The need is satisfied by the attainment of a goal perceived by the person himself and learning results from action directed towards the attainment of that goal. An example will make the matters clear. The child, who has an appetite for candy, feels a need and if a challenging problem is placed before him to find out the candy which is hidden under a book placed in a shelf in an almirah he feels a kind of tension and is motivated to search it out. Till he does not discover the book under which the piece of candy lies, he remains in the state of tension. The stronger is the appetite for candy, and the stronger is the desire to find it out, and the stronger is the motivation to learn. Other definitions of motivation and motives are given below:

1. Motivation is the process of arousing, sustaining and regulating activity.—Good

2. A motive is particular internal factor or condition that tends to initiate and sustain activity.—J.P. Guilford

3. Motives are conditions physiological and psychological within the organism that dispose it to act in certain ways.—McDougall

4. A motive is a state or set of the individual which disposes him for certain behaviour and for seeking certain goal.—Woodworth

The place of Motivation in Learning: Motivation, arouses, sustains, directs and determines the intensity of learning effort. Therefore, it is said that without motivation learning is not possible at any level. Motivation is at the heart of learning. It is *sin qua non* for learning. And no teacher who hopes to induce learning can ignore motivation. The central problem faced by the school involves motivational status of its students. Various ways and means that have been devised to motivate the students to learn are given below:

(1) Intrinsic and Extrinsic Forms of Motivation: Motivation has been classified as intrinsic and extrinsic. The intrinsically motivated child does an act, because the mere performance of the act pleases him and because its outcome satisfies him. For example, he solves a problem because he has a strong desire to do so and he does so whether his teacher requires him to do or not. He solves even the most difficult mathematical problems because finding a solution appeals to him as an end in itself.

Intrinsic Motivation is a state of impulsion in which the learner wants to learn something for its own sake. The teacher, who impresses upon the child the idea that learning a particular subject has its own rewards, is using the most powerful weapon. If all our activities were intrinsically motivated we would have derived very great satisfaction in life. Very few learners learn a thing for its own sake. Hence intrinsic motivation is unrealistic in practice.

Extrinsic Motivation is defined as a state in which a child learns something not for his own sake, but as a means of obtaining some desirable goal which is artificially related to the activity. For example, the child, who solves a problem in algebra or who does his home assignments not for his own sake but either to avoid his teacher's sarcasm, is extrinsically motivated. Many students learn a lesson or master a subject because they want to gain approval or prestige or regard from their teachers or their parents or their class-mates. In reality, most of the behaviour of children in schools or adults in general is extrinsically motivated. A boy, who wants to learn how to deliver a speech in the public both for his own sake and for the cup he will win, is in a fortunate position.

Some of the common forms of extrinsic motivation are as under:

(a) Purposive striving, goals and ideals—The goal and purposes of learning clearly perceived by the individual give strong motivation for better action.

(b) Knowledge of results—Knowledge of results in terms of success and failure provides incentive for greater efforts on the part of the student.

(c) Punishment and rewards—Punishment is an act of inflicting pain deliberately with the purpose of affecting the future conduct of an individual being punished. Thus, punishment is one of the common and obvious methods of keeping under control and guiding the student. Thorn-dike showed that generally punishment speeds up learning and reduces the number of errors.

Rewards are certainly better and positive incentives to learning. They are responsible for initiative, energy, competition, self-expression and creative ability. Reward may be in the form of gifts, money, badges, cups, certificates of merit or other objects of some value.

(d) Praise and blame—Praise stimulates average and inferior children. However girls seem more susceptible to praise than do boys. Regardless of age, sex or initial ability, praise is the most effective of the incentives. Ghase (1932) reported praise to be effective than blame with young children Horlock (1926) generalized that praise is more effective stimulus in motivating both immediate and long continued tasks.

(e) Rivalry—The rivalry between students which leads to resentment, jealously etc. as rivalry between groups of students which creates hatred is the least desirable type of incentive to be encouraged in the schools.

Functions: The functions of motivation in learning are as follows:

1. To select behaviour,

2. To direct behaviour,

3. To energise the students in learning,

4. To develop social qualities,

5. To help in character formation.

6. To help in acquiring knowledge,

7. To help capture the attention.

Q18. Discuss the environmental factor of learning. [June-07, Q3(v)]

Ans. Environmental Factors of Learning: The influence of environment begin since the time of the conception of the child in the womb of the mother. Foetus in the womb is influenced by mother's mental, physical and emotional conditions. The external environment starts from the time of birth of the child. The external environment refers to the surroundings which prevail in home, school and locality. At these places the child interacts with other members of the family teachers classmates or peers and neighbours. He establishes relationship with them. Some of the environmental factors are as under:

Surroundings : Chief surroundings are as under :

(1) Natural surroundings – covers the climatic and atmospheric conditions. For a limited time, humidity and high temperature can be tolerated but prolonged humidity and high temperature become unbearable. They decrease mental efficiency. The intellectual productivity and creativeness of people living in hot regions are much low. Likewise, the morning time is always better for mastering difficult tasks. Studies on the academic progress of evening school students show losses of efficiency varying from one to six percent.

(2) Social surroundings – includes especially the environment of home, school and locality. Learning is affected by physical conditions at home such as large family, small family (specific family of the study) insufficient ventilation, improper lighting, uncomfortable temperature, noisy home environment due to use of radio, and TV etc.

The socio-emotional factors such as child rearing practices, reward and punishment, scope for freedom in activities are decision making play and study facilities, disorganization and discord among birth positions such as eldest or youngest child has his definite influence on learning.

Cultural Demands and Social Expectation : They influence learning deeply, the spirit of culture is reflected in its social and educational institutions. For instance, in an industrialized culture, the emphasis mostly centers mechanical science and preparing children for highly mechanized vocations. Likewise, in an agriculture based community, the educational process focuses on preparing its members for those skills which are suited to the needs of an agrarian community.

Relationship with Teachers, Parents and Peers: This relationship can be explained as under:

(1) The setup of learning – The teacher is an important constituent in the instructional process. The way he teaches and manages the students has an effect on their learning. An authoritarian teacher will create an aggression and hostility among students. On the contrary for it a democratic teacher will create a participatory climate for learning. The democratic environment leads students to constructive and cooperative behaviour. Generally, students learn better in a democratic setup because they like democratic procedures.

(2) Relationship with parents – It plays a vital role in the learning process of the student. If the child-parents relationship is based on mutual respect and faith, it can facilitate his or her learning. On the contrary to it a distorted and unhealthy environment, adversely affects the learning of the student. The upward mobility brings resistance on the part of the student to learn. Students belongings to such families find themselves unable to cope up.

(3) A healthy peer group – This relationship also plays an important role in learning. Student-student relationship in the classroom, school, society, etc., create a particular type of emotional climate. The climate solely depends upon their relationships. A sound relationship provides a tension free environment to the student enabling him to learn more and to complete in the class. If the relationship among peers is not good, it adversely affects their learning.

Media influence of Learning : According to the psychologists, the media is an important component of transmitting information. Media can be divided into two broad categories. Print and non-print media. Their brief description is as under:

1. Print media – It refers to texts or printed materials. It is economical and has traditionally been used for the pedagogical purposes.

2. Non-Print media – It is also known as modern electronic media. It has certain unique qualities which in certain cases facilities learning much far faster than the print media.

Certain non-print media formats and delivery systems contribute a lot to students learning activities. For example, audio tapes or computer can be used effectively to drill and practice in language and learning arithmetic. Electronic media can contribute a lot to promote the discovery approach to learning. Non print media performs following functions

1. Arouse motivation

2. Direct mention

3. Help them actively involved in the learning process.

4. Increase student's concentration.

Q19. What do you mean by 'Laws of Association?' Discuss with suitable examples.

Ans. As we know that if we learn anything by associating it with other things or if we learn concepts linking together in consciousness two or more mental products as sensations, images, precepts, ideas concepts etc., then we can learn them permanently and can recall them according to needs. There are some laws of association –

A. Law of contiguity or nearness : The law of nearness controls the ideas in two ways, one with regard to space and other with regard to time. For example regarding nearness of space we can define many things or ideas which have nearness of space as engine and bogies of train etc. While regarding nearness of time we can learn or know about rain after black clouds in the sky.

B. Law of similarity : We should link up similar facts, things and ideas with each other so that one could easily recall the other. For example we can remind moon after seeing a circled light similar to the moon. We can teach and student can learn and recall similar events and facts easily.

C. Law of contrast : This law states the contrasted characters get associated with each other so that one reminds the other that stands in contrast to it. For example after seeing mouse a child can recall cat also. We can learn opposite events/facts easily by associating them.

Facilitating Learning and Development

Q1. What do you mean by adjustment? Write the characteristics of a well adjusted person.

Ans. Adjustment – Meaning, Characteristics : Adjustment is originated from the biological term adaptation. Biologists used the term adaptation strictly for the physical demands of the environments. However psychologists, use the term 'adjustment' for varying conditions of special or inter-personal relation in the society. According to Dr. Vibasi Adjustment means the reactions to the demands and pressure of social environment imposed upon the individual. The demand to which the individual has to react may be external or internal. Psychologists have viewed 'adjustment' from two important perspective as under:

1. For one, adjustment is an achievement.

2. For another adjustment is a process.

(1) The first point of view emphasizes the quality as efficiency of adjustment.

(2) The second point of view lays emphasis on the process by which an individual adjusts to his external environment.

1. Adjustment as achievement : Adjustment as achievement means how efficiently an individual can do his duties under different circumstances. If we perceive adjustment as achievement, we have to set criteria to judge the quality of adjustment. No universal criteria can be set for all times to come.

However some are as under:

(i) Physical health

(ii) Psychological comfort

(iii) Work efficiency

(iv) Social acceptance

2. Adjustment as process : Adjustment as a process is important for teachers. Students adjustment largely depends on their interaction with the external environment in which they live. They always try to adjust to it. Piaget uses the term assimilation and accommodation to represent the alternation of oneself or environment as a means of adjustment.

(i) Assimilation : A person who carries his value and standard of conduct without any change and maintains these in spite of major changes in the social climate is called assimilator.

(ii) Accommodation : The person who takes his standards from his social context and changes his benefits in accordance with the altered values of the society is called accommodator.

Successful Adjustment : For a successful adjustment a person has to resort to both the devices i.e. assimilation and accommodation.

Characteristics of a Well-Adjusted Person : A healthy and well-adjusted person should possess some observable behavioural patterns. These behavioural patterns must be according to the social expectations of an individual. Some of these patterns are as under:

1. Emotional balance

2. Maturity in thinking

3. Independence in decision making

4. Free from tension due to routine events

5. Warm and understanding towards others

Elements of Adjustment : The prime elements for fulfillment of needs necessary for healthy adjustment of a person are as follows:

1. Absence of obstacle in achieving needs

2. Satisfaction of needs

3. Strong motive in realizing needs

4. Feasible geographical atmosphere to fulfill needs.

Q2. Define Maladjustment. What are the usual forms or characteristics of maladjustment?

Ans. The Maladjusted Person : Mental illness, emotional instability, mental disorders, emotional disorders, personality disorders, behaviour disorders, psychological disorders—all these terms denote one and the same thing. They are interchangeably used to describe what we call maladjustment. They denote conditions of tension and nervousness and the characteristic features of maladjustment and deviations in feelings, acting and thinking. The more serious the disorder, the more radical are the disturbances until a point is reached when the individual becomes almost incapable of adjusting to life.

The Adjusted Person : Most people have to face frustrations conflicts and such situations as may cause concern, anxiety and nervousness at times. They are able to overcome their troubles and adjust themselves to such situations. But there are people who cannot overcome their troubles and cannot compromise with them. They develop behaviour disorders in the form of exaggerated, persistent reactions which tend to incapacitate them and distort their feelings and behaviour. They are maladjusted persons. They create another world in which they can live more comfortably and with real life situations they are in gross disharmony.

Two distinct types of persons have been described above—the normal and the maladjusted. But it must be remembered that the distinction between the adjusted and the maladjusted is very subtle. The line between the two is very thin, for no person is completely adjusted. He is adjusted to a degree. A normal person may be emotionally hyperactive at times and he may be so depressed that he can hardly live with himself. He may at times regress to childish behaviour and still be a normal man. A well-adjusted person maintains a favourable orientation towards reality. "His life is like a ship riding the waves. He may be swayed this way or that by wind or weather but he always returns to an even keel. This even keel is his fundamental balance in life that enables him to withstand the thousands of disturbing stimuli which assail him and still keep his bearings and continue to move towards the goals he has set for himself."

The maladjusted child may either show nervousness or may exhibit emotional over-reactions and deviations or may be emotionally immature. His behaviour may be exhibitionistic or antisocial. He may be suffering from psychosomatic disturbances. Many of the symptoms which are being detailed below may appear in normal children but whenever a combination of these symptoms appear frequently and consistently we should suspect maladjustment.

Symptoms :

(1) Nervousness in the child is exhibited by habitual biting and wetting of lips, nail, biting, stammering, blushing, turning pale, constant restlessness, body rocking, nervous finger movements, frequent urination.

(2) The maladjusted child shows *undue anxiety over mistakes*, marked distress over failures, absent-mindedness, day-dreaming; he refuses to accept any recognition or reward, evades responsibility, withdraws from anything that looks new or difficult: he has lack of concentration, is unusually sensitive to all annoyances is suitable to work when distracted and has emotional tone in argument and feel hurt when others disagree; he makes frequent efforts to gain attention of the teacher. Such are the emotional over-reactions and deviations.

(3) The child, having *emotional disorders*, is unable to work alone, and rely on his own judgment; he is suffering from complexes; he is either unusually self-conscious or over-critical of others, either too docile or too suggestive; such are his characteristic traits exhibiting his emotional in stability.

(4) The child who cannot adjust himself in the school environment shows *exhibitionistic behaviour*. He tends to tease, push and shove other pupils; he wants to be too funny or over-conspicuous; he is either found bluffing, or refusing to accept any lack of personal knowledge; he agrees markedly with whatever the teacher says or does and shows exaggerated courtesy.

(5) The maladjusted child has behaviour disorders which are generally seen in his *antisocial behaviour*. He is cruel to others, bullies them, uses obscene language, shows undue interest in sex, tells offensive stories, dislikes school work, resents authority, reacts badly to discipline, runs away from the class, shows complete lack of interest in school work suddenly. He has *psychosomatic disturbances* also. When he is emotionally distressed, he begins to vomit or develops constipation and diarrhoea or tends to overeat and shows other feeling disturbances.

Conclusion : Many of these symptoms may be seen in normal children but frequent occurrence of a number of these symptoms indicates that the child is mentally ill or maladjusted. Traits that mark the maladjusted child are: Carelessness, Cheating, Cruelty, Destroying material, Disobedience, Domineering, Dreams, Enuresis, Fearfulness, Heterosexuality, Imaginative lying, Impertinence, Inquisitiveness, Interrupting, Masturbation, Profanity,

Obscene notes, Restlessness, Shyness, Silliness, Smoking, Stealing, Stubbornness, Suggestible sulleness, Suspiciousness, Tradiness, Taunting, Temper Tantrums, Thoughtlessness, Truancy, Unhappiness, Unreliability, Unsocial withdrawing, Untruthfulness, Whispering.

Q3. Discuss the main causes of maladjustment.

Ans. Causes of Maladjustment: The causes of maladjusted behaviour of adolescent is under five i.e., main categories.

(i) Family : The family as an institution has various functions to perform various causes e.g. social, economic and psychological, contribute immensely to maladjusted behaviour in children.

(a) Social causes : Gibbian says that the social problem of one generation is the psychological problem of the next generation. Children coming from homes that have been broken due to death, divorce, desertion, separation etc., are often maladjusted in their behaviour. Such children feel insecure and become maladjusted. With the tremendous growth in population, it is extremely difficult for parents to provide even the basic necessities like food, clothing and shelter to their children. It invariably results in greater degree of frustration and hostility amongst them.

(b) Economic causes : The occupational status of parents problems of unemployment poverty and low economic status breed maladjustment amongst children.

(c) Psychological causes: If parents are over-possessive highly authoritative, unrealistic in their expectations incompatible and abusive, this will have an adverse effect upon their children. When the psychological needs are not met, children get frustrated and develop problems like nail biting fear of dark, lack of self confidence.

(ii) Personal causes : The individuals who are physically, mentally and visually handicapped react abnormally to the situation. When they cannot score well academically compared to their peers, they develop an inferiority complex. Finally they isolate themselves from others and indulge in day-dreaming.

(iii) School-related causes : When growing children do not find ways and means to channelise their energy in a purposeful manner in the school they exhibit in maladjusted behaviour.

(iv) Teacher-related causes : If the teacher is unfair, biased or not involved with the student it certainly affects the mental health of the children in the school.

(v) Peer-group related causes : Another important factor that disturbs the psycho-equilibrium of students is an unhealthy relationship with their peer group.

Q4. What is conflict? How will you recognize mental conflicts in children? [Dec-05, Q3(v)]

Ans. Conflict is a general type of thwarting in which the satisfaction of two or more motives is blocked. For example, a child has a need for mastery, prestige and recognition which can be satisfied if he can play hockey well. On the other hand, he has a need of protecting his body from being hurt in the game. The child is faced with two needs, the satisfaction of which is comparable. He desires to have mastery in the game and thus achieve recognition and prestige of his peers. At the same time, he wants that he should not be hurt. He is torn between the two. Conflicting situations are generally of three types:

(a) Approach-approach
(b) Avoidance-avoidance
(c) Approach-avoidance.

(a) Approach-approach Conflicts : When the child is placed in an environment with two equally strong positive valences, he is said to be in an approach-approach conflicting situation. For example, he may, on the one hand, like to read an interesting novel and on the other he may like to go out for playing football. It the desire to go out for playing football is stronger than the desire to read the interesting novel, he will resolve his mental conflict by postponing reading of the novel and vice versa. Such a conflict rarely disturbs behaviour because any one of the two alternative valences of equal strength becomes less strong and the individual proceeds in the direction of the more powerful one.

(b) Avoidance-avoidance Conflicts : The avoidance-avoidance situation arises when both the valences are negative. For example, the child may read the difficult mathematical sums but at the same time he wants to avoid the threat of being beaten by his teacher if he does not solve them. He avoids doing the difficult sums and simultaneously avoids his teacher's rebuke. In such a conflicting situation the only way out is to leave the field and take a third course by adopting a defence mechanism. He may develop headache and avoid both the difficult task and the teacher's punishment. He thus resolves the mental conflict, though temporarily. If he is unable to solve an avoidance-avoidance situation at all, he remains constantly in an insecure condition and develops symptoms of anxiety, nervousness and neurosis.

(c) Approach-avoidance Conflicts : Lastly, when the child wants to play football, but fears being hurt, he is in an approach-avoidance conflicting situation. He wants to approach one and avoid the other. Other instances of such conflicting situations are loving one's mother and fearing her also, desiring to enjoy the forbidden candy and avoiding parents' rebuke, performing an irksome duty and getting approval of parents or teachers or associates. Such a conflicting situation becomes very serious when the child loves and fears the same person or when he is dependent upon and aggressive to the same body. When the child is unable to resolve such a mental conflict either he adopts inferior adjustment mechanism or he suffers from unreduced anxiety. So far, we have theoretically analysed the various forms of mental conflicts. Conflicts are caused by the interaction of the organism and the environment. The behaviour of an individual is the function of what goes on between the individual and the environment. Where there is harmony between the individual and the environment there is adjustment and the reverse happens when there is disharmony between the two.

(d) How to Recognise Mental Conflict in Children : If mental conflicts are not resolved they make enduring changes in personality. When a person is unable to resolve his mental conflicts for a longer period of time, and goes on adopting inferior non adjustive responses, behaviour disorder, mental ill-health, personality distortion may occur. The general ability to adjust becomes reduced and symptoms of maladjustment begin to appear. In brief, they are seen in nervous behaviour, emotional over-reactions and deviations, emotional immaturity, psychosomatic disturbances and antisocial behaviour. Nervousness, excessive anxiety, adjustive defence mechanisms are some of the simple symptoms of mental conflicts in children.

Q5. What is defence mechanism? Discuss in brief types of defence mechanism used by a tensed/frustrated students. [Dec-05, Q3(vi)]

Ans. Defence Mechanism: Defence Mechanism is contrary to the adaptive measures. It may not assist an individual to solve his problem in a constructive way. Instead it may impede the constructive activity and become disruptive. It is a technique adopted by individuals to cope with tension. Stress and anxiety aroused by conflicts. When an individual meets with such a problem, instead of developing and insight to solve it, he may give a totally different explanation for it and escape. However, psychologists are of the view that a defence mechanism rescues the individual from maladjusted behaviour. However excessive use of such techniques may again lead to maladjustment.

Types : Various types of defence mechanism are as under:

(1) Denial to Reality : The child turns away from unpleasant sites, refuses to talk of or listen to unpleasant topics, ignores and denies criticism, and thus he protects himself from traumatic situations.

(2) Fantasy : Fantasies act like safety valves and provide the child some amount of gratification. He imagines himself suffering from some handicap or terrible affliction. To explain away his failure at an examination he imagines a visitation from just fate. When a child's desires are frustrated he thus enters a world of imagination.

(3) Repression : Painful and threatening thoughts are not liked by anyone. We want to exclude from our consciousness disheartening urges, memories and emotions. Repression is the way of forgetting all these. The man who has seen his best friend's head blown off may find the experience so terribly painful that he would like to exclude it from his consciousness altogether. The repression screens out stressful experiences from consciousness.

(4) Rationalization : The irrational behaviour of a person is disapproved by the society he lives in. This causes a stress. The person provides logical and socially acceptable reasons for his past, present and proposed behaviours and justifies them. Thus he persuades himself and others that his actions were correct. This is rationalization. The young boy who fails in a pre-medical test says a doctor's life is no life. Grapes are sour, when the fox is unable to reach them. Sometimes very great personalities have been found to be rationalizing. Hitler regarded it his patriotic duty to exterminate the Jews.

(5) Projection : We place the blame of our shortcomings, mistakes and misdeeds on others and attribute to others our own thoughts, desires and impulses. The boy who fails in a test says that the teacher has not been teaching properly. The boy who is punished for fighting protests 'He hit me first'. Homosexuals with a feeling of guilt others of trying to seduce them, while they remain unaware of their own homosexual inclinations.

(6) Reaction Formation : Troublesome, urges, emotions, feelings and attitudes are excluded from consciousness by repression. They are also removed from consciousness by thoroughly disguising them by adopting an opposite attitude. For example, a child becomes an angel when his parents or teachers are unduly intolerant of his aggressive behaviour. This is reaction formation. The child protects himself from a dangerous situation by trying to develop just the opposite behaviour-pattern on the conscious level.

(7) Regression : A frustrated person returns to an earlier and more serious period of life. For example, the adult adopts the manners of the adolescence or the adolescent adopts the behaviour-patterns of childhood to protect himself from painful realities of the present life. Returning to the protected existence of one's childhood or some other earlier period is regression. A person goes back to the old habits of adjustment such as weeping, crying or other emotional displays which worked in the past well, but which are hardly adequate for solving the problems at the present.

(8) Compensation : When we meet a failure in on activity we have a painful feeling of inferiority which is counter-balanced if we enter into some other sphere of activity in which we can find success. The child who is physically unattractive fails to get social esteem and in order to counter-balance this painful feeling he develops charming manners and learns to be an interesting conversationalist. Thus, he tries to get social approval through compensation.

(9) Sublimation : Most of the defense mechanisms discussed above are ways to get temporary relief and when such defense mechanisms become fixed features of a person's behaviour they cause a serious harm to his development. The least harmful of all defense mechanisms is sublimation through which urges potentially harmful to the person are given a socially acceptable expression. For example, aggressive impulses are potentially harmful. But when a young aggressive boy is given military training and is deployed in a useful profession as a military man, his aggressive urges are sublimated.

Q6. Define sentiments. What is self regarding sentiments? Explain the role of self regarding sentiment in the formation of character.

Ans. Sentiments : The word sentiment is synonymous with passion. Yet we do not use passion in place of sentiment. Love and hate are typical sentiments and are generally calm and cool. Yet they sometimes become pronounceable passionate. When love generates violent emotions and impulses of great intensity, it becomes passion. So we do not use passion in place of sentiment because it implies violence and intensity of excitement.

Self-regarding Sentiments : 'Self' means 'oneself' identity one's personality *i.e.* what one is self can be defined roughly as the elaboration of such statement as—'I am this sort of a person' self refers to the image of total personality of an individual, including bodily self and the sense of identity.

(i) Self-Concept : A human being is aware of himself. He is aware of his past and future and of other people. As he is aware of his own life and ultimate death, he must establish a firm identity and a purpose and meaning for his life. Self concept is the totality of the perceptions that one has about himself, his attitude towards himself, the language he uses to describe himself.

(ii) Self-Esteem : The child's self-esteem is, especially his-self judgment of his own abilities, influence and popularity. To a certain extent, it is a mirror image of the judgment of others. Self esteem is a positive attitude towards oneself and one's behaviour. Quite often, it is a lasting personal disposition.

(iii) Self-Image : The perfect and ideal self which the individual imagines himself or herself to be often identification with an idealized conception of what he or she should be.

Self-regarding sentiments and formation of character : Self-regarding sentiments results from the regard a person attach to himself as a result of learnings from role models like parents, teachers and other strong influences. Self-regarding sentiments provide stability to the person's life. Therefore, the small dissatisfaction or frustration may lead to a conflict. To overcome such conflicts the person needs strong will-power. Thus high regard for self due to chosen standards of conduct alongwith strong will-power can actually frustrate a character that make meaningful changes to the society.

Q7. Discuss the formation of character. List five types of character.

Ans. Formation of Character : Character is related to morality in some respects. How moral sentiments are formed is easy to explain. The moral qualities, which the child develops, are developed through imitative process. The way, in which elders react emotionally to actions, becomes the way in which the child reacts to them. He takes up as model the qualities which his parents or teachers appear to like in their conduct. The qualities which they condemn, are condemned by the child also. But perhaps more influential is the group, the family, the school, the community and the church which have certain moral sentiments in common, *e.g.*, a common hatred for lying, stealing, deceiving or a common admiration for courage, justice, honesty and fair play. The other way, in which moral sentiments are acquired by the child, relates to the formation of the sentiment of self-regard. Through a very long and subtle process the child begins to conceive self clearly and distinctly. Self-regard means self-respect, self-esteem, self-love, self-pride and self-ambition. Many acute satisfaction and sufferings, many emotional experiences, are the product of the working of this sentiment of self-regard; for example, many people are forced to commit suicide because of fear of shame or disgrace. Self-regarding sentiment motivates them to do such crimes. The person, who has a feeling of self-respect, asserts himself. He has a feeling of pride in himself, a tendency for dominance over others. At the same time he has a propensity for submission also. Whatever be the nature of self-regarding sentiment, it is the sense of self-esteem that forces us not to do immoral acts.

Types of Character : Peck has identified five types of character. These types fall in line with Kohlburg's six stages of moral reasoning. The types of character are as follows:

(1) Amoral : Such type of students are self-centered and act on impulses. There is no sense of discriminating right and wrong, no feeling of guilt, mere self-gratification. They may conceal and give a charming appearance to other.

(2) Expedient : Such types of students are self-centered and always strive to gain reward and avoid punishment. They are inconsistent in their behaviour and concerned about their own welfare only.

(3) Conformist : Some students act in accordance with social demands. They are basically immature in nature, but superficially appear to be conforming to societal norms and pretend to be model citizens.

(4) Irrational conscientious : Such types of students have a set of standard and moral code of their own, but conform quite rigidly. They are bound to their conscience and feel guilty if they violate it. They have a sense of right and wrong, and certain acts may be considered right and certain wrong.

(5) Rational altruistic : Such students have a stable set of morals, principles. They understand, evaluate, accept and habitually act upon principles. They may tend to change their principles according to their insights and welfare of other human beings. They may act in a socially constructive way but in accordance with their personal convictions. They are unselfish persons.

Q8. Discuss the educational implication of Adjustment.

Ans. Adjustment – Educational implications : The implications of adjustment are analysed and discussed as follows. Our role is to do as under:

1. To identity problem and maladjusted children : Children with personal inadequacies and who are maladjusted in the school environment should be identified or recognized. The problem children require special attention. Students who suffer from physical disability should be asked to sit in the front row so that they are under direct observations of the teacher. It would enable the teacher to understand them and solve their problems.

2. To reinforce the isolated : Special care should be given to students who isolate themselves from others. School activities should be designed in such a way that every student receives due attention from the teacher.

3. To reform the inferior : We should identify that students who are poor in specific subjects like maths and science and diagnose their specific problems.

4. To transform aggression : The aggressive and hostile feeling of maladjusted students should be converted to athletic contest, painting, dramatise and stage plays.

5. To encourage healthy development of self : If we as a teacher possess values like honesty, truthfulness, sincerity and perseverance the student will develop same sentiment towards us and admire us. By immolating the personality of such teachers, they develop master sentiment in themselves.

6. To train in will power : The generation gap between parents and children creates conflicts in the family. Adolescents often experience conflicts, dilemmas, whether in observing the traditional familial values or in adhering to new emerging values. In such a situation, we can adopt certain new approaches to develop value judgement amongst students. The approaches like value analysis value, discussion and jurisprudential inquiry will develop will power, reasoning, ability and rational judgment amongst students.

7. To refurbish the skills of counseling : A teacher should motivate to acquire extra knowledge about counseling and refurbishing it. The National Justice of Mental Health and Neuro-sciences (NIMHANS) in Bangalore has been actively engaged in orienting and organizing counseling programmes for the benefit of school teachers.

8. To refer to counselors : Teachers may refer the problem children to professional counselors. The trained counselors may diagnose the case and provide appropriate guidance and counseling to students.

Q9. Define social adjustment. Discuss its various process.

Ans. Social Adjustment : Social adjustment is an effort made by an individual to cope with standards, values and needs of a society in order to be accepted. It can be defined as a psychological process. It involves coping with new standard and value. In the technical language of psychology "getting along with the members of society as best one can" is called adjustment.

Nature of Social Adjustment : As Plato says 'Man is a social animal.' We live in a society and form opinion about others and others have opinions about us. We try to behave according to the norms of the society so that we can adjust with others. But it is not an easy talk because the personality of each individual is a unique organization. This organization has to make special efforts to adjust with other unique organization which we all society. Social adjustment is the direction, we, the teacher try to instill adjustment skill in our students: Teacher should emphasise on the adjustment of the student in the school. They should help the student scope with the existing situations of the school. They should contribute to improving the social environment of the school.

Psychologists use the term adjustment of varying conditions of social and interpersonal relation in the society. Thus adjustment can be called the reaction to the demands and pressures of the social environment imposed upon the individual.

Perception and Social Adjustment : There is need of impractical perception for social adjustment. The processes of behaviour *e.g.* learning, maturation, sensation, perception and motivation contribute to the process of adjustment. The way we interact with people depends, to a great extent, upon how we perceive them and how we interpret their behaviour. The perceptions about people—what we think, what they like—influence the way we respond to them. Our social perceptions of others are initially based on the information we obtain about them—in some instances the attribution inference we make about the cause for their behaviour. It is of course, important to have accurate knowledge of others before deciding on the kind of possible interaction with them.

Impression Formation and Social Adjustment : Impression formation is the process by which information about others is converted into more or less enduring cognition or thoughts about them. When we first meet someone, we usually have access to information how the person looks and where he or she works and what he or she says. There facts form the basic cognitive framework by which we understand others and try to adjust with them.

Other Processes in Social Adjustment : There are certain other processes which we can use for social adjustment as under:

(i) Stress and Adaptation: Environmental factors which make it hard for an individual to live are called stress. The stress is experienced as irritation as discomfort. At a slightly more advanced level stress is explained as the anticipation of harm. In human beings certain kind of stresses produce anxiety. Anxiety some times produces defensive response. Defenses are generally regarded as poor methods of adjustment.

(ii) Social Influence: The process of social influence contains two critical elements. These are as under:

(a) Someone's intervention

(b) Inducing change in other person.

The phenomena of influence, which also includes imitation conformity and obedience always contain an agent which has caused a change in the focal person (FP). Influence situations can be differentiated by noticing the different characteristics of agent and of the behaviour that makes up the intervention.

The following five concepts help us understand the process of social influence better.

1. Social Facilitation : In a group situation the presence of others would always influence performance and thus the efforts to bring changes in performance of an individual are called social facilitation. The presence of others increases an individual's arousal level which in turn, enhances performance of well learned responses. For example, a well trained singer would, according to this theory *i.e.* social facilitation, performs better when others are present but a beginning would make more mistakes when giving a recital in front of others than when practicing at home.

2. Imitation : Imitation involves change in focal person's behaviour that matches as copies others' behaviour. Student imitate the behaviour of social personalities for getting the recognition.

3. Compliance to Others : Human being as a social being has to adjust himself in the social environment in his daily life, he commands others and works according to his one or other's rules and regulations. In a family every member is dependent on each other. Sometimes even parents obey the rules of their children. This type of situation influences them to adjust in social environment.

4. Conformity to Norms : Conformity is the situation wherein individuals change their behaviour so that they may become more similar to those of the other members of the group.

5. Obedience : Obedience is the situation wherein the agent has legitimate right to influence the focal person and the focal person has the obligation to obey.

Q10. What do you understand by social maturity? Discuss the nature of social maturity.

Ans. Social maturity means knowing what to do and striving for it by following role models to reach the desired level of acceptable social behaviour.

Social maturity is a long process to be socially mature. Students should be exposed to those people who are socially mature so they can pattern his behaviour accordingly. The students can try to reach the expectations of the social system, parents, teachers, siblings and peers who matter to them.

The Nature of Social Maturity : The maturity of a student is influenced by various social factors as under:

(i) Concept of dependence : Independence; An individual is required to modify his behaviour in terms of asserting his independence and seeking aid or relief in the socio cultural context.

(ii) Self Control : Self control as a part of social maturity is necessary for decision making and facing the consequences. Acquiring self control is partly maturational and partly learnt behaviour. The students studying in a secondary school understands that society does not expect him to regress to childhood behaviour at this age so he attempts at coming up to the expectations of the society and this he achieves by controlling his behaviour.

(iii) Stress : Everybody has to overcome stresses. Every time there is a stress situation. A mature individual mobilizes the available resources and utilizes them to the best of his ability to overcome the stress.

(iv) Social maturation : Socially mature are aware of their roles. During the process of social growth students learn to live up to the expectations of the society in which they live.

Ability to Size Up a Social Situation : Another component of social maturity is to size up a social situation and react to it appropriately.

Social Adjustment and Social Maturity : The behaviour of the individual depends on maturation. Maturation is also helpful in the process of social adjustment. The socialization plays an important role in social maturation, social learning and social adjustment. Much of the behaviour of child determined by the process of socialization.

Q11. Discuss school-related factors which influence student's adjustment. [June 2003 Q7]

Ans. The getting along with the members of the society as best as one can, is called adjustment. These are following school related factors which influence student's adjustment.

1. Classroom climate: Classroom climate influences students' adjustment very much. If classroom climate is democratic, affectionate and cooperative then we can expect that students would adjust themselves sufficiently.

2. Evaluation system of school: If school has supportive and encouraging evaluation system, if school has validity and objectivity in evaluation then it can influence student's adjustment positively.

3. Proper training of teachers: If the teachers of school are well trained in educational psychology, they can help students in making proper adjustment in school. We can see that personality and democratic attitude of teacher influence student's adjustment positively.

4. Proper relationships between administration: There should be a proper relationships between teachers and teachers, principal and teachers. It can produce a positive influence on student's adjustment.

5. Adequate curriculum: The curriculum of school also influence student's adjustment. If the curriculum of school is need based and planned psychologically then students can adjust themselves effectively.

6. Adequate recreational facilities: If students are provided essential and enough opportunity to take part in recreational activities according to their interest, needs and ability then they can adjust themselves positively. So we should organize various co-curricular activities as games and sports, cultural activities, literal activities, field visits etc.

Besides this, the following measures can also help students in adjusting to the school environment:

(1) The school environment should be free from partially and should provide the feeling of security in students, irrespective of their socio-economic status.

(2) School environment should be democratic. Students' representation on various committees should be made.

(3) School should organize various curricular activities for students.

(4) Teachers should know the fundamental principles of human behaviour to solve students' problems. They must be emotionally stable and have positive attitude towards teaching. They should create conducive school climate.

(5) Students should be encouraged to express their views and feelings on various issues related to school freely.

(6) Teachers should develop a variety of interests in students so that they can satisfy their emotions.

(7) Day-to-day problems can be discussed in class.

(8) Sex and moral education should be an integral part of the school curriculum.

(9) School can organize guidance services for students.

(10) There should be flexibility in school activities to accommodate the individual needs of the students.

Q12. What do you mean by group dynamics? How does study of group dynamics help a teacher in classroom transaction? [Dec 2003 Q2]

Ans. Dynamics mean change and group dynamics means the change of behaviour through interaction in the group. As we know that students live in groups in school as their classroom, group of playmates, hobby club, science club, library etc. It is natural that students interact with each other in groups to perform their needs, get informations, provide messages etc. As we know that human behaviour is not static, so when students interact in their group/

groups with other members then the behaviour of members who constantly, interact, undergoes continuous changes. This kind of changing in behaviour of students due to their interaction in group with group members, is called group dynamics.

We see that when teacher organize any group project work in classroom regarding any topic, then he/she formulates various groups and provide them project work/works. Students have to interact with the members of their group to perform various works of project, to get information, to seek help, etc. Every group demands reciprocity among its members. Every group influences, to a great extent, the behaviour of its members. Students interacts with the environment for their development. This development depends on social interaction. A teacher should study group dynamics to deal with various groups of students. Now we shall discuss, how study of group dynamics help a teacher in classroom transaction—

1. To provide appropriate guidance to students for their adjustment : If teacher has basic knowledge of group dynamics then he/she can provide appropriate guidance to his/her students for their adjustment. As we know that education aims to make socially adjustable citizen of the country, we want that our students should have positive adjustment with their friends, classmates, playmates and others. Sometimes students can face certain problems regarding their process of adjustment. If teacher is well-equipped with the basic knowledge of group dynamics, if teacher knows how a student should interact with other members of his/her group positively then he/she (teacher) can provide proper guidance to students about their adjustment.

2. To improve the emotional and social climate of the class : As we know that we can not even imagine to organise participative, effective and aimful teaching-learning process in the class which does not have proper emotional and social climate. If the students of the class have negative attitudes about each other, if they act unsocially as enemies, if they do not care emotions, needs, expectations of others then we cannot expect a successful transaction of teaching-learning process in that kind of class. Through the study of group dynamics, a teacher can guide his/her students for making proper adjustment and healthy interaction with each other. Teacher can improve the emotional and social climate of the class.

3. To improve group relations in the class : We can see some particular patterns of relationship among the students of the class as-stars, isolates, mutual pairs, chains etc. If teacher has basic knowledge of group dynamics then he/she can provide a leadership role. The role of the leader is now shifting from authoritarian to a democratic and participatory one. Teacher should try to encourage participation of students in all the school activities. If teacher has studied about group dynamics, then he/she can improve the climate of the students of his class by taking them into confidence. Teacher can take his/her decisions democratically. By studying group dynamics, he/she can motivate students to participate in learning activities. Since group relation has an important role in teaching-learning process so a teacher should improve group relation in the class. For this improvement he/she should have knowledge of group dynamics.

4. To deal effectively with social groups : Teacher has to organise various activities in various groups. To deal efficiently with social groups in classroom, in playground, in laboratory, in co-curricular activities, teacher should have study about group dynamics.

5. To have a thorough knowledge of the interaction process : As we know that in a class we can not find all the students of same qualities, needs, interests etc. They may be of different socio-economic background. Teacher should try to ascertain positive interaction among these students. For this teacher should have a complete knowledge of group dynamics and the interaction process.

6. To remove conflicts and stresses in the group : As we know that conflicts and stresses in the group, disturb the learning climate of the class. A teacher should try to remove these. For this a teacher should have study the group dynamic process. As a whole, a teacher's work is not only to teach the students but he/she should work to create positive circumstances in the class which could motivate students towards participative and aimful learning. For this kind of creation a teacher should have thorough knowledge of group dynamics which help a teacher in classroom transaction.

Q13. Discuss the classification of students with special needs.

[June-07, Q2]

Ans. As a teacher, we have to acquire necessary information and skills to understand the student as a unique individual in terms of individual differences in learning levels. These differences among individuals may be attributed to a number of factors. These factors force us to understand the learning process in the broader context rather than as an isolated phenomenon or process. One of these contexts is the 'characteristics' of the students themselves.

Students with special needs can be classified into five categories as under:

1. Physical Impairment: Students with Locomotor Disability—Children with physical disabilities may have locomotor problems which are related to muscular and joints of the body affecting mobility of limbs and extremities. The students with such impairment may find difficulty in attempting those learning activities which need physical movement.

We can play an important role in helping students to overcome physical impairment, parents support can be sought in this regard. In case of severe disability, the students can be referred to Distinct Rehabilitation Centres of Primary Health Centres (PHCs).

Suggestions :

1. Suitable seating arrangements should be made in the classroom. Students with crutches and wheelchairs should be provided a seat on the right front space in the classroom, so that the movement of the other students is not blocked or hindered.

2. We should ensure that they get adequate opportunities to participate in physical and recreational activities in the class and the school. Other students should be encouraged to join them in such activities.

3. The disability needs to be taken into consideration. While grading their papers, if they have difficulty in writing, they may be provided with extra time.

2. Students with Visual Impairment: The children who have visual disability can not read the usual text and may need some learning aids such as Braille in case of blindness. Then there are partially sighted students. Some students read only large print say for example, 14 point and above, some require magnifying glasses to read. Some children have restricted field of vision. The teachers should identify such students and provide them special help in their study.

Visual disability can be identified as under :

1. The student asks other students for help when taking notes from the blackboards.

2. He holds objects including the book close to his eyes.

3. Observable deformity in the eyes.

4. He robs eyes frequently.

5. There is frequent reddening of eyes.

6. He covers one eye and tills the head forward.

7. He bumps into people as objects.

8. He complains of headaches.

9. He has watery eyes.

10. He blinks frequently or squints eyelids together.

If child displays any of these types of behaviours we may refer him to the PHC/hospital for eye check-up. Teacher's functions are as under:

1. A teacher should pay special attention to the student with visual disability. He should allow such students to sit in the front rows so that they can read the blackboard with ease.

2. They should be encouraged to glance out of the window now and then while reading for the blackboard.

3. We should write in bold letters which are legible.

4. We should read aloud when we write on the blackboard.

5. Books with bold letters (14 points or more) should be available in the library to cater to the needs of these students.

6. the District Rehabilitation Centres and hospitals may be approached for hand lens, magnifying glasses, etc. For students whose disability is beyond the spectacle lens.

3. Students with Hearing and Speech Impairment: Hearing problems interfere with learning and performance. Hearing problems may also cause speech problems. So we should identify such students and take steps to meet their educational needs.

4. Identification of Hearing Disability: The level of hearing is measured by audiometers in terms of decibels (d b). Mild loss is within the range of 20-30 d b, marginal 30-40 d b, moderate 40-60 d b, severe 60-75 d b, and profound loss is above 75 d b.

The students with hearing problems can be easily identified by observing their behaviours.

The behaviours of students with hearing problem is as under :

1. He has observable deformity in the ear (s).

2. Frequent discharge from the ear (s).

3. Complain of pain in ears frequently.

4. Displays speech difficulty.

5. While listening to the teacher, watches his face carefully.

6. Makes, many errors in taking dictation.

7. Frequently requests teacher to repeat directions and question.

8. Turns head on one side to hear better.

9. Scratches ear(s) frequently.

The student with any of these behaviours may be referred for a medical check-up. It is important to get the help of the professionals to identify the degree of loss and suitability of the hearing aid.

Education of Disabled Students :

1. Students with hearing problems should be asked to sit near the teacher for improved listening.

2. Teacher should use a reasonable level of pitch (voice) while speaking.

3. Teacher should avoid mumbling and speaking too fast.

4. While reading from the text book his lips should be visible to the students so that they are able to supplement listening up lip-reading. While speaking or writing on the blackboard teacher should face the students.

Speeches defects arising out of hearing problems can be corrected through speech training, using reinforced drill and practice.

Students with Low Mental Ability : The performance of the student with low mental ability do not have any physical problems but they are poorly adjusted in the classroom. Some observable behaviour for identifying such students is as follows.

The Low Mental ability student behaves as under:

1. He seeks immediate reward.

2. He displays fear of failure.

3. He displays poor academic achievement.

4. He forgets what he has learnt after a short time.

5. He is inattentive and disturbed.

6. He shows too much reliance on presentation of concrete objects.

7. He has poor self image.

8. He lacks self confidence.

9. He shows too much dependence or concrete examples.

10. He avoids active participation in classroom activities.

11. He has restricted communication.

12. He has poor muscular coordination.

13. He has difficulty in doing things for himself like eating dressing bathing and grooming.

14. He has problem in following what he has been told.

15. He learns at a slow pace.

16. He seeks more repetition and practice as compared to other students.

Teaching the students who have low mental ability : Teacher should provide concrete experience to such students.

1. Such students require repetition and more practice than the normal students.

2. Learning tasks should be presented in small steps.
3. Their attention is to be drawn to important points of the learning tasks.
4. Simple questions may be asked to given them a feeling of success.
5. Immediate Feedback or reward should be the watch world for such students.
6. These students need training in communication skills.
7. The curriculum has to be translated through simple and interesting learning experience.

Students with Learning Disability: Some students may have specific learning problems such as reading, writing, spelling or arithmetic. For example, some students always read and write 'b' as 'd' 'was' as 'saw' '21' as '12'. These students are said to have a learning disability which arises out of the problems in psychological process. These students should be provided with special help in learning.

Identification of Disability: The following are some of the observable behaviours for identification of learning disability.

1. He is always unitedly and late in submitting home work and coming to class.
2. He is destructible and cannot remember his time table.
3. He writes number wrong *e.g.* '12' as '21' as write '69' when asked to write '79'.
4. Makes mistakes in spellings, especially omits letter in words as change their place *e.g.* pat instead of 'tap' or 'felt' as 'left' 'rember' in place of 'remember'.
5. He does not read well although his oral answers are intelligent.
6. Reads individual letters in the words but has difficulty in putting the sounds of the letters together. For example, he may say, the sound b/e/g and say 'Bad' or sound f/o/g say 'frog'.
7. Omits words or lines in reading.
8. He is so excited that he is unable to complete any task.
9. Does not perform well in the examinations although, he is clever and has no physical disability.

Education of students with disability: Such students need help in areas of their disability such as reading arithmetic etc. They can be helped as under:

1. We should adopt suitable teaching strategies to support their learning.
2. We should not criticize the students unnecessarily.
3. Corrective feedback is most important at this stage.

Q14. What is a gifted child? How will you identify him? What should be the nature of education for a gifted child?

OR

Define gifted child or talented students. What is the areas of teacher's intervention for gifted child?

Ans. The gifted, the genius, the talented and the creative are some of the terms used in psychology for those children who stand at the top level. Kolesnik defines the gifted child as one who in his age-group is superior in some ability which may make him an outstanding contributor to the welfare and quality of living in our society. Such a child is at the top, generally in intelligence. His I.Q. ranges from 130 to 140. But the term gifted should not be related to intelligence only.

Terman and Oder regard gifted children as those who rate far above the average in physique, social adjustment, personality traits, school achievements, and who have a variety of interests. In this sense the word gifted has a greater relationship with the natural endowment.

The following are the chief characteristics of the gifted children and their presence may help us in identifying the gifted child.

1. Better Physique : The gifted child is heavier than the normal one. He learns speaking and walking 2 or 3 months earlier than a normal child.

2. Greater Capacity to Learn : The gifted child is not only superior in intelligence, he has a greater capacity to concentrate on a particular subject.

3. Versatility of Interests : In a gifted child there are a number of developed interests.

4. Greater Educational and Social Maturity : The gifted child has a tolerance for disagreeable circumstances, freedom from unreasonable fear, cultivated positive emotions, and inhabited negative ones. He has an ability to make mistakes without feeling disgrace and delay the gratification of impulses. He has greater social maturity and finds better adjustment in the society he keeps.

5. Greater Interest in Abstract Thinking : A gifted child shows an interest in abstract thinking and therefore can solve difficult problems more easily.

6. Greater Vocabulary : The gifted child has a broad vocabulary at his command. His active vocabulary is much greater and can use a large number of words and can speak fluently.

7. Greater General Knowledge : The gifted child has information about his environment. His general knowledge is greater because of greater interest in reading.

8. Greater Achievement : As a gifted child is above average in intelligence and had greater capacity to study and learn his achievement is always superior to that of his classmates.

Areas for Teacher's Intervention/Nature of Education for gifted students: The following are the major areas where your interventions will prove useful for gifted students :

Moral and social issues : At times we do not expect students to be concerned about moral and social issues. It is not unusual to find students with superior abilities to have very strong opinions on moral and social issues.

Emotional problems : Students with superior abilities are subject to same type of emotional problems. Their unusual abilities and other characteristics may lead to emotional problems.

Removing the feeling of isolation : Since these students are different in physical, social and mental development, they may feel left out. At times the feelings of superiority works against their personality adjustment.

Convergent vs divergent thinking : Mostly school work is evaluated on conformity to one right answer. Such evaluation rewards convergent thinking but can be harmful for divergent thinking, where different answers of a problem are possible.

Self-concept : Self-concept refers to one's impression about oneself. Students who generate or express unusual ideas are sometimes criticized in the group. This may result in poor self-concept.

Self-criticism : Many gifted students have high goals and become self-criticism. They may also be communicated expectation on the part of teachers, parents as well as peers. Teachers may expect them to always give the correct answer or be outstanding in class. This induces anxiety and stress in students.

Q15. Discuss the role of a teacher to bring the special child psychology at level with a normal child.

Ans. Special child means the students who have special needs. Teacher should try to fulfill their special needs so that they could not think themselves unfit in the class. Here we shall discuss role of the teacher to bring these special children at level with normal child separately according to their needs:

1. Role of teacher for the special child of physical impairment : Teacher should make arrangement of suitable seating system in classroom for them. The seating arrangement should be such that it allows independent movement of the students. Teacher should ensure that they get adequate opportunities to participate in physical and recreational activities in the class and school. If these type of special child have difficulty in writing. He/She may be provided extra time for it.

2. Role of teacher for the special child of visual impairment : First of all, if we see any visual disability in our student then we should refer him/her to the hospital for check-up. We can allow such students to sit in the front rows so that they could read the black board with ease. We, as a teacher should write in bold letters which are legible. We should also read aloud when we write on the blackboard. Books with bold letters should be available in the library to cater to the needs of these students. Through these efforts we can bring these type of special children psychologically at level with a normal child.

3. Role of teacher of the special child of hearing and speech impairment: Teacher can do a lot of help/work for them. We as a teacher should ask students with hearing problems to sit near us for improved listening. Teacher should use a reasonable level of pitch (voice) while speaking. We should not speak too fast and avoid mumbling. We as a teacher should have our lips visible to the students while we are reading so that they are able to supplement listening by lip-reading. We can correct their some hearing problems through speech training using reinforced drill and practice. We should also send them for medical check-up.

4. Role of teacher for the special child of low mental ability : Every teacher can find special children of low mental ability in his/her class. To bring them at level with a normal child we, as a teacher should provide them concrete experience. These special children require repetition and more practice than the normal students. We can present learning tasks in small steps. We should give them a feeling of success by asking simple questions. We should provide immediate feedback or reward for these kind of students. We should give them training also in communication skills.

5. Role of the teacher for special child of learning disability : To bring them at a level with a normal child, teacher should provide them help in areas of their disability. We as a teacher should adopt suitable teaching strategies to support their learning. We should not criticize these kind of students. Teacher should diagnose their problematic areas and then organise extra classes to solve their problems.

6. Role of the teacher for special child of gifted and talented : We, as a teacher should provide them extra work where they could use their both convergent and divergent thinking. Such kind of students may have superiority complex in themselves. These feeling may arise some emotional problems. Teacher should understand these emotional problems and then try to solve them. Sometimes these gifted and talented students may be criticized in the group. Teacher should solve this problem by giving them group activities so that these special children could not make poor self-concept.

7. Role of the teacher for special child with socially disadvantages : As we know that economic poverty can still be a constraint in the educational development of educationally backward sections of Indian society. Their parents lack motivation towards education. They have low self concept and inadequate educational facilities and the low expectations by the teacher. We, as a teacher should develop an awakening in them towards education and motivate them for education. We, as a teacher should present acceptance and recognition. Teacher should understand their problems and then try to solve them so that they could study at a level with normal children.

8. Role of the teacher for special children from the deprived sections of the society (SC, ST) : These children think that education is not for them and their upward mobility is not possible so they drop out of school. We, as a teacher should fill the feeling in them that education is for them. We should provide them special facilities. We should motivate them toward education. The students of Scheduled Tribes may use local dialects for communication. We, as a teacher should provide and ensure a non-discriminatory attitude and environment in class and school. We as a teacher should become responsible for the developmental activities both educational and social in the tribal areas. We as a teacher should have a major role in motivating parents and the community for sending their children to school and they should be informed them time to time about special schemes for them.

Thus teacher can lot to bring these special children psychologically at a level with normal children. It is the main responsibility of us, as a teacher to understand their special needs and problems and then we should try to solve them so that these special children could take part in teaching learning process whole heartedly and aimfully.

Q16. Discuss education of girls.

Ans. Constitution of India provides equalization of opportunities across gender. Society continues to discriminate between boys and girls. The National Policy on Education 1986, recommended that provisions should be made for equal educational opportunities for girls. It was recommended with a view to removing disparities and attending to their specific needs. The following factors contribute to a negative attitude towards the education of girls in our society.

(i) Considered Backward – Women by and large are still considered incapable of competing with men. Specially in areas of leadership initiative and boldness.

(ii) Incapable of Decisions – It is considered that women are not capable of taking their decisions.

(iii) Expectations – It is based on the role expectations boys and girls are discriminated.

(iv) Social Evils – There are many social evils such as dowry system, bride price, prostitution, child marriage etc. in the society which contribute to lowering the self-concept of the girls.

(v) Stigmas – There are certain stigmas attached to women because of the discriminating perception of the society.

All these factors give birth to certain biases in the society which are unfortunately reflected in the school curriculum, text books and even in our behaviour with the students in classroom.

Areas : Three areas of the discrimination in textual content are as under:

1. Thematic content : We often see more topics dealing with men and their heroic efforts than women.

2. Linguistic content : In language text books some of the expressions degenerate the state of women, for example *do you cry like a girl.*

3. Teacher's behaviour : Sometimes through very subtle behaviour we also contribute to the misconception. For example, we may tell in a co-education class or in a girls class that it does not suit a girl to be a 'tomboy'.

Suggestions to a Teacher : As teacher we may like to reflect on the following to contribute to conveying a positive image of girls.

(i) We should encourage the girls to be self reliant and provide them opportunities for preserving and fighting for self respect.

(ii) We should highlight the capabilities of girls.

(iii) We should encourage healthy competition.

(iv) There should be fair representation of women's image and role.

(v) We should remember that girls are not a burden, bridegrooms need not be bought and brides sold.

(vi) There is nothing like *men's* and work as *women's* and work.

Q17. Define guidance. Discuss the nature, type and basic assumption of guidance.

Ans. To understand guidance it is better to contrast it with what is not guidance. According to Crow and Crow "Guidance is not giving direction, it is not the imposition of one person's point of view upon another person. It is not making decision for an individual which he should make for himself. It is not carrying the burden of another life.

Crow and Crow observes that guidance is an assistance made available by a qualified and adequately trained person to another person to help him to manage his own activities, develop his own point of view, and make his own decision. Whenever a person aided directly or indirectly by a qualified person in knowledge, emotional fitness, mental activity, social and civic adjustment, guidance increases individual's ability to think and act independently or follow his own initiatives.

There are many expressions used to mean guidance *e.g.* to lead, to steer or to direct. But in all these terms we find compulsion, indoctrination and direction. To guide implies help that is more of personal nature than either to steer, to direct, to regulate, or to conduct. The focus of guidance is on the individual and not on the problem, its purpose is to promote the growth of an individual for self-direction.

Emery Stoops holds that guidance is a continuous process of helping the individual to develop on the maximum of his capacity in the direction most beneficial to himself and to society.

An analysis of this definition indicates that the concept of guidance includes several significant characteristics.

Characteristics : Some important characteristics are as under:

1. Guidance is a continuous process.

2. It leads to self development and self direction

3. It leads to discovery of needs assets, plans of action and adjustment of emotional blocking.

4. It focuses attention on individual.

5. It is an assistance rather than direction imposition or compulsion.

6. It is given by technically and professionally trained persons.

Nature and Types and Guidance : The ways in which the guidance practitioners help students are as under:

1. Professionals help students to seek the information needed to make decisions and choose the best alternative out of various choices.

2. Assisting them to secure adequate information and develop techniques that will enable them to develop desirable information as and when they need it.

3. Assisting in choosing an appropriate vocation.

4. They provide tryout and exploratory experience.

5. Assisting them to develop desirable attitude, interest and ideals.

6. In carrying students to follow a balanced programme of physical activities.

7. Assisting students in making effective use of their study time.

8. Helping students in developing leadership qualities.

9. Assisting them in becoming progressively responsible for their own development.

10. Assisting students in attaining emotional stability.

Basic Assumptions of Guidance : Guidance and counseling programmes community represent a wide range of approaches for delivering services. The development and implementation of guidance services is based on certain underlying assumptions and basic principles. Author J. Jones discussed seven basic assumptions as under:

1. Race, colour and sex have little as no relation to aptitude and abilities.

2. Many crises cannot be successfully met by student without assistance.

3. The school is in a strategic position to give the assistance needed.

4. Guidance is not prescriptive instead at progressive ability for self guidance.

5. Variations within the individual are significant.

6. Abilities already existing in individual are not usually specialised.

Q18. What are the domains of guidance? Describe the procedure for educational and vocational guidance.

Ans. There are three major types or domains of guidance as under:

1. Educational Guidance : Educational guidance is concerned with the assistance given to students in their choice and adjustment with relation to school, curriculum courses and school life.

2. Vocational Guidance : Vocational guidance is a process of assisting the individual to choose an occupation, prepare them for or enter upon and progress in it.

3. Personal Guidance : Personal guidance is an assistance given to student to solve their emotional problem and to help them to control their emotions and feelings.

Procedure for Educational and Vocational Guidance : The following procedures are generally adopted for educational and vocational guidance:

(1) In providing educational and vocational guidance several orientation talks are organised for choosing a right type of education and vocation.

(2) Students are encouraged to participate in groups in academic, vocational and recreational activities in order to know their interest, ability and aptitude.

(3) Psychological tests are administered in order to know their personality and abilities.

(4) In order to provide educational and vocational guidance school examination results are also taken into consideration.

(5) Teacher's assessment about individual's ability and other characteristics are also considered.

(6) Parents' opinion about their wards are also taken into consideration.

(7) Occupational-oriented talk and visits are also one of the steps for educational and vocational guidance.

(8) Interviews are also conducted in order to know the educational and vocational plans of the individual.

Q19. Discuss various types of counseling.

Ans. (1) Directive Counseling : This type if counseling is directive in its nature. The counsellor plays an important role in it. He/she is the authority which states a judgment over any problem. In this type of counseling student has not any important role but counsellor has problem in his/her main focus. Student has to cooperate to his/her counsellor. Since it is an authoritative type of counseling so students communicate a little and counsellor does most of talking. In it we can not see democratic environment. Student has to work under the counsellor not with him. We can give counseling regarding intellectual aspects in it.

(2) Non-directive counseling : In this type of counseling, student is provided a great opportunity for free expression in which he/she could give information to counsellor completely. In this type of counseling, student works with counsellor not under him/her. It is democratic in behaviour where counseling develops further insight, a more complete and accurate understanding of the problem. Since student plays a central role in it so we can also say it client centered counseling.

(3) Electic counseling : In this type of counseling, counsellor offers many alternative solutions of a problem from which student could select the most appropriate one. Counsellor has the need of individual in his/her view at the time of counseling. Counsellor has the effect of counseling on student in his/her mind.

A teacher should use these type of counseling according to need and nature of students as well as problems.

Q20. How will you organise counseling services in your school? Explain with example.

Ans. Providing help by a trained person to students for solving their problems is called counseling. Counseling is the activity where all the facts are gathered together and the experiences of the students are focused upon the particular problem to be solved by him, where he is given direct and personal help in solving his problems.

We can organise counseling services in our school. We can use counseling services for solving various problems of our students. For this class teacher will play a role of counsellor because he/she knows students more deeply than subject teacher. We can organise both directive and non-directive counseling services. In directive counseling, we can provide counseling to students by having their problems in main focus. As for example, a student is facing some particular problems in completing project work. The student is not doing well in this project work due to his/her personal problem. We can solve these problems by providing him counseling service. In non-directive counseling student goes to get help to counsellor. For this work we can give special period once in a week for such kind of service where students could seek help of counsellor in solving their problems. Thus we could organise counseling services in our school successfully.

Q21. Explain the process of guiding students.

Ans. The major responsibilities of the teacher is to create, provide conducive environment in the school for optimal learning. It is agreed that education should reach to all children irrespective of their caste, creed and religion. In order to provide guidance to special learners, it is important to identify them systematically based on teacher observation, academic records, creative activities and performance in mental ability tests. The following strategies are suggested for providing guidance to those students who have learning difficulties :-

1. To identify the students for guidance purpose.

2. To administer specially designed diagnostic test.

3. To analyse the causes of learning difficulties.

4. To plan cooperatively the approaches for removing the difficulties.

5. To implement the approaches.

6. To evaluate the approaches.

Guiding Backward Students : After identifying the backward children we should first decide one of three possible ways for the education of backward and children.

(i) Whether they should be given education in a regular class.

(ii) They should be thought in a separate class in the same school.

(iii) They should be provided education in a separate school.

The following principles of learning must be kept in mind while teaching the backward children in classroom:

1. To be taught in simple steps so that they can achieve mastery in their learning at their one pace.
2. Given immediate reinforcement for their success.
3. To be given the opportunity to practise knowledge and skills.
4. To be provided with immediate knowledge of results.
5. Given a variety of stimulation.

Guiding Gifted Students : The following steps may be followed while guiding the gifted children:
1. Identify the gifted children on the basis of observation of their characteristics.
2. Administer intelligence test.
3. Select the most appropriate approach for catering the gifted children. These approaches are—
(a) Segregation of gifted children and arranging classes exclusively for them.
(b) Acceleration through which the gifted children may be allowed to complete the prescribed course of study in a shorter period.
(c) Enrichment programme suggesting additional books and journals for their study.

Guiding Creative Students : The teacher in the class and outside the class may encourage the spirit of enquiry in the students. For it, following points should be kept in mind:
1. Full freedom should be provided for coming out with new ideas.
2. Psychological freedom and psychological safety are essential for creative expression.
3. The technique of brainstorming or creative problem solving can be conveniently used in small group of students.
4. They should be given full freedom for the development of their imagination.
5. They should be encouraged to think on the courses and consequences of an action.
6. They should be encouraged to think different approaches and alternatives.

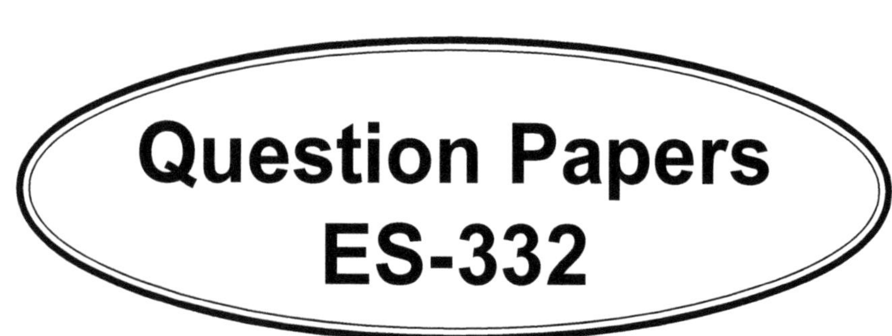
Question Papers
ES-332

ES-332 : PSYCHOLOGY OF LEARNING AND DEVELOPMENT
June, 2002

Note : All the questions are compulsory. All the questions carry equal weightage.

1. Give your answer in about 600 words.

Discuss, with suitable examples, the various principles of human development.

OR

Discuss, with the help of suitable examples, various theories of motivation. How can these theories help you motivate your students?

2. Write your answer in about 600 words.

Discuss the principles of learning. How will you use these principles in your classroom?

OR

What do you mean by humanistic approach to learning? Critically discuss its educational implications.

3. Attempt any *five* of the following. Answer each question in about 120 words.

(i) Discuss Kohlberg's stages of moral growth.

(ii) Discuss the problems related to cognitive development. What measures will you suggest to overcome cognitive development problems of your students?

(iii) Discuss misconceptions regarding heredity and environment. Give examples from your experiences as a teacher.

(iv) Discuss educational implications of operant conditioning. Support your answer with suitable examples from your classroom experience.

(v) What do you mean by 'Laws of Association'? Discuss with suitable examples.

(vi) Discuss social, economic and psychological causes of maladjustment.

(vii) What do you mean by 'conflict'? How will you help your students resolve their conflicts?

(viii) Discuss differences between guidance, counselling and psychotherapy.

4. Write your answer in about 600 words.

Hema is a bright student and always tops in the class. Her I.Q. reveals that she is a gifted student. She often feels that regular classroom teaching is not challenging and does not meet her intellectual curiosity. She also often feels bored and at times considers herself as being a misfit in the class.

Which instructional strategies would you suggest to help Hema? Support your answer with convincing arguments.

ES-332 : PSYCHOLOGY OF LEARNING AND DEVELOPMENT
December, 2002

Note : All the questions are compulsory. All the questions carry equal weightage.

1. Answer the following question in about 600 words.
'Teachers can do a lot to help adolescents develop a balanced personality.' How? Discuss your experiences in this regard.

OR

Discuss critically various modes of learning. Support your discussion with examples.

2. Answer the following question in about 600 words.
Critically discuss the influence of environmental factors on personality development of children.

OR

Discuss principles of learning deduced from learning theories.

3. Answer any *four* of the following questions in about 150 words each.
(i) How will you, as a teacher, facilitate social development of your students?
(ii) What is meant by divergent thinking? Discuss the important conditions which can foster students' divergent thinking.
(iii) Discuss the nature of values. How are they learnt or acquired?
(iv) Discuss, with the help of suitable examples, the implications of gender issues for teachers.
(v) Discuss the characteristics of learning.
(vi) Discuss, with the help of examples, implications of domains of learning (cognitive, affective and psycho-motor) for the teaching-learning process.
(vii) What is meant by defence mechanism? Discuss, in brief, various types of defence mechanisms used by tensed/frustrated students.
(viii) What is meant by 'counselling in school'? Differentiate between directive and non-directive counseling.

4. Write your answer in about 600 words.
Discuss your role as a teacher to bring the special child psychologically at level with a normal child.

ES-332 : PSYCHOLOGY OF LEARNING AND DEVELOPMENT
June, 2003

Note : (i) All the questions are compulsory.
(ii) All the questions carry equal weightage.

1. Answer the following question in about 600 words.
Discuss the implications of heredity and environmental factors for the teaching-learning process. Support your answer with suitable examples.

OR

Do individuals differ in their intelligence? Discuss the instructional strategies you will use for handling individual differences in intelligence in your class.

2. Answer the following question in about 600 words.
Compare and discuss the educational implications of behaviourist and cognitive approaches to learning.

OR

What do you mean by the humanistic approach to learning? Discuss its implications for classroom practices.

3. Answer any *four* of the following questions in about 150 words each:
(i) Why is physical education necessary in schools? How would you facilitate physical development of your students?
(ii) What is meant by creativity? How can creativity be fostered?
(iii) Define 'interest' as an aspect of the affective domain. Why should a teacher trainee study various aspects of 'interest'?
(iv) 'Maturation is an important factor which influences learning.' Discuss this statement with the help of examples.
(v) 'Motivation is the heart of learning.' Discus this statement with examples.
(vi) Discuss the measures you will take for resolving conflicts.
(vii) Discuss school-related factors which influence students' adjustment.
(viii) Discuss the following methods of learning:
(a) Spaced v/s Unspaced learning
(b) Mediating method

(c) Memory systems

4. Answer the following question in about 600 words.

You might have observed in your class that some students, though intelligent, do not fare well in the term-end examinations. How will you identify such students and help them secure better marks?

ES-332 : PSYCHOLOGY OF LEARNING AND DEVELOPMENT
December, 2003

Note : (i) All the questions are compulsory.
(ii) All the questions carry equal weightage.

1. Give your answer in about 600 words.

Compare the educational implications of cognitive and behaviouristic approaches to learning. Support your answer with suitable examples.

OR

Discuss the strategies to foster creativity among Secondary School students.

2. Give your answer in about 600 words.

What do you mean by group dynamics? How does study of group dynamics help a teacher in classroom transaction?

OR

'Adolescence is a period of storm and stress.' Discuss the statement with convincing arguments.

3. Attempt any *four* of the following. Answer each question in about 150 words each.

(i) Discuss the laws of association in learning.

(ii) How can you as a teacher help students resolve conflicts? Discuss.

(iii) What do you mean by social maturity? Discuss its nature giving suitable examples.

(iv) How will you identify students with learning disability? Discuss the measures you will use to help students overcome their learning disability.

(v) How will you organise counselling services in your school? Explain with examples.

(vi) Discuss social, economic and psychological causes of maladjustment.

(vii) Discuss the problems related to emotional development. What measures will you suggest to overcome emotional problems of your children?

4. Write your answer in about 600 words.

There are students in your class having different learning capabilities

or outcomes. Based on your experience, discuss the conditions/factors responsible for their differential learning outcomes.

ES-332 : PSYCHOLOGY OF LEARNING AND DEVELOPMENT
June, 2005

Note : (i) All the **four** questions are compulsory.
(ii) All the questions carry equal weightage.

---

1. Answer the following in about 600 words.
Clarify the concepts of growth and development. Discuss the role of a teacher in facilitating the growth and development of the higher secondary school students.
Refer to Chapter-1, Q.No.-2&3

OR

What do you mean by Cognitive Development? Explain Piaget's theory of cognitive development.
Refer to Chapter-1, Q.No.-16

2. Answer the following in about 600 words.
Explain different factors that affect the development of personality. Describe the impact of mass media on the personality development of adolescents.
Ans. Personality - Concepts and Meaning : Personality is the most abstract word used in English language. Its connotative significance is very broad but denotative significance, negligible. Scarcely any word is more versatile. There is no single definition which may be regarded as correct. Some of the definitions are psychological, some are not. The first task is to distinguish between them and the second task is to select from among available psychological definitions one that best fits the phenomenon one wants to assess.
The word personality has been derived from the word 'persona' which means theatrical mask. 'Persona' has four distinct meanings:
(a) What one appears to others and not what one really is.
(b) The part one plays in life.
(c) The sum total of qualities.
(d) Distinction and dignity as in style of writing.
According to the first meaning personality may be thought as external appearance and not the true self. The second meaning of persona regards personality as a role which the player assumes. The third involves distinctive personal qualities in the personality and the last derivative has significance of

prestige and dignity.

As personality is a complex concept we have an interaction of a number of factors that go to shape the personality of an individual. Some of the general factors are:

1. Genetic factors.

2. Physique.

3. Environmental factors.

4. Personal response.

Both the inherited factors and the environment determine what a child would be. The environmental factors that include parental circumstances, infantile, experiences, home conditions, parent-child relationships, school and society, cultural and sub-cultural influences exerted by school, church and community, all play an effective role in the shaping of personality characteristics.

Genetic Factors : The effect of genetic factors on personality is not direct as there is little evidence that there is a causal relationship between inherited factors and personality traits, such as co-operativeness, aggressiveness and honesty. Hereditary factors exert their effect upon the organism through the constitution make-up. The organism responds to the external world with his psychological mechanisms which the hereditary factors control. Heredity affects the endocrine gland structure which in turn affects the behavioural traits of an individual. Hereditary plays an important role in endocrine structure and its functioning. The endocrines such as thyroid, pituitary, pancreas, gonads and adrenals pour hormones directly into blood stream.

Effect of Body-build on Personality : The laymen believes that the big muscular boy is dominant and aggressive, the fat girl is jolly and easy going and that the lean and thin person is serious and tense. Some psychologists have tried to relate body structure to personality traits.

Body build has a relationship with personality trait, but it should be remembered that in most cases the relationship between physique and behaviour is a result of social behaviour; for example, a child who is suffering from some physical handicap is rebuffed by his peers and is considered loss worthy than the normal one. No direct causal relationship can be assumed to exist between body structure and personality traits.

Environmental Factors : The environmental factors that play a significant role in shaping the personality of an individual are his home, his socio-economic status, community's educational institutions, government, community, religious institutions, local customs and mores.

Home is the most important environmental factor that shapes the personality traits of children.

Socio-economic status of children and youths affects their personality traits through different social goals, ideals and attitudes.

The School can also improve the home conditions by giving parents proper guidance as regards in improvement in nutritional standards and beautification of homes and other sanitary conditions.

Society : The neighbourhood, sub-culture and general culture have also a potent influence upon what a child will be.

Sibling relations : Brothers and sisters are called sibling.

(a) It is seen that a sibling-less only child tends to become overprotected and self-centered unless the parents deal with the child differently.

(b) The eldest child happens to be an only child till the second is born when the first is "dethroned" from the function of solitary affection. It generally develops jealousy in him or her.

(c) Children in intermediate positions have mixed experiences they may tend to suffer more from inferiority feelings generated by comparison. The youngest child is never deprived of the affections of parents and may turn into a spoilt if "babied" child.

Effect of Mass Media : -

Mass-media : The mass media radio, television, the newspaper and the magazine or the comic, etc. communicate to the child the styles of the various sub-cultures in the total culture. Certainly the variety makes the child aware of other forms, objects and styles and creative tensions in him.

Thus we see that the personality development is a resultant of two main factors:

(i) What we are (heritage)

(ii) What we have (environment)

But there is also another factor which should not be lost sight of. It is the individual's response. Two persons perceive the same stimuli but they react to them in quite different ways. One's response is an outcome of one's potential (heritage) as acted upon by environment. Thus, one's personality is the resultant of three forces; what one is, what one has, and what one does.

OR

Explain the concept of learning and briefly describe its different theories.

Refer to Chapter-3, Q.No.-1

3. Attempt any *four* of the following questions in about 150 words each:

(i) Explain with examples emotional development of an individual.

Refer to Chapter-1, Q.No.-10

(ii) What is humanistic approach to learning? Describe its characteristics.

Refer to Chapter-3, Q.No.-9

(iii) What do you mean by domains of learning? Give suitable examples for different domains.

Refer to Dec-2005, Q.No.-3(ii)

(iv) Explain the concepts of intelligence, aptitude and creativity, with suitable examples.

Refer to Chapter-2, Q.No.-2&5

(v) Explain intrinsic and extrinsic motivation with suitable examples.

Refer to Dec-2007, Q.No.-3(iii)

(vi) Define the concepts of heredity and environment. How do heredity and environment influence the growth and development of an individual?

Refer to June-2006, Q.No.-3(iii)

(vii) Explain the nature and process of verbal learning.

Refer to Dec-2007, Q.No.-3(iv)

4. Answer the following in about 600 words.

How will you identify maladjusted students in your class? How will you as a teacher solve the psychological and social problems of such students? Explain.

Refer to June-2007, Q.No.-2

ES-332 : PSYCHOLOGY OF LEARNING AND DEVELOPMENT
December, 2005

Note : (i) All the **four** questions are compulsory.
(ii) All the questions carry equal weightage.

---

1. Answer the following question in about 600 words.
Explain the concept of development. Discuss the role of the teacher in facilitating human development.
Refer to Chapter-1, Q.No.-2

OR

Explain the concept of cognitive development with special reference to Piaget's framework for conceptualising child development. Discuss factors facilitating cognitive development.
Refer to Chapter-1, Q.No.-16

2. Answer the following question in about 600 words.
Discuss Bio-social and Psychoanalytical approaches to personality giving propositions of prominent propounders of these approaches.
Refer to Chapter-1, Q.No.-22

OR

List major tenets of the Humanistic approach to learning. Discuss the contributions of Maslow towards Humanistic Psychology.
Refer to Chapter-2, Q.No.-14

3. Attempt any *four* of the following questions in about 150 words each:
(i) Discuss personal factors influencing the process of learning.
Refer to Chapter-3, Q.No.-16

(ii) Explain any three levels of cognitive domain or area.
Refer to Chapter-3, Q.No.-11

(iii) Discuss in brief the nature and development of values in school system.
Refer to Chapter-2, Q.No.-11

(iv) Define the concept of 'Locus of Control' and explain its dimensions

giving examples.

Ans. Locus of control: The concept identifies the type of personal control used by an individual. When the locus of control is internal, individual views himself as personally in charge of his own destinies. When the locus of control is external, the person feels he is at the mercy of external circumstances.

Locus of control has two dimensions: External locus of control and internal locus of control. In external locus of control, the student perceives having little control over fate and fails to perceive a cause-and-effect relationship between actions and their consequences. Students with an internal locus of control are likely to attribute their success to ability and effort and their failure to lack of effort. Students with an external locus of control are likely to believe that their successes and failures are governed by task difficulty, chance, lack of ability, mood, bias or unusual help from others.

(v) Explain the nature and types of psychological conflicts.

Refer to Chapter-4, Q.No.-4

(vi) What is meant by 'Defence Mechanism'? Discuss any three defence mechanisms giving suitable examples.

Refer to Chapter-4, Q.No.-5

(vii) What do you understand by 'Social Maturity'? Explain briefly its relationship with social adjustment.

Refer to Chapter-3, Q.No.-4

4. Answer the following questions in about 600 words.

Suppose you have identified one backward and one gifted student in your class. Describe the method you used to identify each of them. Discuss the principles you would follow in guiding: A — the backward student and B — the gifted student. Summarise the contrasting characteristics of A and B.

Refer to June-2006, Q.No.-4

ES-332 : PSYCHOLOGY OF LEARNING AND DEVELOPMENT
June, 2006

Note : (i) All the **four** questions are compulsory.
(ii) All the questions carry equal weightage.

---

1. Answer the following question in about 600 words.
Differentiate between the concepts of growth and development. Discuss adolescence as the crucial stage of human development.
Refer to Chapter-1, Q.No.-1&5

OR

Explain the concept and nature of personality. Discuss the psychoanalytical and psychosocial approaches in understanding personality.
Refer to Chapter-1, Q.No.-21&22

2. Answer the following question in about 600 words.
Explain the psychometric approach to understand the concept of intelligence. Discuss appropriate instructional strategies for handling individual differences of the learners at various levels of intelligence.
Refer to Chapter-2, Q.No.-2

OR

Explain the concept of learning. Discuss various characteristics of learning with suitable examples.
Refer to Chapter-3, Q.No.-1

3. Attempt any *four* of the following questions in about 150 words each:
(i) Explain the principles of learning deduced from the learning theory of Thorndike.
Refer to Chapter-3, Q.No.-1

(ii) Explain nature of social adjustment and social maturity with examples.
Refer to Chapter-2, Q.No.-12

(iii) Discuss briefly the relationship between heredity and environment on growth and development of the individual.

Refer to Chapter-2, Q.No.-17

(iv) Define the concept of motivation and explain its role in learning.
Refer to Chapter2, Q.No.-14

(v) Discuss teachers' role in improving group relationship in a school.

Ans. Teachers' Role in Improving Group Relationship: In a classroom situation, generally two types of roles are identified: teacher's role and student's role. In group dynamics the teachers can provide a leadership role. The role of the leader is now shifting from authoritarian to a democratic and participatory one. Teachers must, therefore, encourage participation of students in all the school activities. To improve the climate of the classroom students should be taken into confidence and decisions taken democratically. Teachers' role is to facilitate the learning process. They are no more the instructor and the director of learning; they are facilitators of learning of their students. In teaching-learning process teachers should act as guides to promote learning. They should motivate students to participate in learning activities. Students' participation in learning activities individually or in groups enhances their learning.

(vi) Briefly discuss broad classification of students with special needs with reference to physical and mental aspects.

Ans. Students with Special Needs : We, as a teacher, might have come across a large number of students. Some of them we remember; others we forget over a period of time. These characteristics may be those of appearance, mannerism, performance or even of our special relationship triggered off by some important incident. We may like to refer to them by some grouping nouns.

Now we will see that students are characterized by some speciality. This 'special' characteristics calls for considerations from we so that these children may be able to learn without any strain. In other words, if we consider education to be a process of developing every individual to the best of his/her capability, we need to facilitate the process of capability building in each child, more so in those who need such consideration because of special characteristics. For example, a student with short height needs to be seated in the first row. The student with hearing problem needs to be nearer to the teacher. The differences in students are much more complex than what generally seem to be, on the surface. Special needs refer to reflecting the special requirements of a student

calling for specific adjustment in the regular education programme.
These adjustments may be in terms of the size of the letters, height of the furniture, lighting arrangement in the classroom or quality of communication. Special needs may arise out of a child's body/physique, mental level at which a child operates, attitudes or any disadvantage which may effect the student.

(vii) Discuss impact of various mass media on personality development of school children.
Refer to Chapter-1, Q.No.-25

4. Answer the following question in about 600 words.
One of your students has secured 95% in the Board's examination. How will you find out whether he is gifted or creative? In case you have identified him as a gifted student, what steps would you follow while guiding him in the school?
Ans. So far we have see that special characteristics of students that make them different from other students in the classrooms or in our experiences as teachers over a period of time. Sometimes the special needs of students arise not the so-called deficits either in their personality behaviour or performance but from their high mental level.
Gifted children are those who show consistently remarkable performance in educational endeavours. They possess superior intellectual ability within the range of the upper two to three percent of the population. According to some psychologists, academically gifted students are those who are within the top 15% to 20% in the schools.

Gifted students may have the following characteristics :
1. Knowing about things of which other students are unaware
2. High ability for abstract and symbolic thinking
3. Curiosity indicated by asking serious questions
4. Large vocabulary and mature expressive ability
5. Learning commensurates with that expected of older students, often reading at an earlier than average age
6. Requiring limited exposure and fewer repetitions to learn
7. Often thinking faster than they write (can result in sloppy work), or
8. Poor study habits that may result in careless work.
The following are the major areas where our intervention will prove useful for gifted students:

Removing the feeling of isolation : Since these students are different in physical, social and mental developments, they may feel left out. At times the feelings of superiority works against their personality adjustment.

Self-criticism : Many gifted students have high goals and become self-critical. They may also be communicated expectation on the part of teachers, parents as well as peers. Teachers may expect them to always give the correct answer or be outstanding in class. Their induces anxiety and stress in students.

Convergent vs divergent thinking : Mostly school work is evaluated on conformity to one right answer. Such evaluation rewards convergent thinking but can be harmful for divergent thinking, where different answers of a problem are possible.

Moral and social issues : At times we do not expect students to be concerned about moral and social issues. It is not unusual to find students with superior abilities to have very strong opinions on moral and social issues.

Self-concept : Self-concept refers to one's impression about oneself. Students who generate or express unusual ideas are sometimes criticized in the group. This may result in poor self-concept.

Emotional problems : Students with superior abilities are subject to same type of emotional problems. Their unusual abilities and other characteristics may lead to emotional problems.

ES-332 : PSYCHOLOGY OF LEARNING AND DEVELOPMENT
June, 2007

Note : (i) All the **four** questions are compulsory.
(ii) All the questions carry equal weightage.

1. Answer the following question in about 600 words.
Describe various stages of human development. Discuss the role of teacher in facilitating the development of the learners.
Refer to Chapter-1, Q.No.-3&8

OR

What is meant by 'individual differences'? Discuss the factors producing individual differences.
Refer to Chapter-2, Q.No.-1

2. Answer the following question in about 600 words.
Define the students with special educational needs. Describe the teacher's role in meeting the educational, social and psychological needs of such students.
Refer to Chapter-4, Q.No.-13

OR

Explain the concept of learning. Discuss personal factors that influence learning with suitable examples.
Refer to Chapter-3, Q.No.-16

3. Attempt any *four* of the following questions in about 150 words each:
(i) Explain Piaget's views on moral development.
Refer to Chapter-3, Q.No.-10

(ii) Discuss the role of teacher in the development of adolescent personality.
Refer to Chapter-1, Q.No.-7

(iii) Explain the meaning of interest and its development in studies at school.
Refer to Chapter-2, Q.No.-9

(iv) Discuss the implications of verbal learning for class-room practice.
Refer to Chapter-3, Q.No.-15

(v) Briefly discuss the environmental factors influencing learning.
Refer to Chapter-3, Q.No.-18

(vi) Mention the different types of conflicts and explain the measures for resolving them.

Ans. Conflict is a general type of thwarting in which the satisfaction of two or more motives is blocked. For example, a child has a need for mastery, prestige and recognition which can be satisfied if he can play hockey well. On the other hand, he has a need of protecting his body from being hurt in the game. The child is faced with two needs, the satisfaction of which is comparable. He desires to have mastery in the game and thus achieve recognition and prestige of his peers. At the same time, he wants that he should not be hurt. He is torn between the two. Conflicting situations are generally of three types:

(a) Approach-approach
(b) Avoidance-avoidance
(c) Approach-avoidance.

(a) Approach-approach Conflicts : When the child is placed in an environment with two equally strong positive valences, he is said to be in an approach-approach conflicting situation. For example, he may, on the one hand, like to read an interesting novel and on the other he may like to go out for playing football. It the desire to go out for playing football is stronger than the desire to read the interesting novel, he will resolve his mental conflict by postponing reading of the novel and vice versa. Such a conflict rarely disturbs behaviour because any one of the two alternative valences of equal strength becomes less strong and the individual proceeds in the direction of the more powerful one.

(b) Avoidance-avoidance Conflicts : The avoidance-avoidance situation arises when both the valences are negative. For example, the child may read the difficult mathematical sums but at the same time he wants to avoid the threat of being beaten by his teacher if he does not solve them. He avoids doing the difficult sums and simultaneously avoids his teacher's rebuke. In such a conflicting situation the only way out is to leave the field and take a third course by adopting a defence mechanism. He may develop headache and avoid both the difficult task and the teacher's punishment. He thus resolves the mental conflict, though temporarily. If he is unable to solve an avoidance-

avoidance situation at all, he remains constantly in an insecure condition and develops symptoms of anxiety, nervousness and neurosis.

(c) Approach-avoidance Conflicts : Lastly, when the child wants to play football, but fears being hurt, he is in an approach-avoidance conflicting situation. He wants to approach one and avoid the other. Other instances of such conflicting situations are loving one's mother and fearing her also, desiring to enjoy the forbidden candy and avoiding parents' rebuke, performing an irksome duty and getting approval of parents or teachers or associates. Such a conflicting situation becomes very serious when the child loves and fears the same person or when he is dependent upon and aggressive to the same body. When the child is unable to resolve such a mental conflict either he adopts inferior adjustment mechanism or he suffers from unreduced anxiety. So far, we have theoretically analysed the various forms of mental conflicts. Conflicts are caused by the interaction of the organism and the environment. The behaviour of an individual is the function of what goes on between the individual and the environment. Where there is harmony between the individual and the environment there is adjustment and the reverse happens when there is disharmony between the two.

(d) How to Recognise Mental Conflict in Children : If mental conflicts are not resolved they make enduring changes in personality. When a person is unable to resolve his mental conflicts for a longer period of time, and goes on adopting inferior non adjustive responses, behaviour disorder, mental ill-health, personality distortion may occur. The general ability to adjust becomes reduced and symptoms of maladjustment begin to appear. In brief, they are seen in nervous behaviour, emotional over-reactions and deviations, emotional immaturity, psychosomatic disturbances and antisocial behaviour. Nervousness, excessive anxiety, adjustive defence mechanisms are some of the simple symptoms of mental conflicts in children.

(vii) Differentiate between Guidance, Counselling and Psycotherapy.

Ans. Differentiate Between Guidance, Counselling and Psychotherapy: Guidance is a relatively broader term than counseling. Counseling is supposed to be one of the services under the broad scheme of the guidance programnme. Techniques of guidance and counseling fail to make an adjustment between the individual's self and environment. Psychotherapy is the treatment of a problem characterized by an extreme form of emotional nature where the intellectual powers of the individual fail to work. The techniques used in these three fields are different. In psychotherapy the treatment used is quite often physical, that is, it is either through the administration of drugs, electro-conclusive therapy or psychosurgery. On the other hand, in counseling, psychological techniques are adopted to help the client gain insight and confidence. A further distinction is made in terms of the nature of the problems. Reality-oriented educational and vocational problems have been considered as the province of guidance and counseling. Personality problems of the individual are the province of psychotherapy. In short a guidance practitioner works with a normal individual, counselor works with the normal but emotionally charged (normal anxiety) and psychotherapists with patients who have neurotic anxieties.

4. Answer the following question in about 600 words.
Discuss some effective methods of learning which you would like your students to practice in the class and home. Illustrate your answer with relevant examples.

Refer to Chapter-3, Q.No.-6

ES-332 : PSYCHOLOGY OF LEARNING AND DEVELOPMENT
December, 2007

Note : (i) All the **four** questions are compulsory.
(ii) All the questions carry equal weightage.

---

1. Answer the following question in about 600 words.
Explain the characteristics of socio-emotional development of secondary and senior secondary school students. Discuss teacher's role in facilitating their development.

Ans. Secondary and Senior Secondary School Students – An adolescent has the tendency to think about what is going on in one's own mind and to study oneself. He looks more closely at himself and defines himself differently. The adolescents realise that these are differences between what they think and feel and, how they behave. They are dissatisfied with themselves. They critically examine their personal characteristics and compare themselves to others. This process goes on.

Adolescents try to think whether other people see and think about the world in the same way as they themselves do. They learn that other people cannot know fully what they think and feel. Thus they consider themselves knowing better than others.

1. Identity : The adolescents have cognitive ability to relate the past to the present. They think about the future. This characteristic presents the young adolescents with the problem of understanding the continuity of experience across time and projecting that continuity into the future. To accomplish the adolescents depend on several activities, some of the important activities are as under:

(i) The adolescents pay great attention on how other people view them. This is the reason why they listen carefully to their peers, parents, teachers and other adults for any information that indicates how these people view them.

(ii) The adolescents search the past and often want to know about their ancestors, family tree, their own infancy and childhood experiences.

(iii) The adolescents act on their feelings and express their beliefs and opinions accordingly. They place a high value on being honest and behave in the ways that are true to oneself.

(iv) The adolescents try to find out what kind of persons they are. For this purpose they adopt different ways. They adopt the characteristic of other people to see if those characteristic fit in them. It is found that they take on and quickly cast off the traits of peers, teachers and other acquaintances.

Erikson has given the name identity diffusion to the experience of not having sense of one's identity. This is the unpleasant awareness of continual change in oneself and of the difference between one's self-concept and how others see one to escape this troubling situation.

2. Autonomy : Adolescents have an increase in demands for autonomy that is, for self-determination. As adolescents, awareness of their increasing similarity to adults grow. It becomes increasingly difficult for them to accept adult directions. It is well known to the adolescents that they will have to take responsibility for actions as adults and they need to practice that responsibility in more and more arenas.

It is often observed that those adults who work with adolescents happen to give more advice than is necessary. It should be kept in mind that the sensitivity to the need of adolescents to maintain their autonomy is a valuable characteristic for teachers to keep in mind while dealing with them. The adolescents should be given proper guidance sometimes even firmly, without stopping them for exercising their choice. By allowing choices a teacher, can help the adolescents to develop both responsibility and independence. A teacher can prepare them for adulthood by expecting them to gradually take on more responsibility and to face the consequences of their choices.

3. Conformity : At the time when adolescents seek autonomy from their parents and other adults, they often seek to conform to their group. To gain peers acceptance the adolescents copy one another's style of dress, language and behaviour. Sometimes adolescents are seen forming a group that excludes all those who do not wear similar clothes and use similar languages.

4. Interpersonal development : Peers are the focus of adolescence. Various activities link friendship popularity, conflict with peers, dating and sexual relationships all take a tremendous amount of the adolescents time and energy. Adolescents who have similar interests and values form groups. The friendship made in adolescence may endure through life.

5. Intimacy : In early adolescence, two new needs arise as under:

(i) The need for intimacy, for a relationship with a person to share their feelings and thoughts.

(ii) The need for sexual gratification. Intimacy is first felt and needed by adolescents. There should be someone with whom they can share their feelings and emotions. They try to have intimacy first with peers, usually drown from the same sex, classmates, etc.

To communicate intimacy needs learning to talk about one's feeling and thoughts in an appealing way. Such communication needs trust in the partner's goodwill and tolerance. Learning to develop intimate communication with peers of the other sex is one of their major interpersonal attributes. They find that intimacy with the same sex is easier to achieve because they go through similar changes and are more familiar. This is the reason why the other sex is less familiar for most adolescents. The adolescents who manage to develop relationship with the other sex successfully are those ones who can separate their needs for intimacy and for sexual gratification. They give priority to developing friendship with peers of both sexes. They have great control over themselves and do not confuse sexual intimacies with intimacy that does not include sex.

Now Refer Chapter-1, Q.No.-13

OR

Explain the concept of personality. Discuss the main hereditary and environmental factors which influence the personality development.

Refer to Chapter-1, Q.No.-21&23

2. Answer the following question in about 600 words.

Explain the concept of learning. Discuss main characteristics of Piaget's cognitive approach to learning.

Ans. According to Burner, cognitive development occurs in three phases- enactive (doing), ikonic (object models or pictures) and symbolic (signs and symbols).

Piaget's Concept of Cognitive Development : Jean Piaget offers a rich framework for conceptualizing the development of the child's thinking and cognition during the span of his growing/development to an adult. To him, cognitive development means how knowledge is acquired and developed through successive stages and at various age levels. Hence his theory of cognition is sometimes called **genetic epistemology**. It focuses attention on the interaction between his biological inheritance and his environment for cognitive development.

(a) Underlying Mental Process : In order to progress further into Piaget's cognitive development processes, we could cognisize or understand the fact that all cognition takes place due to two processes:

(i) Assimilation which means taking in or absorbing stimuli/information from the environment, and

(ii) Accommodation which means making room for or adjusting to incoming stimuli/information.

These twin processes together facilitate adaptation. Adaptation is an ongoing process which helps the individual internalize or store in all that one comprehends. This then, forms schemes or mental representations or maps of the world.

All learning is adaptive as an infant learns to cry when hungry or an adult learns to speak a native language in a foreign land. All these have adaptive value.

(b) Stages of Cognitive Development and Accomplishments : Early in life (0 – 2 years) the child learns by touching and sensing. We must have observed little babies holding the objects of their attention and putting it in their mouth. This is a stage called sensori-motor stage. As the child grows he develops some amount of reasoning. He tends to imitate in order to learn, though he himself is the centre of all attention. This is the pre-operational stage.

At the concrete operational stage the child learns enough to make transformations in what he observes. His imagination power moves to propel him to the formal operational stage. At this stage he can apply logic to hypothesize to build relationships and to infer from the relationship.

(c) Methodology of Studying Cognitive Development : Piaget's method of studying cognition is a one-to-one verbal interactive, inquiry-oriented method, popularly known as the **clinical method**. Certain mental-operation tasks, in accordance with age and stage of development with supporting material, are prepared. For example, a typical Piaget task on probabilistic reasoning for a 14-year-old student is given below:

(i) Purpose of the task : To assess the child's comprehension of probability.

(ii) Materials : 96 one-inch wooden blocks of 4 different colours (36 red, 36 blue, 20 yellow and 4 green), a paper bag, a box.

(iii) Procedure : Separate blocks into four colour groups, divide each colour group into half. Give one half to the child and instruct him to put them in the paper bag or box. Keep the other half in front of the child as a reference test.

(iv) Factors Facilitating Cognitive Development : Factors facilitating cognition are internal readiness, environmental experiences, social experience and equilibration.

For Piaget and other cognitivists such as Wadsworth, Flavell, Sullivan etc., the important thing is interactions and equilibration. The key to cognitive development as it relates to educational practice is the activity of the students, their actions on objects, events and other people. While interaction refers to internal organismic readiness, environmental experience is obtained through physical experiences or repetition reinforcement, manipulation of things in the environment and logic-mathematical experiences. Social interaction relates to cognition through interactive modes with people where one learns about relationships, concepts, namely cooperation, competition, cultural mores and practices, etc. Language is the medium of social experiences (verbal and non-verbal). Equilibration refers to a self-regulatory process and assimilation and adaptation where a balance is struck and a new cognition takes place or a new schema comes into being.

OR

Explain the concept of adjustment. Discuss characteristics of a well-adjusted and a maladjusted person giving suitable examples.

Ans. Social adjustment can be defined as a psychological process. It frequently involves coping with new standards and values. In the technical language of psychology, getting along with the members of the society as best as one can is called adjustment. Adjustment maintains peace and harmony in home, school, society and in the country.

Psychologists use the term adjustment of varying conditions of social and interpersonal relations in the society. Thus we see that adjustment means reaction to the demands and pressures of the social environment imposed upon the individual. Whenever two types of demands come into conflict with each other and resultant in an adjustment being made, a complicated process for the individual, then some special problems of adjustment arise.

For instance, we see that role of a teacher is important in the process of social adjustment because teacher have to train his students to face personal, social and economic problems in their life. Students' adjustment with society or in school largely depends on their interaction with the external environment in which they live. A class as a group gives students opportunities to interact with each other. Students in social situations mostly interact in groups in classroom and on the playground. To deal effectively with social groups one must study the dynamics of group behaviour.

Now Refer Chapter-4, Q.No.-2

3. Attempt any four of the following questions. Answer each questions in about 150 words:

(i) "Adolescence is a period of stress and strain" Explain.
Refer to Chapter-1, Q.No.-5

(ii) Explain the characteristics of language development in children.
Ans. Characteristics of language development: The following are the characteristics of language development:

- **Semanticity:** The quality of language in which words are used as symbols for objects, events or ideas.
- **Syntax:** The rules in a language for placing words in proper order to form meaningful sentences.
- **Productivity:** The capacity to combine words into original sentences.
- **Displacement:** The quality of language that makes one communicate information about objects and events in another time and place. Language makes possible the efficient transmission of large amounts of complex knowledge from one person to another, and from one generation to another. Displacement permits parents to warn children of their own mistakes. Displacement allows children to tell their parents what they did in school.

(iii) Explain the nature and types of motivation.
Refer to Chapter-2, Q.No.-14

(iv) Briefly discuss the misconnects regarding heredity and environment.
Ans. Interaction of Heredity and Environment : A large number of individual differences are caused by the interactive process of heredity and environment. To each child heredity provides a potential and the dynamic forces of environment act upon that a potential in a different way. Let us illustrate how the interactive forces of heredity and environment produce differences in individuals. We may have for the sake of illustration one trait (intelligence) and at one end of the diagram we place the rod measuring the rate of mental maturity (I.Q.).

There are three children of the same percentage X and Y each. The hereditary potential for these children A, B, C or for P, Q, R is the same being represented by the equality of height of the cones. But as environmental factors influence members' sets differently, the hereditary potential is realised in different amounts or degrees. With least stimulating environments only a part of the potential is realised (A, P) and with very stimulating environments we have full realisation of the potential (C, R). The differences between the six children are due to interaction of hereditary potential and the environment.

Misconception regarding heredity and environment.

We have many misconceptions regarding heredity and environment due to lake of proper knowledge. People uses two terms in born and heredity interchangeably. It is usually believed that whatever is in inborn in heredity. Some think that taking birth is the end of the heredity. We should not consider birth as the end or beginning of one type of influence as it is only a stage of development. We should understand that heredity does not necessarily results in resemblance of offsprings to their parents. Heredity does not refer to any transmission as these skills or behaviours are consciously learned by the parents and do not fall within the purview of heredity. We have many other misconceptions too. It is believed that if a heredity origin is identified under a given condition, nothing or very little can be done to improve it. Really this is not true. Many heredity diseases are curable. Some people think that all heredity characteristics cannot be changed but it is not totally true. There are very few heredity characteristics that be changed by any known environmental factors.

(v) Explain the main factors that influence classroom learning.

Refer to Chapter-3, Q.No.-5

(vi) Explain the characteristics of the gifted and talented students.

Refer to Chapter-3

(vii) Differentiate between guidance and counseling with suitable examples.

Ans. Guidance : According to Crow and Crow, "Guidance is not giving direction, it is not the imposition of one person's point of view upon another person. It is not making decisions for an individual which he should make for himself. It is not carrying the burden of another's life". Crow and Crow observe that guidance is an assistance made available by a qualified and adequately trained person to another person to help him manage his own activities, develop his own point of view and make his own decisions. Guidance cannot be given by everyone and anyone; the person should be a qualified practitioner. Whenever a person is aided directly or indirectly by a qualified person in knowledge, emotional fitness, mental acuity, social and civic adjustments, guidance increases individual's ability to think and act independently or follow his own initiatives.

There are many expressions used to mean guidance. These expressions are to lead, to steer or to direct. But in all these terms we find compulsion, indoctrination and direction. In general, to guide implies help that is more of personal nature than either to steer, to direct, to regulate or to conduct. The focus of guidance is on the individual and not on the problem. Its purpose is to promote the growth of an individual for self-direction. This help may be given to a person as an individual or in a group.

Counselling: The Concept : Counselling has been defined in different ways by different people. It implies a personal relationship between two individuals in which one gives certain kind of help to the other. Counseling is, thus, the activity where all the facts are gathered together and the experiences of the students are focused upon the particular problem to be solved by him, where he is given direct and personal help in solving his problems. Counseling is aimed at the progressive development of the individual to solve problems. Carl Rogers is of the view that counseling is definitely a structured, permissive and dynamic relationship which allows the student to gain an understanding of himself to a certain degree which enables him to take positive step in the light of his new orientation. The help must be given in such a way so that it encourages the growth in the individual for self direction.

4. Answer the following question in about 600 words.

Explain the concept of group dynamics. Describe five activities which you would like to undertake in the class for improving the group relationship among your students.

Ans. Concept of group dynamics : A teacher deals with groups of students for five to six hours everyday. In order to make our teaching effective, we should study group dynamics. A class is a group of students with different socio-economic background. We, as a teacher, should have a thorough knowledge of the interaction process among the students. If we are well-equipped with the basic knowledge of group dynamics, we can provide appropriate guidance to students for their adjustment. By doing so we can also improve the emotional and social climate of the class.

The teacher must know how adolescents form groups and what is the structure of groups and other mechanisms operating in the group situation. Students seek love and motivation from their groups. Smooth functioning of the group is important for effective learning. If there are conflicts and stresses in the group, learning will be disturbed. A teacher's knowledge of group dynamics can improve the social and emotional climate of the school/class. She/he can improve group relations to maintain proper mental health of the individual members and group relationship in the class.

Group Relationship in the Class : Analysis of sociometric studies shows the following patterns of relationship among the students of the class:

1. Stars : Stars are the students in the class whom majority of the students like.

2. Isolates : The students whom no member of the class likes or wants to associate. They are rejected by all.

3. Mutual pairs : There are the students who like each other. There is reciprocal relationship among mutual pairs of students.

4. Chains : There are chains of relationship among students where A chooses B and B chooses C. There is a closed circle where A likes B, B likes C and C likes A.

Teachers' Role in Improving Group Relationship : In a classroom situation, generally two types of roles are identified: teacher's role and student's role. In group dynamics the teachers can provide a leadership role. The role of the leader is now shifting from authoritarian to a democratic and participatory one. Teachers must, therefore, encourage participation of students in all the school activities. To improve the climate of the classroom students should be taken into confidence and decisions taken democratically.

Teacher's role is to facilitate the learning process. They are no more the instructor and the director of learning; they are facilitators of learning of their students. In teaching-learning process teachers should act as guides to promote learning. They should motivate students to participate in learning activities. Students' participation in learning activities individually or in groups enhances their learning.

ES – 332: PSYCHOLOGY OF LEARNING AND DEVELOPMENT
June, 2008

Note : *(i) All the* ***four*** *questions are compulsory.*
(ii) ***All*** *the questions carry equal weightage.*

Q1. Answer the following question in about 600 words.
Differentiate between growth and development with the help of suitable examples. Why should a teacher study the principles governing growth and development?

OR

Explain the concept of individual differences. Discuss the individual differences in intelligence and creativity with suitable examples.

Q2. Answer the following question in about 600 words.
Explain the concept and type of motivation. How does motivation contribute to enhance children's academic achievement?

OR

Discuss the influence of personal and environmental factors on classroom learning. Give examples.

Q3. Answer any four of the following questions in about 150 words each:
(i) "Adolescence is a period of storm and stress." Elaborate.
(ii) What should a school do to ensure healthy social development of children?
(iii) How do children attain new concepts?
(iv) How does cognitive domain of learning differ from affective domain?
(v) How will you facilitate students' adjustment in schools? Discuss.
(vi) Explain the meaning and nature of guidance. How is it related to counseling?
(vii) Explain the suitable in which you can use the method of spaced and unspaced learning.

Q4. Answer the following question in about 600 words.
Prepare a plan for the identification of emotionally maladjusted children in your class. Discuss the strategies you shall devise to help such children.

ES – 332: PSYCHOLOGY OF LEARNING AND DEVELOPMENT
December, 2008

Note : *(i) All the* ***four*** *questions are compulsory.*
(ii) ***All*** *the questions carry equal weightage.*

Q1. Answer the following question in about 600 words.
"Different aspects of development of children are inter-related and inter-dependent." Discuss the statement with the help of suitable examples.

OR

Explain the importance of affective domain of personality. Discuss the role of school for the inculcation of moral and social values in children.

Q2. Answer the following question in about 600 words.
Differentiate between learning and maturation. Describe conditions which affect learning.

OR

Explain the meaning and nature of 'conflicts'. What measures can teachers adopt to resolve different types of conflicts in students?

Q3. Answer any *four* of the following questions in about 150 words each:
(i) How is divergent thinking different from convergent thinking? Explain.
(ii) "No two individuals are alike." Illustrate.
(iii) Describe the nature of transfer of learning.
(iv) Describe Kohlberg's stages of moral growth.
(v) Explain special needs of socially disadvantaged children.
(vi) How does law of association influence learning? Explain.
(vii) Define learning outcomes. How are learning outcomes related to objectives of learning?

Q4. Answer the following question in about 600 words.
You might have observed your students using various defence mechanisms in the class. Discuss specific situations in which your students have used defence mechanisms. Illustrate your answer with suitable illustrations.

ES-332 : PSYCHOLOGY OF LEARNING AND DEVELOPMENT
June, 2009

Note : (i) All the ***four*** *questions are* ***compulsory.***
(ii) All the questions carry ***equal*** *weightage.*

Q1. Answer the following question about 600 words'
Discuss the concept of creativity and its components. How can a teacher develop students' creativity through the teaching of school subjects? Explain with the help of suitable examples from any subject of secondary school curriculum.

OR

Explain briefly the broad components of affective domain of personality. How do individuals differ from each other with regards to the development of affective aspect of their Personality? Discuss with reference to any one aspect of affective domain.

Q2. Answer the following question in about 600 wards.
Explain the concept of learning. Discuss principles of learning and their implications for classroom practices.

OR

Define maladjustment. Explain the school related factors which cause maladjustment among children.

Q3. Answer any four questions of the following in about 150 words each
(a) How does Television affect development of child's personality? Explain.
(b) Explain Piaget's concept of assimilation and accommodation in cognitive development.
(c) Early childhood period is a time of rapid growth and development in all areas. Elaborate.
(d) Explain the main characteristics of gifted children.
(e) Discuss briefly the components of aptitude.
(f) What is academic achievement? Is it possible for all students to have the same level of achievement? Discuss briefly.
(g) Explain briefly Maslow's theory of motivation.
(h) Differentiate between directive and nondirective counselling.

Q4. Answer the following question in about 600 words.
You are a teacher in a secondary school. Prepare a plan for organising school guidance service in your school.

ES-332 : PSYCHOLOGY OF LEARNING AND DEVELOPMENT
December, 2009

Note : (i) All the ***four*** *questions are* ***compulsory.***
(ii) All the questions carry ***equal*** *weightage.*

Q1. Answer the following question in about *600* words :
Differentiate between intrinsic and extrinsic motivation. What should a teacher do in a class to ensure students' motivation for learning ? Discuss.

OR

Discuss the socio-emotional development in adolescents.

Q2. Answer the following question in about *600* words :
Explain the concept and nature of social maturity. Discuss the factors responsible for social adjustment in schools.

OR

Explain the concept of socially disadvantaged children and their education. Illustrate your answer with suitable examples.

Q3. Answer *any four* of the following questions in about 150 words each
(a) Explain briefly, the adaptive mechanism to resolve conflicts.
(b) How do children's interests influence their learning? Explain
(c) Explain the concept of transfer of learning and its implications for schools.
(d) Explain the concept of individual differences. Illustrate with the help of suitable examples from the cognitive domain of personality.
(e) Explain reasons to study the principles of human growth and development by teachers.
(f) Differentiate between emotional characteristics of primary and upper primary school children.
(g) Explain briefly the problems which children generally face in their language development.
(h) Explain the process of concept attainment in learners.

Q4. Answer the following question in about *600* words :
You are a teacher of Class IX and X. Prepare an action plan for the nurturance of students' creative potential through teaching of the subject of your specialisation.

ES-332 : PSYCHOLOGY OF LEARNING AND DEVELOPMENT
June, 2010

*Note: (i) All the **four** questions are compulsory.*
*(ii) All the questions carry **equal** weightage.*

Q1. Answer the following question:

Explain the concept of human development. Discuss various stages of development with special emphasis on adolescence.

Refer to Chapter-1, Q.No.-2 & Q.No.-7

OR

Explain the specific nature, characteristics and problems of language development. Discuss its implications for classroom teachers.

Refer to Chapter-1, Q.No.-20

Q2. Answer the following question:

Explain the concept of intelligence. Discuss the instructional strategies in handling individual differences in intelligence.

Refer to Chapter-2, Q.No.-2 & Page No. 61[Strategies for handling]

OR

Discuss the cognitive approach to learning and its educational implications.

Ans. Concept of Cognitive Approach to Learning

The word 'cognition' is derived from the Latin word cognoscrere which means to know, or to perceive. Cognitive theories discuss how people gain an understanding of themselves and their environment and how, in using this, they act in relation to their environment. According to cognitive theorists, teaching is a process of developing understanding or insight in the learner. Learning is the organization of percepts and purposes by the learner. Classroom experiences are related to the individual goals of students. These experiences are encouraged to discover relationship to create the consequences of their efforts. Cognitive approach emphasizes and given importance to cognition (perception) in learning. According to this approach, learning is a complex process and it is viewed as acquiring changes in the cognitive structure. In other words, learning is the change in the cognitive structure. These changes (learning) take place generally in basically three ways. They are:

· Differentiation
· Generalization, and
· Restructurisation

In differentiation learning begins by differentiating specific aspects of oneself and of one's environment. For example, an infant perceives every woman as his mother. Later on the differentiates between mother, aunt, sister, etc. Thus the cognitive structure becomes more specific.

In generalization concrete and particular instances are given and the children reach general conclusions or generalizations. After differentiating the concepts, the child gradually categorizes the differentiated concepts on the basis of specific unifying characteristics known as generalization. For example, the child first learns to differentiate between various things as men, women, animals, birds, etc. and later on he unify these differentiated concepts to form a single concept – living things, and thus generalization is reached.

Restructurisation, as the processes of differentiation and generalization take place, the individual restructures his cognitive structure to accommodate these differentiated and generalized concepts to gain control of himself and the world. The child learns that all living things do not behave as human beings do. Thus, the concept of living things is restructured.

Characteristics of Cognitive Approach

The main characteristics of the cognitive approach are as follows:

• Earlier cognitivists gave more emphasis on insight while the modern cognitivists place more importance on the human mental process, similar to a computer system *n* operation.

• In the cognitive approach, learning is considered as an active and dynamic process.

• In the approach the perceptions of the learner are processed through differentiation. Generalization and restructurisation which helps the learner in reacting to the specific cognitive structure to get a clear picture of the environment.

• The cognitive approach is represented by a dynamic system.

• The learner is purposive, and interacting within the field of his/her goals.

• It is the most suited for concept formation, problem solving and other higher mental processes.

Educational Implications

The following important direct/indirect educational implications of Piaget' approach to cognitive development are given below:

• Piaget's description of cognition (as a result of interaction of the individual with environment, accompanied by the process of assimilation and accommodation) indicates that cognitive development is a continuous process from birth to adulthood. This theory believes in gradual progression from one stage to another. Therefore, the teacher should try to determine the levels/stages of development of learners and accordingly he should plan his instruction/teaching.

• The relationship between the educational system and the child will be a unilateral and reciprocal one.

• Childhood is accepted as a necessary and important phase in the development of logical thinking.

• Science and mathematics are taught with actions and operations. Such instructions should begin in nursery school with concrete exercises.

• Experimental procedures and free activity through training should be introduced for both liberal arts science students.

• Active methods that require the students to rediscover or reconstruct the truths to be learned should be used. The teacher also provides counter examples to the students that lead to reflection of their often hasty solutions.

• Audio-visual aids can serve only as accessories in the student's personal investigations of truth.

• Give-and-take can be developed in the group.

• Spontaneous activity with small group of students brought together by means of their mutual interest in a particular activity should be the major feature of classroom learning. The classroom should be a centre of real activities carried out in common so that logical intelligence may be elaborated through action and social change.

• Students must be permitted to make their own mistakes and to correct these errors themselves. Therefore, classroom instruction must be planned to facilitate the processes of construction, assimilation and accommodation through which physical/ empirical abstraction and reflective abstraction can occur.

• The process of experimentation by students at all ages is important. Only through experimentation the learner can acquire the skills that are necessary for formal operational thought. More importantly, experimentation often gives birth to new ideas. For young children, their first new ideas may not seem so original to adults. But such a practice in which children are encouraged to develop new idea s can lead to original discoveries. The more we can help children to have their own wonderful ideas and feel good about themselves for having them, the more likely it is that they will someday happen upon wonderful ideas that no one else happened upon before.

• The cognitive activity that is generated by experimentation is essential. A child can be mentally active without physical manipulation, just as he can be mentally passive while actually manipulating objects.

• Many activities in pre-school curricula can provide opportunities for cognitive development. Block painting, finger painting, musical games, cooking, dramatic plays, etc. engage the children in empirical and logico-mathematical abstraction.

• The classroom should provide situations to children in constructing their own knowledge so that the children can comprehend the world in new ways at different cognitive levels.

• Classroom activities should maximize the child's opportunities to construct and coordinate many relationships that he or she is capable of exercising.

• At the pre-school level the child is more interested in the observable effects of his or her actions than in relating the result to an organized cognitive structure.

• The implications for educational practice are important. First, a variety of activities, games and experiences should be provided so that the learner can exercise his or her developing subsystems. One suggestion is to use individualized mathematics laboratories that utilize a variety of materials for measurement and experimentation. Examples include blocks, dried peas, matchboxes, drinking straws, pipe cleaners and so on.

• Games and activities that can provide experience with classification and seriation are also needed. Classification games can be developed using blocks or pieces of plastic or felt that vary in two properties. Such as colour and shape. Circles, squares and triangles in red, blue, yellow and green for example, may be used in a variety of ways. Card games in which shapes and/or colours are to be matched is one example.

• Drill and practice should be given in the classroom to make teaching-learning effective.

Q3. Answer any four of the following questions:

(a) Adolescence is a period of stress and strain. Elaborate.

Refer to Chapter-1, Q.No.-5

(b) Differentiate between Intrinsic and Extrinsic motivation with suitable examples.

Refer to Page No. 81, Q.No.-14

(c) Explain the impact of mass media on personality of school children.

Refer to Page No. 50, Q.No.-25

(d) Describe briefly the factors which influence learning.

Refer to Page No. 125, Q.No.-16

(e) Explain meaning of guidance and counseling. How is counseling related to guidance?

Refer to Page No. 192(vii)

(f) How can a teacher facilitate students' adjustment in school?

Refer to Page No. 146, Q.No.-11

Q4. Answer the following question:

As a teacher you face certain problems related to student's adjustment in the classroom and school. Describe strategies you would adopt to improve the overall group relationships among students of your school.

Ans. We, as a teacher, are more concerned with the adjustment of students in school because the primary purpose of education is to train students to be successful in their social life. They are trained to face social and economic problems. The process of adjustment starts right from the birth of the child and continues till death. Human beings have the highest capacity to adapt to new situations. They not only adapt to physical demands but also adjust to social pressures.

Teachers have important role in modifying and shaping the personality of students in accordance with natural objectives of life. The greatest contribution of teachers will be to channelize the energy of students to reconstruction in their social life. One of the challenges hurled at teachers is to maintain the mental and physical health of the children and youth of the nation. The teacher has to emphasize on the harmonious development of students' personality so that they can contribute to the welfare of the country. You can facilitate their adjustment in their life. You can also help them in maintaining their mental health because proper mental health leads to social adjustment. There are some school-related factors which influence students' adjustment in school. Important factors are as follows:

(i) Proper training to teachers: Teachers who are properly trained in educational psychology may help students in their adjustment. Teachers' personality and democratic attitude are also important factors which can promote adjustment in students.

(ii) Adequate curriculum: Curriculum should be planned and transacted in such a way that it should fulfil psychological and social needs of students. Need fulfilment leads to better adjustment.

(iii) Adequate recreational facilities: Facilities, such as sports, library, debate and excursion may help students in their adjustment. We should provide proper recreational facilities to them in the school.

(iv) Classroom climate: If the classroom climate is affectionate and cooperative enough, it can facilitate better adjustment in students.

(v) Proper relationships between administration: Cordial relations between the Principal and teachers, and teachers and teachers, and teachers and office staff also play an important role in creating harmonious and congenial environment in the school.

(vi) Evaluation system of the school: Evaluation should be rigid cum flexible. Too much subjectivity and unreliability should be avoided. Numerical marking should he avoided and grades should be given to students. Due to low marks, students lose confidence in their life which then affects in their mental health. The world 'fail' should not be used by the teachers.

An adjustment mechanism is a habitual method of overcoming blocks, reaching goals, satisfying motives, relieving frustration and maintaining equilibrium. Every individual uses his own mechanism to maintain a balance in his own personality.

- The school environment should be free from partiality and should provide the feeling of security in students, irrespective of their socio-economic status.
- School environment should be democratic. Students' representation on various committees should be made.
- School should organize various curricular activities for students.
- Teachers should know the fundamental principles of human behaviour to solve students' problems. They must be emotionally stable and have positive attitude towards teaching. They should create conducive school climate.
- Students should be encouraged to express their views and feelings on various issues related to school freely.
- Teachers should develop a variety of interests in students so that they can satisfy their emotions.
- Day-to-day problems can be discussed in class.
- Sex and moral education should be an integral part of the school curriculum.
- School can organize guidance services for students.
- There should be flexibility in school activities to accommodate the individual needs of the students.

ES-332 : PSYCHOLOGY OF LEARNING AND DEVELOPMENT
December, 2010

Note: *(i) All the* ***four*** *questions are* ***compulsory.***
(ii) ***All*** *the questions carry* ***equal weightage.***

Q1. Answer the following question in about 600 words:
Explain the concept of development and its principles. Discuss the role of teacher in facilitating development of students.

OR

Explain the meaning of moral development. Discuss Kohlberg's stages of moral development giving suitable examples.

Q2. Answer the following question in about 600 words:
Distinguish between heredity and environment; discuss them as factors influencing personality development with examples.

OR

Discuss Maslow's theory of motivation. How is it important for learning? Explain common devices that can be used for increasing extrinsic motivation in students.

Q3. Answer any four of the following questions in about 150 words each:
(i).Explain the concept of creativity and individual differences with regard to creativity.
(ii). Explain the meaning and types of locus of control with suitable examples.
(iii). Discuss briefly the nature and characteristics of language development.
(iv). Explain any three domains of learning as per Bloom's Taxonomy.
(v). What do you understand by social adjustment? Explain the process of social influence.
(vi). Briefly describe the problems faced in the education of girls at the school stage.

Q4. Answer the following question in about 600 words:
Students face problems related to their studies, choice of vocations and/ or personal adjustment. What activities will you carry out as a teacher in a secondary school to help your students solve their problems? Prepare a plan of guidance activities and discuss the procedure of organising these activities.

ES-332 : PSYCHOLOGY OF LEARNING AND DEVELOPMENT
June, 2011

Note: *(i) All questions are* ***compulsory.***
(ii) All questions carry ***equal*** *weightage.*

Q1. Answer the following question:

Explain the principles of development. Describe the role of teacher in facilitating student development.

Refer to Chapter-1, Q.No.-2 & Page No.-26, Q.No.-13

OR

Explain the concept of cognitive development. Discuss Piaget's stage of cognitive development.

Refer to Page No.-30, Q.No.-16

Q2. Answer the following question:

Explain the concept of 'individual differences'. Describe the role of school in value formation among students.

Ans. Refer to Chapter-2, Q.No.-1 & Page No.- 78 [Value and the school]

OR

Explain the nature and meaning of motivation. Discuss Maslow's hierarchy of basic needs, giving suitable examples.

Refer to Page No.-81, Q.No.-14 & Page No.-83 [Maslow's Theory]

Q3. Answer any four of the following questions:

(a) Explain the concept of gender issues.

Refer to Page No.-87, Q.No.-16

(b) Describe briefly the factors influencing personality development.

Refer to June-2005, Q.No.-2

(c) Explain the concept of behaviouristic approach to learning.

Refer to Page No.-111, Q.No.-8

(d) Describe media influence on learning.

Refer to Page No.-130 [Media Influence of learning]

(e) Explain the concept of emotional maturity.

Refer to Page No. 9 [Emotional Development]

(f) Discuss psychological cases of Maladjustment.

Refer to Page No. 136 [Psychological causes]

Q4. Answer the following question:

As a teacher, in a secondary school, having inclusive setting, you teach children with special needs who come from deprived section of our society. Describe the specific points you would keep in mind to understand the special educational needs of those children, specially the girls.

Refer to Page No. 155, Q.No.-15 & Page No. 157, Q.No.-16

ES-332 : PSYCHOLOGY OF LEARNING AND DEVELOPMENT
December, 2011

Note: (i) All four questions are ***compulsory.***
(ii) All questions carry ***equal*** *weightage.*

Q1. Answer the following question in about 600 words:
Explain the stages of human development. Discuss the major changes during adolescence stage.

OR

Explain the nature and meaning of language development. Discuss the role of an effective teacher in acquisition of language competency by students.

Q2. Answer the following question in about 600 words:
Explain the concept of personality development. Discuss main factors which influence personality development of children.

OR

Explain the meaning and nature of academic achievement. Describe instructional strategies to cope with differences in academic achievement.

Q3. Answer any four of the following questions in about 150 words each:
(a) Explain Kohlberg's concept of moral growth.
(b) Explain the concept of divergent thinking and creativity.
(c) Explain the concept of cognitive approach to learning.
(d) Explain the meaning and nature of group dynamics.
(e) How will you identify children with learning disability?
(f) Differentiate between guidance and counseling.

Q4. Answer the following question in about 600 words:
As a teacher in a secondary school you have students in your class who face adjustment problems. Give concrete examples to illustrate your role in helping children with adjustment problems.

ES-332 : PSYCHOLOGY OF LEARNING AND DEVELOPMENT
June, 2012

*Note: (i) All four questions are **compulsory.***
*(ii) All questions carry **equal** weightage.*

Q1. Answer the following question in about 600 words:
Examine Kohlberg's theory of moral development. How can teachers facilitate children's moral growth?
Refer to Chapter-1, Q.No.-12 & Q.No.-13

OR

Explain the concept of individual differences. In what ways individuals differ from one another. Illustrate your answer with suitable examples.
Refer to Chapter-2, Q.No.-1, Q.No.-5 & Q.No.-6

Q2. Answer the following question in about 600 words:
Explain any three laws of learning. How will you make use of these laws of learning in the teaching of your subject at secondary level? Illustrate your answer with suitable examples.
Refer to Chapter-3, Q.No.-2

OR

How do children's needs and interests affect their learning? Illustrate your answer with suitable examples.

Ans. You, as a teacher, might have come across a large number of student. Some of them we remember; others we forget over a period of time. If you try to remember students of, say last one or two years, there is a great chance that you would remember only those children who have some special characteristics. These characteristics may be those of appearance, mannerism, performance or even of your special relationship triggered off by some important incident. You may like to refer to them by some grouping nouns. Try to recollect some such characteristics and use one word/phrase to explain some of these groupings.

Now you will see that students are characterised by some speciality. This 'special' characteristics calls for considerations from you so that these children may be able to learn without any strain. In other words, if you consider education to be a process of developing every individual to the best of his/her capability, you need to facilitate the process of capability building in each child, more so in those who need such consideration because of special characteristics. For example, a student with short height needs to be seated in the first row. The student with hearing problem needs to be nearer to the teacher. The differences in students are much more complex than what generally seem to seem to be, on the surface. Special needs refer to reflecting the special requirements of student calling for specific adjustment in the regular education programmes.

Q3. Answer any four of the following question in about 150 words each:

(a) Explain the relationship between language and culture.

Refer to Page No.-40 [Language and Culture]

(b) What is achievement motivation? Explain the difference between children with high and low achievement motivation.

Ans. Refer to Chapter-2, Q.No.-14 and Page.No.-46 [Achievement Motivation]

Difference between children with high and low achievement motivation

High	Low
Learns to be learned.	Works appear to have learned.
Put purposes in middle difficulties.	Put purposes too easy or too difficult.
Qualification feelings have been developed.	Qualification feeling have not been developed.
Makes installation to the effort.	Makes installation to the external factors.
It tries to overcome the difficulties encountered.	Barely be in defeat when faced difficulty.

(c) Discuss the role of mass media in the development of values among students.

Ans. Media has been considered an important component of transmitting information. Media can be divided into broad categories–print and non-print media. Print media refers to texts or printed materials. It is economical and has traditionally been used for pedagogical purposes.

But, it may not be the only or the perfect medium to impart education. Non-print media, also known as modern electronic media, have certain unique qualities, which, in certain cases, facilitate learning much more faster that the print medium. These help to meet diverse learning objectives more efficiently than the printed matter.

Certain non-print media formats and delivery systems contribute well to student's learning activities. For example, audio tapes or computers can be used effectively to drill and practice in language and learning arithmetic. Electronic media can help promote the discovery approach to learning. For example, a film can be exploited for discovery teaching in the physical sciences.

Students keep watching the various sections of the film until they perceive the relationships between the visuals. Then they are curious to find out the principles that explain those relationships. Likewise, in the social sciences various media can be used to present students with visual and auditory experiences that provide related inquiry. Films and stimulation are often used to present real-life or laboratory learning situation to students.

The role of the electronic media has proved effective for teaching students. These excite the student psychologically and prepare/motivate them to participate in teaching-learning activities. Non-print media perform following functions:

- direct attention,
- arouse motivation,
- increase student's concentration, and
- help them actively in the learning process.

(d) Describe the characteristics of 'maladjusted person'.

Ans. There are some basic characteristics of maladjusted person:

- **Withdrawn and timid:** Frequent withdrawals from difficult situation may make individual timid and weak in facing real life situations.
- **Shy and self-conscious:** Shyness is usually associated with the self-consciousness, concern with the impression one gives to other people, and concern with their negative evaluation. A shy individual has low self-esteem and tends to anticipate adversities. Thus often keeping silent and avoiding eye contact.
- **Fearful:** Fear is a strong emotion involving perception of danger, unpleasant agitation and often a desire to hide from meeting student of higher classes, being along in a room, and fear of doge, strange noises, the dark, etc.
- **Anxious:** Anxiety is personality trait. It results from conflict, which is an inevitable part of life. Anxiety describes individual's level of emotionality. We see many students who are tense and worried (highly anxious) and those who are cool (hardly anxious). Since anxiety is an inferred emotional state of an individual, it cannot be directly observed. It can be measured through psychological tests/techniques.
- **Delusions:** Delusion is an irrational and obstinate that the individual actively defends, e.g. a child does not work hard for the find examination and thinks that it is the God only who can get him through the examination and he fails. This shows the delusion in him which makes him maladjusted.
- **Extremely aggressive:** Aggressive students show enterprising or energetic behaviour or tendency to be dominating in the class or the school. Sometimes an individual fails to show the tendency of dominating in a social situation and hurts herself instead, e.g. a child beats her doll, kicks the dog, or other objects.

• **Tension:** When a person does not feel a kind of inner freedom, the strain which results from muscular contradiction and through which muscles, tendons, etc., are stretched under a threatening situation.

• **High aspirations:** A person has high hopes and aspirations for his future life. When the hopes are not achieved, he becomes unrealistic in life.

• **Feeling of inferiority:** A feeling of inferiority, arising from the sense of imperfection and incompletion in a particular sphere of life, which motivates the individual to strive for a higher level of development and such, are the cause of all improvement in life situations. Each time a new level of achievement is reached, inferiority feelings reappear, continuing to stimulate upward movement. If inferiority feelings become exaggerated by adverse condition at the home, physical or mental disorders on inferiority complex may develop which makes an individual maladjusted.

• **Emotionally disturbed:** If the internal and external adjustment of a child are not achieve, he becomes emotional, e.g. weeping, nail biting, thumb sucking, etc. and becomes maladjusted.

• **Isolated:** Maladjusted children suffer from a feeling of isolation. This feeling does not allow them to mix and interact with other members of class, class, school, family or society. In families where parents are extremely busy and neglect their children, the children develop a feeling of isolation or dejection. This makes them maladjusted.

• **Sensitivity:** Maladjusted children are very sensitive. They get hurt easily, e.g. on being teased by teacher in the classroom or parents in the family, sarcastic remarks by peers, unwelcome advice by others, etc.

(e) How will you identify a visually impaired child?

Refer to Page.No.-150 [Student with Visual Impairment]

(f) Discuss the characteristics of a socially mature person.

Ans. Characteristics of a socially mature person

The socially mature person:

(1) has capacity for friendship and rarely makes enemies. He has friends and likes to be with people.

(2) has a good control over his emotions, a pleasant disposition and a tolerant and understanding attitude. He rarely shows offensive feelings or aggressive behaviour.

(3) has a power of leadership. This power shows itself in early childhood and becomes stronger as the person grows older.

(4) has the ability and desire to co-operate with others. While leading in some spheres, he should be equally willing to co-operate and follow leadership in other spheres.

(5) learn to become economically independent. The desire to become economically independent shows itself during the teens and should be pursued.
(6) becomes weaned away, from the parental roof and establishes his own home and family. This parallels the achievement of economic independence.
(7) has play interests and engages in recreational activities suitable to his age.
(8) lives according to high social and moral standards and is not delinquent.
(9) is mannerly, courteous and gentle in personal relationships.
(10) achieves good heterosexual relationships and gets along well with members of the opposite sex.

Q4. Answer the following question in about 600 words:
You have to organise a workshop on career guidance for students of class XII in your school. Prepare a plan for the organisation of the workshop. Also write the content of the presentation on 'Career Options after class XII'.

Ans. The workshops assist one to:
- to identify his/her skills and qualifications
- to envisage his/her career goals and develop career plans
- to learn about standards and expectations of application processes in science and economy
- to enhance his/her qualification and professional knowledge for future job responsibilities

Plan for organisation of Workshop

Conduction: The whole workshop should highly interactive & informal. English predominantly & Hindi when required should be used.
Place: Audio-Visual Room or similar room.
Requirement:
- One table or hand held mike
- One collar mike
- Blackboard on a stand
- Chalks
- Table & chairs
- One Overhead projector
- One teacher during the workshop. His or her role shall be non-participatory and shall be limited to maintain discipline.

Duration: 3-4 hours or more depending on the problems of the students.
Seating: Much close proximity to the students as possible. The students in the last row should be able to see the projections on the screen clearly and also hear distinctly.
Number of Students: 25-30 or less and as homogeneous (from class XII) as possible.

The Workshop Schedule

A two-person team shall conduct the workshop. The class composition can be changed for, e.g. boys & girls can sit together.

Day 1: Generating Awareness & Creating Atmosphere For The Workshop (Explain the children what career counselling and vocational guidance is.)

Day 2: Workshop for XII class girls. (Commerce group).

Day 3: Workshop for XII class boys. (Commerce group).

Day 4: Workshop for XII class girls. (Science group).

Day 5: Workshop for XII class boys. (Science group).

Day 6: Workshop for XII class girls. (Art Group).

Day 7: Workshop for XII class boys. (Art Group).

Career Workshop Topics

(1) Introduction & Instructions.

(2) How people (students) take decisions?

(3) Planning & Budgeting: Importance and Relevance.

(4) Career: What? & Why? Characteristics & Types.

(5) The Right Career.

(6) Consequences of having a Wrong Career: A Chronological Journey.

(7) Why People take wrong decisions? What makes people choose a wrong career?

(8) Comment on questions: Something to ponder.

(9) Inherent Interest: Path to Right Career.

(10) The Grand Plan.

(11) Discover Your Right Career:

(a) Self Realisation

(b) Finding your inherent interest

(c) Making a list of Interests

(d) Correcting & Completing list

(e) Narrowing the corrected & completed list.

(f) Mapping (Generalisation, Deletion & Distortion)

(g) Reverse Engineering

(h) The Ultimate Question

(12) Summary.

ES-332 : PSYCHOLOGY OF LEARNING AND DEVELOPMENT

December, 2012

Note: (i) All questions are ***compulsory.***
(ii) All questions carry ***equal*** *weightage.*

Q1. Answer the following question in about 600 words:
Why should teachers study principles of human growth and development? Describe major characteristics of human development during adolescence period.

OR

Explain the difference between convergent and divergent thinking. As a teacher, what will you do to develop divergent thinking ability among your students?

Q2. Answer the following question in about 600 words:
Examine the role of heredity and environment in individual differences among children. Illustrate your answer citing examples of students in your school.

OR

What is cognitive approach to learning? Describe Piaget's stages of cognitive development and their implications for the development of school curriculum.

Q3. Answer any four of the following questions in about 150 words each:
(a) Discuss the characteristics of inter-personal development of secondary school students.
(b) How does mass media impact the personality of an adolescent?
(c) Explain the meaning and nature of attitudes.
(d) How do girls differ from boys in language development?
(e) As a teacher, how will you help your students to resolve the conflicts they experience in schools?
(f) Describe the characteristics of an emotionally mature individual.

Q4. Answer the following question in about 600 words:
You have identified two students in your class who are not socially well adjusted. Prepare a report on the status of their social adjustment. The report may have the following three sections:
(a) Bases for the identification of the students.
(b) Reasons for their lack of social adjustment.
(c) Your plans to help the students.

ES-332 : PSYCHOLOGY OF LEARNING AND DEVELOPMENT
June, 2013

Note: (i) All the four questions are ***compulsory.***
(ii) All questions carry ***equal*** *weightage.*

Q1. Answer the following questions in about 600 words:
How can you, as a teacher, facilitate socio-emotional development of secondary school students? Discuss with examples.

OR

'Individual differences are crucial for teachers who are responsible for guiding all forms of learning.' Discuss the statement with the help of relevant examples.

Q2. Answer the following question in about 600 words:
What is meant by transfer of learning? How will you facilitate transfer of learning in your students? Discuss.

OR

Discuss the implications of conflicts among students in the classroom situation with suitable examples.

Q3. Answer any four of the following in about 150 words each:
(a) Why should a teacher trainee study the process of human development? Discuss its implications.
(b) Discuss the classroom implications of language development for teachers.
(c) How will you foster creativity in children? Discuss.
(d) Describe the characteristics of learning.
(e) Describe the role of the 'memory system' as a method of learning.
(f) What do you mean by 'group dynamics'? Describe the role of teachers in improving group dynamics.

Q4. Answer the following question in about 600 words:
A heterogenous class comprises gifted, average and below average children. How will you cater to the learning needs of such a heterogenous group of children in your class? Give convincing illustrations in support of your answer.

ES-332 : PSYCHOLOGY OF LEARNING AND DEVELOPMENT
December, 2013

Note: (i) All the four questions are ***compulsory.***
(ii) All the questions carry ***equal*** *weightage.*

Q1. Answer the following question in about 600 words:
How will you, as a teacher, develop holistic personality of your students? Discuss with suitable examples.

OR

Discuss the impact of non - cognitive factors on student's learning and development. Support your answer with examples.

Q2. Answer the following question in about 600 words:
Which approach to learning; behaviourist or cognitivist, do you prefer while teaching your students? Support your answer with convincing arguments.

OR

How will you describe the students with special needs? Discuss the areas where you, as a teacher, will intervene to cater to their learning needs.

Q3. Answer any four of the following in about 150 words each:
(a) Discuss the following principles of development:
(i) Sequentiality
(ii) Differentiality
(b) Discuss specific instructional strategies for handling individual differences in intelligence.
(c) Explain the relevance of gender issues to teachers and teaching.
(d) Describe the principles of learning.
(e) How will you identify maladjusted students in your class? Discuss.
(f) How will you organise guidance services in your school? Discuss.

Q4. Answer the following question in about 600 words:
Select a topic of your choice and prepare a lesson plan for the students of class IX incorporating the following principles of learning:
(a) Law of effect
(b) Law of practice
Highlight as to how the lesson plan is based on these principles of learning.

ES-332 : PSYCHOLOGY OF LEARNING AND DEVELOPMENT
June, 2014

Note: *(i) All four questions are* ***compulsory.***
(ii) All questions carry ***equal*** *weightage.*

Q1. Answer the following question in about 600 words:
Explain the concept of human development. Describe briefly the principles on which human development is based. Why should a teacher study the process and principal of child development? Discuss.

OR

What is meant by moral by morel development? Describe Kohlberg's stages of moral development. How far do you agree with Kohlderg's theory of moral development?

Q2. Answer the following question in about 600 words:
Define creativity and explain its dimensions. How shall you identify creative children in your class? Explain.

OR

'No two individuals are alike'. Discuss the statement in the context of intelligence and creativity.

Q3. Answer any four of the following questions in about 150 words each:
(a) Examine the role of heredity in producing individual differences among human beings.
(b) How do children's interests affect their learning in schools?
(c) Explain the relationship between language and culture.
(d) How does child's self concept affect child's social development.
(e) Discuss some special needs of children belonging to scheduled castes and scheduled tribes.
(f) Explain the difference between Guidance and Counselling.

Q4. Answer the following question in about 600 words;
You have observed that there are a few socially maladjusted children in your class. Prepare a plan to identify the causes of their maladjustment and to help them to overcome their problems.

ES-332 : PSYCHOLOGY OF LEARNING AND DEVELOPMENT
December, 2014

Note: (i) All four questions are ***compulsory.***
(ii) All questions carry ***equal*** *weightage.*

Q1. Answer the following question in about 600 words:
Explain the concept of cognitive development and factors facilitating its development.

OR

Home and school play a mutually reinforcing role in the development of child's personality. Discuss.

Q2. Answer the following question in about 600 words:
Define academic achievement. Examine the factors affecting children's academic achievement in elementary schools in rural and urban settings.

OR

What is maladjustment? Discuss characteristics of maladjusted persons. What should a teacher do to help a maladjusted child in her/his class?

Q3. Answer any four of the following questions in about 150 words each:
(a) What should teachers do to improve interpersonal communication among children?
(b) Learning is goal directed and purposive. Discuss.
(c) Explain the concept of emotional maturity.
(d) How can teachers help children with visual impairment? Explain.
(e) Explain the relationship between learning and maturation.
(f) Discuss special needs of gifted children.

Q4. Answer the following question in about 600 words:
You are a teacher in a secondary school and you have been asked to organise a seminar for the students of class X on the theme 'What after Class X?'. Prepare a detailed plan for the organisation of the seminar describing its objectives, scope, content, strategy, etc.

ES-332 : PSYCHOLOGY OF LEARNING AND DEVELOPMENT
June, 2015

Note: (i) All four questions are ***compulsory.***
(ii) All questions carry ***equal*** *weightage.*

Q1. Answer the following question in about 600 words:
Explain the nature and concept of moral development. Discuss Kohlberg's stages of moral development.

OR

Explain the concept of cognitive development. Discuss Piaget's stages of cognitive development.

Q2. Answer the following question in about 600 words:
Explain the nature of personality. Discuss the important factors which influence development of personality, giving illustrations.

OR

Explain the meaning of learning process. Discuss main principles of learning with suitable illustrations.

Q3. Answer any four of the following questions in about 150 words each:
(a) Explain main characteristics of language development.
(b) Explain the impact of media on personality development.
(c) Describe briefly the nature of gender issues in schooling.
(d) Differentiate between low and high achieving students.
(e) Differentiate between directive and non-directive counselling.
(f) Explain the concept of emotional maturity.

Q4. Answer the following question in about 600 words:
How will you identify children with special needs such as mild visual impairment and/or hearing and speech impairment in inclusive setting? What will you do in meeting the educational and psychological needs of these children?